T0365940

RE-ENTRY

Classical Apologetics Deciphered

Frederic-John Herriott

RE-ENTRY
CLASSICAL APOLOGETICS DECIPHERED

iUniverse books may be ordered through booksellers or by contacting:

iUniverse
1663 Liberty Drive
Bloomington, IN 47403
www.iuniverse.com
844-349-9409

ISBN: 978-1-5320-1965-4 (sc)
ISBN: 978-1-5320-1964-7 (e)

Library of Congress Control Number: 2017903750

Print information available on the last page.

iUniverse rev. date: 09/22/2021

How hard to know where it all starts
And harder still to see the end
Should one be brave, and face the truth
Or weave a million cobwebbed dreams?

– fjh

This book is dedicated to the memory of four steadfast and faithful friends in whose company over the years many happy hours have been spent.

Dan Byrne, Dalkey, 1910 - 1997 RIP

Peter Doyle, Shillelagh, 1912 – 1988 RIP

Paul Brienza, La Jolla, 1917 – 1998 RIP

Joe Foyle, Ranelagh, 1935 –

ACKNOWLEDGEMENTS

My thanks to all those who read the text and offered advice and encouragement especially Francis Hyland, Matt Lillis & Mark Waggoner. Further thanks must go to my clerical confreres, Fr Arthur O'Neill PP and Fr Ramon Angles SSPX.

Sincere thanks are also due to Maeve Fleischmann, Enda Whelan and Harriet Duffin who legitimized the text and especially my script editor Linda O'Rafferty whose support and backup never wavered from beginning to end.

Lastly and especially my wife Joan and all the family whose inexhaustible supply of patience and endurance withstood many dark clouds, my love and deepest thanks.

INTRODUCTION

If one were to judge a book by its cover, then this one would stand out as a prime example of why never to purchase a book on this basis.

It has little to do with Space, and even less to do with the RE-ENTRY process each home-ward bound space vehicle must make. Instead, as a book it has more to do with you, the reader, than perhaps any other book you are likely to read this year.

Thanks to the four men mentioned overleaf, and a host of other conversations with various people over the years, the truth I had been looking for for very many years dawned for me one day in realizing that the great dust covers, the window blinds, the drawn curtains and the bolted shutters must all be thrown open finally if the spiritual truths and deep knowledge of the church founded by Jesus Christ 2000 years ago were again to be made available and shared widely, enthusing the many while inspiring the few.

I firmly believe this was the sentiment that motivated Pope St John XXIII in conceiving the idea of a 2nd Vatican Council in 1958. Once he realised in his latter years that a better Church could only lead to a better world, he could think of nothing else. With such a positive and progressive plan in mind, he went ahead and called the Council which opened in Rome on 11th October 1962, and concluded on December 8th 1965.

Living with the results of this Vatican Council as one looks around the world now more than a half century later, one only sees a world containing a host of countries and societies far removed from the one the then pope envisaged. If anything, it is perhaps the antithesis of everything he had hoped for. How and why the legacy of the Council spawned the Catholic Church of today only time and history will tell. What concerns mankind today however, is what the state of the Church and what the state of the planet will be fifty years hence. How together they will both meet the needs of our descendents.

How this book addresses this scenario and where we are heading depends very much on you. If you are a Roman Catholic, a member of the Universal Church of Rome, faithful or unfaithful, practising or non-practising you will be challenged by its contents. If you are a person still searching for the truth then this book will provide you with much food for thought. If on the other hand you are an easy going, fairly well laid back type of person perhaps now is a good time to reflect on your life as, there is every chance you may find your name already inscribed here, and your future contained in the following pages.

Contents

CHAPTER

I

Whatever it is, there is something about throwing pebbles into very still water that is hauntingly, beautiful yet mysterious. The elliptical arches, the sound, the ripples all combine to produce a tantalizing effect which seems to elicit in each of us a momentary pause. A moment suspended in time, as if seeking to extract an answer of unique awareness.

Pondering this tranquil scene presents one with a mind game or self-analysis whereby a person's life could be compared to a set or series of pebbles, always arching, moving, sounding, echoing and splashing either into some deep gloomy pool or a hidden sun-drenched pond.

Would the number of pebbles relate to days, weeks, months or perhaps only major events during one's life? Would there be clusters of happy pebbles in between sad pebbles, in different colors and sizes? Would other people's pebbles and their ripples interface or interfere? At what stages would the control or lack of control over one's pebbles be lessened or increased? How or why would one designate the throwing of them to somebody else, and who might that someone be?

Who among us, walking with someone in the street have not passed a stranger, only to be told by our companion that "that person has thrown their life away?." Very frightening to hear, as the stranger more often than not looks quite normal, yet the intrigue has been provoked, and one waits in trepidation to hear the story behind the lost life.

Considering all the friends, acquaintances, relations and colleagues we meet over the years, have we not ourselves consigned some misfortunate individual to oblivion, or aided in their downfall by our actions, or worse, by our lack of them? It could well be that the tragedy and wounds of the person are often much closer to us than we would like to believe, let alone acknowledge. Saddest of all is the realization one day that the person one pities and rejects most of all, is the one staring back with empty eyes from the mirror on the wall.

For a lot of people, life is little more than a four-letter word. It is transitory, it is secular, it has a beginning, middle and an end, and it consists of the sum total one makes of it. The belief in a living and loving God has for many been revamped or reoriented into nothing other than an image of an infant at Christmas or a crucified Christ on a cross at Easter. For others, if heaven exists it is now a place for all to participate in rather like a favourite country club teeming with people over a hectic weekend. With the passing of time and the acquisitions of life secured, the fulcrum of care gets lighter and more distant, and the process of living a material life becomes the route one chooses. The affluent person assumes it is their 'God given right,' and it is acknowledged by their families and friends as such.

The modern world of competitiveness promises the maximum reward for the most ambitious members of society. Shakespeare, in his time was far more circumspect as he chose to see individuals as actors and actresses appearing briefly on the stage of life; this theme has long since been repeated, as it guarantees each and every 'ordinary' person some modicum of fame or glory, however short-lived either may be. Life, on the other hand would be very cruel without the capacity to hope, and it is this common bond that unites every individual person to 'live together in hope'. To deny this capacity for hope is a cruel blow but to shatter it in whatever dream a person chooses, is tantamount to blowing out a candle. In today's world millions upon millions of such candles are threatened by the menacing winds of change neither understood nor recognized for what they are by those who are living their lives in hope.

The health services, economic and educational disadvantages inflicted on vast numbers of populations are destroyers of human hope. Whether one lives in the slums of Sao Paulo or the back streets of Detroit, the dawn of each day heralds a degree of hope for even the poorest beggar, the one who dares to cling to a life which to all but him is unrecognisable as having any value whatsoever.

The great unfathomable mystery which gives one the lifestyle of an observer and another the life of a player, perhaps, never will be solved. How one is chosen to live and work enjoying all the pleasures a first world city has to offer, while another fights every inch of the way from South America through Central America and Mexico, to end up picking avocados in Fallbrook CA is truly amazing in its perversity, yet, it is a riddle this book somehow hopes to address.

There are many today who see life in terms of astrological signs, luck, fate, chance, tarot cards. They move their allegiance from one area of influence to another, abdicating their own individual control to whatever the present collectiveness seeks to encourage or promote. This "Friends" TV soap sic type of existence tends to make life more comfortable and somehow understandable particularly to young adults preferring to act more in unison rather than alone. This herd instinct offers a comfort zone to those who forever seek to go with one person or with others but never on their own, as they are too insecure to venture out, as an individual, alone. They need the security experienced when travelling in numbers to give them a sense of shared confidence and credibility.

Jigsaws, puzzles, and indeed multidimensional games are all similies, easily comparable to life. The mystical 'hand of cards' dealt to each person at birth is a great favourite of many. Yet such a predetermined fate must, by its nature be disregarded. However, when all has been said and done on this subject, there is something incredibly enjoyable and exciting about the realisation of chance, opportunity, talent and technique, all contributing to the order of life.

Imagine the excitement of watching small infants building with colored bricks and blocks. Their shapes, sizes, colors and uses allow each toddler to work to his/her own designs, skills, and plans, engrossed in their own private little world. Frequently some well-meaning adult may feel the need to offer assistance but their contribution seldom, if ever, adds to the child's field of dreams. It is also not unusual to see one child in a group kick or knock over a little buddy's best attempt-just for fun, or for the sheer delight in the resulting destruction. The happiness or unhappiness that surrounds such a scene is a warning of the life that lies ahead for all of them, yet it is seldom recognized as such. The cubes and triangles, pillars and arches, blues and yellows are all very essential, as they fit here and fail to fit there, in the building or plan referred to as 'life'. What use is a triangle when a square is needed, especially one which has been hurled in frustration across the room? All the pieces are relevant and are there to be used, if not as originally planned, certainly in another positive or constructive manner.

What is important is that the missing piece, lost, misplaced or hidden earlier must be found and effectively incorporated before the final task can be completed. When this takes place the tears, joy and happiness are finally realized. This seemingly childish amusement or attempt to accomplish a basic task is elemental, yet essential, if one is to make onward progress through life. The need to come to terms with the advantages and disadvantages life brings to each and every one are not only similar but in many ways are duplicate sets of keys in how most people deal with their adult lives.

For this reason the closeness of siblings, the relationships between uncles and nieces, aunts and nephews and the whole spectrum of inter-family ties matter enormously. The new partnerships, the alternate lifestyles, the non-biological bonds, however strong, can seldom, if ever, equate to the primal union in which "blood is always thicker than water". To console, to show sympathy for, to express concern, to offer understanding are all qualities that reflect the true Christian. Without these qualities it is hard to accept the person one meets as having any likeness whatsoever to Christ. If the views expressed by an individual are harsh, self-centered or critical, it is not uncommon to hear the person being referred to as 'unchristian'. Without some very basic elementary blocks in place, the life one begins to build can be off-centred and flawed, making it prone to future structural problems.

'It is essential that the original course of blocks be laid on solid foundations to sustain the onslaughts which will be ongoing and unavoidable through the passage of time. Infants and children are so greatly advantaged and genuinely fortunate if they begin life's journey nurtured in a true Christian home.

It is well established by experts and research analysts that children go through a number of developmental stages until they reach the age of six or seven. By this time 85% per cent of the normal growth patterns have been well established. Subsequent events will either assist or impede in their on-going development but the formative years will forever remain as the primary life-blocks crucial for whatever lies ahead.

No matter what happens during the teenage years and into young adulthood, the formative years will be the resource from which they will draw their life's strengths. What is even more crucial is a deeply personal, spiritual courage strong enough to sustain them in their everyday lives.

In today's world many people are tied to the emotions, skills and educational experiences they were introduced to as infants and young children. For those who were born into Christian families where caring and sharing values were promoted as natural, the early years are those which will prove extremely beneficial. For others less fortunate who may have been locked in an acrimonious albeit affluent situation, or a serious poverty-trap, they are barely or rarely equipped for what lies ahead. The relevant outlook and abilities needed to move through adolescence and college are often seriously impaired from early childhood by scars of grief or despair. Denied one or more building blocks needed to lay the foundations to secure a purpose-driven, life the alternative or shallow-based existence may often produce an emotionally disadvantaged person with serious psychological flaws.

A sum total of 5, 10 or 15 years spent in a harsh, dysfunctional background can take a heavy toll that will almost inevitably lead to a frustrating and meaningless life, riddled with lifelong disappointments and despair. Juvenile courts on a daily basis give testimony to the gross injustices children are forced to endure because of circumstances totally outside their control.

If life and especially a life lived in a difficult home environment is the seed bed for a confused young adult, it must be the primary task of the educational authority to provide a counterbalance or guidance system to correct such a negative growth pattern. Regrettably for many reasons self-righting educational systems rarely function very efficiently and the very opposite of what should take place for the good of the child often transpires.

It is perhaps easy to understand why the system may fail in a secular or state run institution, but why this may also be the case in many Catholic schools and colleges is totally contrary to what should be the case. The challenge today is not just to stop, reverse and introduce the Catholic way of life, it is to re-define it in a far more powerful light, presenting it with arguments and discussions that will inspire those who seek the tangible reality of living the Catholic life in as full and as faithful a way as possible. It is not difficult to comprehend how Christian schools today can produce so very many unchristian students. The advent of personal gratification, individual achievement, control and prosperity, are now all clearly defined goals. It is certainly difficult to present a Christian lifestyle as the preferential one to which all Catholics are expected and encouraged to adhere to, however, it is this primary and basic misdirection of ambition which has been allowed to grow and develop into such a messed-up values system that it is now almost impossible to challenge or confront the 'status quo'. The need for such a reordering of today's young adult Catholics cannot be over emphasized. Unless there are such committed, vibrant, enthusiastic Catholics evangelizing the church today it cannot successfully hope to perform the role it is mandated to play.

Of all the Christian churches in the world today, the Catholic Church, usually referred to as the Roman Catholic Church, is the largest and most influential. Its claim as the original Church founded by Jesus Christ purports to contain the fullness and totality of Christ's life and teachings from its origins 2000 years ago. The Christ-given authority it claims as its sole brand enables the Catholic Church to identify itself as the 'Living Bride' of Christ on Earth and as such is ordered to proclaim the Gospel, the 'good news,' to all persons. Pope Pius XI was totally committed to this instruction and declared,

6

"The Church has no other reason for its existence than
to extend over the Earth the Kingdom of Christ and
so to render people sharers of His saving Redemption."

Many other Christian communities and groups also claim the right as followers of Christ to preach the Gospel in many varied biblical and fundamental ways. These Christian sects, under whatever guidance or direction they have chosen, nevertheless have their origins in the one true universal Church of Rome. At whatever stage or under whatever influence they severed their connection with Rome it was a choice that was made and taken by them.

The definitive work, A History of the Protestant Reformation in England and Ireland, written between 1824 and 1827 by William Cobbett, a Protestant himself no less, portrays the great rift in all its brutality and shame. To have a preacher representing today's Pope referring to the "great theological and spiritual enrichment that came from the Reformation" to the General Synod in Westminster Abbey is quite extraordinary. Or as some observers would prefer to say, quite disgraceful. It maybe not possible today to attribute all matters such as divorce, abortion, contraception and euthanasia to many well-meaning reformed churches, societies and communities, yet without any doubt there are millions of Christians who choose to believe that, given certain circumstances, these areas are not sinful and indeed justifiable.

The Catholic Church allows no such ambiguity and those who seek to practice their faith diligently in union with the Church are not in a position to entertain, encourage or condone such matters. The choice of Catholicism, carefully made, is Christianity in its most authoritative and purest form. It is a difficult choice to make and a difficult choice to pursue, and most of all, an extremely difficult choice in which to persevere. Nevertheless the exuberant and eminent Catholic writer of the last century Hilaire Belloc said it most succinctly when he vehemently proclaimed,

"This is the faith into which I was born, and this is the
faith in which I hope to die."

7

The omniplex cinema screen attracts the viewer from the very beginning to the very end. It produces the Alpha and the Omega and the viewer leaves content with a certain degree of satisfaction or fulfilment. Faith also needs to be seen on such a mega-wide band- width or vision. The Faith of solitary highlights, contained in individual Sacraments, Baptism, Confirmation and Marriage makes little sense when presented and viewed in such individual isolation. It is only when faith is seen as a complete castle, a citadel, a cathedral of immense beauty and power in which every sacrament is witnessed in its true continuity and setting, that one even begins to sense the mystery and awe Catholicism inspires.

Religion for many today has not only ceased to be a cornerstone in their life, but rather it has become more like a few minor bricks in their wall. It is of little real significance or importance, and its purpose has become almost totally non-functional, serving only to be seen as a somewhat inconsequential decorative item, to be displayed on a few glamorous occasions. The essentials of living in today's world have become for the most part purely secular and pluralistic. Good is now something to be self-decided, social advancement is for the betterment of self, all barriers removed can only bring advanced freedoms, and a higher standard of living for all, ensuring a stable and happy society. This juvenile outlook of course generates the Midas myth in which the person who first reaches the age of 80 with the most toys wins.

Such is the popular concept of the good life that millions of people will spend every working day of their lives trying to achieve it. To the practising Catholic, it is a totally meaningless juvenile and self-destructive lifestyle, and only serves the needs of those for whom there will never be enough. The temptation of greed will forever see to that. Modern man however has little if any interest in religion and seeks instead to demean and diminish it, claiming it will be in the fields of science, technology, medicine, and space exploration that all the answers mankind is seeking, will be found.

Since the second half of the last century, the world has evolved into a far more dangerous place. It has continued to become more polarized and more competitive; it has become more demanding and decadent;

and it has also become considerably more totalitarian. The constraints and conditions fashioned more and more via high-speed definitive communications have formed and fostered in each layer of society an acceptance to be controlled by fewer and fewer people. In addition to the political and or banking structures of individual countries, the transnational corporations and the monetary mandarins who control the world's money markets are themselves under threat. Organizations now meet and operate almost independently of nations, regardless of national aspirations or national ideals. Much has already been written about such powerful entities as the Council on Foreign Relations, The Bilderberg Group and The Trilateral Commission, yet a host of other inter-governmental bodies and stealth agencies also exist and move behind the scenes manipulating the planet's resources of food, water, energy and everything that adds to or subtracts from the quality of life of countless millions of people throughout the world.

It is becoming more evident every passing decade, that decisions are being taken by such influential and transnational groupings, as to how the vast majority of sections of mankind need to be directed individually and collectively. These international foundations seek the advancement of the human race only insofar as it meets their own criteria. Such topics as population control, the responsibility for the collection and distribution of world financial markets and the legislative power of sovereign countries are all areas where the adherence of the individual to the system he or she is part of is the primary objective. By controlling the individual many are controlled and the exercise of the common franchise in the direction one is given becomes no more than an exercise in sophisticated slavery.

How then can the Catholic faith best be portrayed and presented as the most meaningful and authentic religion for those who genuinely want each person to be treated as equal? How can one live a life exemplifying from within that each person through their faith is encouraged to practice and believe? How can a personal loving relationship with God in a life dedicated to following Him faithfully be possible? These and many similar questions are seldom posed in school, and sadly for many never posed within their entire lives. Without being asked, addressed and answered, a vacuum of life exists, and for many, life manifests itself as the wanderings of a person lost in a vast wilderness.

The Catholic Church was founded by Jesus Christ to show people the way, the truth and the light to rescue people from darkness, to bring people back from the desert, to direct them to salvation. So how can one begin again to realize that it is only in accepting the invitation to follow Christ that one gains one's spiritual freedom? To follow is to know and to know is to love, there is no other way. The path or the way contains the trials and tribulations but the choice is clear. The problems of life will be there to be dealt with as best one can, and one can choose to do so with God's help or without God's help; it is for every person to exercise their own free will in making their decision. In loving God one must love His Church, the bride of Christ. It is inconceivable to claim a love of God while ignoring or disrespecting His Church. Institutionalized as it may have become it remains the Bride of Christ and all Catholics must remain faithful and true to it, regardless of how badly it has been managed over the past few decades by some of its most senior sons.

Today the Catholic Church teaches the fullness and the sacredness of life in all its forms as the common denominator for all men, regardless of race, creed or color. It is unequivocal in its stance that from pre-birth through after-birth and from pre-death through after-death man is born in the image of God. Pope Emeritus, Benedict XVI, in his first encyclical entitled, Deus Caritas Est given on December 25th 2005 in St Peter's Basilica, chose for his theme the 'Meaning of Love' because for him it was the most obvious place to start. It was reasonable to assume that it would be the foundation stone on which he would build his future teachings, through subsequent encyclicals. What more appropriate title could he have chosen to introduce his papacy than an encyclical based primarily on love? Whilst he continued his papacy and sought to overcome the onslaught of clerical abuse and scandals while at the same time adjust and redirect liturgical authenticity, others were seeking to promote devious agendas by releasing confidential documents to the press. That such a climate of treachery to alter the course of his papacy by such foul means were been taken, must only be deplored and whether the work of one person or a group of people their motive can only have been one loaded with bad intent. The subsequent resignation of Pope Benedict XVI today remains to be clarified and in the fulness of time, if it is God's will, it will be. Under the reign of Pope Benedict's successor, Pope Francis I, the 'Bishop of Rome' as he prefers to be called, his decisions to radically change some of the Church's management structures and controls is quite clear. These changes show a new and distinct direction he wishes the church to undertake and follow whilst under his authority. Already, it is clear the winds of change are being clearly felt in Rome. It is impossible to predict where this papacy age will attempt to lead the faithful but already the murmurings of some bishops globally indicate that an-uneasiness exists now as never before. Indeed it would appear that the opinions and deliberations of perhaps a group of ten or twelve theologians may seriously decide to reinterpret the dogma and doctrine of two thousand years endorsed by all councils up to the inauguration of Vatican II

How the Church must again find its full vigour and validity in preaching the Gospel, as was intended by Christ is the great task that appears to be dividing bishops from bishops and cardinals from cardinals. In today's world of advanced communications spreading the good news and drawing all persons of goodwill closer to Christ must become the key goals of Pope Francis' mission. It is only his authority that unites just as it is his lack of authority that divides. The internal need to re-evangelize the Church in order for it to be fully united is perhaps the greatest challenge facing the present Holy Father. In a similar way the time is also for the Clergy to reach out to the laity as never before in bringing them to the altar of the Lord. It is only by sharing with them the Mysteries of Faith that the support and confidence the laity are obliged to offer them will be reborn and re-established. That the Church comprises 2% clerical and 98% lay members means that the mutual respect and love of one section for the other must be both genuine and meaningful. Unless this clarity of the Faith and its meaning is accepted, ensuing spiritual doubts and confusion will continue to cause more and more people to stray and the Church to crumble.

The Church is crystal clear that God is for all and that God's word is to be addressed to every person in their own right. There is no exclusivity: every individual person matters to God. This truth cannot be overstated, and its deliverance is essential to anybody who wishes to re-ignite his/her spiritual flame. This prime truth gives an insight into the mind and heart of Christ, the true Supreme Shepherd who laid down his own life so those who seek Him may have eternal salvation. This truth is so real and so important that it can never be over-emphasized or diminished in any way.

In a world where everyone is entitled to birth, dignity, education, health care and sanitation, there should be no industries of death, no means or opportunity for transnational monolithic companies to exploit vast areas of natural resources, no governments which facilitate fringe groups of terrorists or banking systems that can cripple and destroy the financial lives of millions. Without the Gospel, without the living Catholic Church there to combat such global inequalities and injustices, vast populations will have no voice to speak for them.

The Holy Father, elected by the College of Cardinals, is chosen by them to represent God on Earth.

The choice is man-made yet from the first moment of his election he is understood to be under the guidance of the Holy Spirit. How the Pope conforms to this guidance or how he chooses to seek advice from other sources will be the hallmark of his Pontificate. How well he accomplishes his role is the cross he alone must bear. On a daily basis he expresses views that are the thoughts and aspirations of many holy priests and bishops; the great difference being that when the Holy Father speaks everybody listens. It maybe only once or twice, if at all, in his entire Pontificate that he may exercise his power to speak "ex cathedra". When this occurs the words he speaks are believed to be the very thoughts of God Himself, and are binding on all faithful Catholics as defined dogma and must be accepted as such. In the affairs of the world and the Catholic Church itself many curious persons choose to listen to what the Holy Father has to say yet few leaders and politicians have the courage to publicly unite their views with his and promote the official Catholic viewpoint as, is their own, to follow.

The Church as a body is expected to foster, promote and uphold such views however unpopular or demanding they may be, yet sometimes it seems the supportive silence is deafening Once the views of the Pope are in conflict with the policies of some governments or legislatures they are usually brushed to one side as if of no weight or validity. Nevertheless they are the views he is obliged to preach to his own flock in particular and to people of good will throughout the world who are prepared to listen. As for the forces of Evil, in whatever guise or industry they operate, their opposition to many Papal statements are voiced daily in much of the world's press or fashioned in such a way as to appear supportive knowing all the while the situation can be turned to their advantage.

To alter, obscure and in any way possible distort and dismantle Church teaching is the general policy for most of the secular media in developed countries. Their agenda is to continuously present the Catholic Church and its views as an authoritarian, draconian, and interfering institution forever exploiting the weak and in the process allowing the spread of HIV and AIDS, or especially, restricting the rights of women. They seek to portray this package using the power of constant media repetition designed to penetrate the belief system of the individual until it will become completely absorbed by the masses. Such is this hostile media stream that it becomes responsible for undermining the true nature of the relationship between man and woman. Created and perfectly designed by God whereby each could fully complement enjoy and respect each other forming the bedrock of the family and society into which they would introduce their own newborn infants. The havoc being created within the Domestic Church, the Christian family, redefined now as un-natural rather than natural, is becoming more evident day by day as society increasingly mutates from its true original function. Today, to facilitate the abnormal changes and roles evolving within human relationships and so recognize them as somehow or other authentic and alternate, certain senior members of national hierarchies are now prepared to consider changing fundamental church teachings. In the modern world there are those who seek to speak in terms of a restructured Church amended to meet the needs of a new unity in diversity of a new age. The most basic keystone of society the very 'family' itself is under a serious attack which in time may well lead to its disestablishment as it exists today. This polarization is being engineered from all angles both within and without the Church and quite often promoted sadly by those whose primary function is supposedly to protect and guard it from all errors and dangers.

It may be that the harm being inflicted is for the most part without malice or intent; nevertheless there are those who choose not to distinguish the genuine doctrine of the Church from the mere speculation of certain professional scholars. This attitude of preference and individual interpretation of sacred scripture is as dangerous as a cancerous growth in a healthy body. A further development in radical thinking is the constant drive to promote as the primary role of the Church that of a global aid agency interested in man's temporal needs rather than his spiritual salvation.

This modern solicitude for the geopolitical rights of man and the environmental state of the planet of course has got to concern the Church but it is the on-going spiritual survival of mankind individually and collectively which is and must always remain its primary objective. The spiritual warfare that exists between the forces of Evil and the love of God never ceases, even momentarily, yet today its very existence is barely acknowledged. The Kingship of Christ as supreme ruler of all mankind is seldom if ever even preached.

A single drop of ink in a glass of milk will change the nature of the drink in form, texture and color, add many more drops and eventually the milk ceases to be drinkable. By polluting the Church's teachings little by little over the years, the inevitable outcome is that a significant percentage of confused Catholics are now spiritually illiterate of essential church doctrine. A proportion of today's generation on the other hand is totally confident enough to embrace modern innovations and views expressed by doubtful theologians given the refinement of presentation.

The quick-read download indoctrination is being accepted at an alarming rate as a valid substitute for genuine religious knowledge. This cursory spreadsheet overview integrates well with the fast moving lifestyles based on the TV image of a feel-good, appear-good lifestyle. It however is illusory and serves to do only more damage to one's spiritual well-being. A seminal case in point is that of a young Catholic attending a funeral Mass for a recently deceased neighbour or acquaintance. The deceased person whose lifestyle of self- interest and materialism may have left a lot to be desired nevertheless receives the most glowing praise from the priest on the altar. This cannot make any logical sense to the young person who is then forced to consider why he or she should then choose to take religion seriously? In fact, why bother at all to contemplate a more disciplined Catholic lifestyle if one consistently witnessed the terrible inadequacies or clerical scandals which appear in turn to be appallingly dealt with by those in authority?

For members of other faiths and religions who choose to misinterpret the Gospel liberally, their indifference to Catholicism is understandable, yet such indifference is not an option open to Catholics. Practising members of the church should be well aware that it is the private and hidden lifestyle of the deviants, rather than the church as a divine institution itself, that will continue to have their behaviour inflict injury after injury upon it.

For Catholics who claim to be active followers of Christ yet behave in terms of discrediting their Church and who chip away at the very doctrines themselves, there is a great urgency and need to reintroduce them to the true light. The Church does have a hierarchy, it has a curia, it has a college of cardinals, it has a congregation of bishops, it has numerous orders of religious, it has archdioceses, dioceses, and parishes, lay apostles, prelatures, priests, nuns, brothers, deacons and a vast laity of hundreds of millions. It is mammoth, it is diverse, it is political, it is practical, it is like all autocracies made up of people, some excellent, some terrible, some humble, some self-seeking. This vast enormous body therefore is led and directed in the Gospel by a whole command structure centralized in Rome. Its teachings and rulings are conveyed to national, local and parish level for the laity desiring to lead their lives in union with the Church's teachings.

The question of such core teachings and their acceptance must therefore be of primary importance to the well-being of the Church. The area of teaching, of preaching, and indeed the whole area of spreading the truth of Christ throughout the world must ultimately rest on the Holy Father's shoulders, and his closest cardinals. There appears in today's Church separate and distinct groups of clergy both in favour and not in favour of the Pope's ministry.

Today's great need to protect family life, from the very adverse effects of birth control, the unjust consequences of unfair world trade agreements, the unequal distribution of natural resources are all challenges which must be confronted through Catholicism. The vast amoral amounts of money being spent on the armaments, drugs, pornography and other industries are everyday facts of life which must not continue to be considered acceptable by first world countries, any more than the whole plethora of other social and domestic evils which are somehow or other seldom seriously challenged by our Church. Our responses to date are perhaps too pluralistic: or over-lenient as we seek to appease rather than take the necessary, courageous action that is so urgently needed. In a world of harsh economics it is perhaps because we seek solutions of a material kind rather than put our trust in God that we fail again and again to make our prayers and presence real. Is it possible that in the Papacy of Francis I a rallying call for a major renaissance of Catholic faith will be heeded? If such a mission were to be undertaken then surely one should have to look no further than the Jesuits themselves, the Society of Jesus, to lead such a wonderful unification. Yet even here there must be doubt that the church is again almost being denied by its own.

The Jesuits, one of the most illustrious of religious orders, founded in 1558 by St Ignatius of Loyola, was awarded its prelature to safeguard, affirm and protect Papal authority and teaching. Over the latter half of the twentieth century it seemed to have chosen to negate this role. After Vatican II the protection of the Pope, his authority and catholic teaching began to play second fiddle as the twin tenet calls of 'Justice & Peace' rang out and the Jesuits saw themselves assuming a more meaningful and glamorous role. Needless to say this fledgling self-appointed identity did not sit well with Papal favour and storm clouds began gathering.

Not for the first time in its history the Society moved into uncharted waters as it began to try and establish for itself a new image, a different role, a progressive way forward almost totally alien to the one envisaged by its founder. The Jesuits' change of emphasis, their collective mindset, their active interest in the emerging school of Liberation Theology were all causing concern and Pope St John Paul II was not prepared to tolerate such independence. He choose a respected Jesuit scholar Fr Paolo Dezza SJ to take control of the Order as a special Papal Delegate, and bring the Order back into fidelity. It can be said that during the papacy of Pope Benedict XVI the relationship between the Holy See and the Jesuit Order, like many other relationships, was once more improved and re-established but, not to the comparable depth of its original prelature. How the present Holy Father, himself a Jesuit, oversees the on-going role of the Order remains to be seen. Regardless of their great successes in some of the developing countries their inability to attract first-world vocations has led to their demise as one of the Church's premier religious Orders. The purity of their mission which for over 400 years never failed to attract the finest young men with courage and conviction has somehow lost itself and the flame of the order burns lower and lower. Today there is perhaps a necessity for a new society of Ignatian inspired priests to once more defend the Papacy and give to it the complete loyalty, protection and courage its founder intended.

The role of the Holy Father as shepherd to the flock, as servant to fellow bishops, as Successor to Peter seems to be a somewhat unacceptable authority for today's Church and world. How this can be so is unclear as the role, the office and the mission never appears to be directly challenged. Nevertheless the college of cardinals and his select intimate groups chosen from his most senior members of the Church's hierarchy are without doubt the movers and shakers in the halls of disparate views.

The addresses of the Pope attract constant opposition from various quarters as he preaches relatively popular lectures beneficial to all mankind. He preaches to promote a new evangelization, he preaches for more reconciliation between Christian churches, he preaches for clearer dialogue with the leaders of different faiths, and all the while addresses all men and women as sons and daughters of God. For many his views are too bound to the more neo-modernist viewpoint formulated by the Second Vatican Council and as such are seen as alien by those to whom classical Catholicism remains the apogee of truth and fidelity.

Those who disagree and seek to promote further liberalism and ecumenism at all levels within the church are pressing forward as they see in Francis a Pope who will not only listen to their ultra modern views but will in fact endorse them. This Jesuit Papacy then needs to be one of firm determination firstly with its own hierarchy as the disparate views expressed in the Synod of the Family so clearly demonstrated. Without doubt it needs to address its own governance. As it is only when this is done, can a genuine reconciliation of its clergy take place. Paradoxically if or when this actually happens it seems hard to visualise how those who have defended Church liturgy and doctrine in its purist form for over fifty years can then not only be joyfully reconciled but recognised for their years spent in the wilderness.

The need to understand the Church and the formative role it seeks to maintain in today's world has never been greater. To realize such dimensions it is important to understand why it matters so much to the Church as more than the receptacle of great importance, such as Humanae Vitae rightly shows. This seminal document was the turning point in the late 1960s for many Catholics, clergy and laity alike who chose to rebel and challenge the fact that Papal instruction, discourse, and teaching could be easily set aside and repudiated. This encyclical of such momentous consequences was the glory of Pope Paul VI, and was intended to be recognised as the shining light of his Pontifical reign. Sadly, its non-acceptance was due to many reasons, the primary one being it was never presented or taught by those who were entrusted with that role, and its true message was almost entirely distorted and basically lost to the Catholic world. People of goodwill for whom it was intended were consequently denied it.

Decades later with the wisdom of hindsight, the 'sacredness of life' being more clearly understood the encyclical has, if anything, grown in stature and become even more relevant and meaningful in today's world. In a world of in-vitro fertilisation, embryo research, dna gene manipulation and a whole host of the most advanced generic projects which are pushing back further and further the boundaries of what today constitutes a human being. The distance or the destination such research will bring to the human race is unknown. If one considers how seeds vegetables and crops are being genetically modified today is a foretaste of what science may very soon be able to accomplish in the infant of the first or second trimester some years from now one has every reason to be concerned as to what the geo-engineering of babies will mean to the sanctity of life.

From a more practical viewpoint the very low birth rate in some European countries means that they are no longer self-sustaining, and are already being forced to rely on a migrant workforce from other countries if they are to continue to function as viable nation's, growing their economies. Likewise health care services in many European countries are already dependent on Philippine, Indian and Asian migrant workers. Regardless of the abortion figures and pro-euthanasia activists' claims, it is not difficult to understand just how clearly Paul VI was trying to teach the real meaning of life to all mankind when he introduced his encyclical. The neo- feminist movements, the liberal groundswell and the secular lobbies all combined to make certain however it was never acceptable, and the Catholic teachers and preachers of the day lacked the skills and courage required to defend and promote it. The pope himself despondent and dejected, was crushed under the opposition of his own fellow bishops to Humanae Vitae. This encyclical, his eighth, also was his last. He wrote no further encyclicals and died ten years after its publication, a frail and broken man.

As is possible in many lives that there is no turning back. Yet it is also clear there may be no way forward either, the happiest outcome in this scenario is that the person simply retires. In the case where this is not possible a person may perhaps put aside some of the workload. Such is the beauty of the encyclical that it clarifies a firm instruction from the pontiff to his bishops around the world advising them of his views on a particular situation or topic instructing them to follow his lead. It is not Catholic doctrine, it is not dogmatic, it is not binding.

It is expected, however, that the bishops of the world would pay attention and listen to the words of their own bishop, the Bishop of Rome, and act accordingly. When it became evident that Pope Paul's encyclical was not being received and supported as he wished it to be, the authority of the Papal office was under serious attack. For a Pope of considerable strength and courage a summons to the Vatican issued to the most renegade group of bishops would have been the true and saintly way to have tackled the situation but sadly Paul VI having had the courage to publish his encyclical failed to insist on its message being fully delivered from the altar and his instructions being followed.

The pope unable to bear the strain to all intents and purposes eased himself into a de- facto abdication. The two-fold tsunami which resulted from this papal upheaval was that disobedience to the Holy Father's wishes was from then on quite possible and furthermore a new form of Protestant evangelicalism began to take place. What it meant was that a consensus of opinion by a number of bishops could hold sway and compete with that of the Holy Father. Today to accept authority, to willingly serve, to seek orders and put oneself in the service of God, can be a difficult path to choose. To pursue an alternative route to authority and look instead for 'fellowship' to promote the popular path of the evangelical Christian is today gaining more and more support. George Weigle, the Vatican affairs scholar, has termed the present Pope, Francis I as an Evangelical Catholic, a title which must be acknowledged as one of the latest and most radical of all of the Holy Father's titles. To try and make some sense of it, a comparative term 50 years ago would have been to describe someone as 'a white blackman'.

For many such reasons then, it is a struggle to evangelize in a true Catholic sense of the word, rather it is easier to join forces and run with the herd as opposed to staying on the pilgrim path, preaching the good news to all who are ready to hear it. Struggling to avoid the many potholes and sharp flints which distract one from looking very far ahead, it is also too easy to avoid giving anyone else a helping hand. Yet this is what we must do. Taking time off to do something good for others, whilst not expecting anything in return is, sadly a little far removed from today's code of living. Today we are inclined to pay as we play, to subscribe to a credit card form of Catholicism as we are usually too busy to engage with even next door neighbors. It also appears we just do not have the time for promoting or proposing any type of meaningful parish projects, so vital in making a neighbourhood a truly faithful community.

The reaction to such shortcomings is to reach into one's pocket or handbag and make a donation or contribution, to salve the conscience and make one feel that one has now done more than their bit. For those who choose this easy method and prefer not to actively participate or become involved, the role model they offer to their children is less than inspirational even when, or if, it is every recognized by members of the family. Young people today are not trapped in some Matrix-type world of cyber-space because that is what they know best, they are there because that is what they themselves choose to relate to. Unreality is a much more enjoyable zone to inhabit than reality and the prefered domain of all web surfers, bloggers and social media networkers. It is the environment and culture into which they were introduced and wish they freely choose to remain and believe in. To enlist them to follow Christ, and to take the hard road, to put others before themselves, to resist being led into the zombie state or slave trap seeking wealth, celebrity and glamour status would seem to be an insurmountable task; nevertheless it must be seen as one worthy of the 'challenge' and welcomed as such.

To gain an understanding or knowledge of the Catholic faith it is essential for any person who seeks to follow Christ to try to identify with Him. In doing so one must somehow attempt to both realize and accept the demands contained and outlined in the beautiful prayer of St Francis of Assisi;

> Lord, make me an instrument of Thy peace;
> Where there is hatred, let me sow love;
> Where there is injury, pardon:
> Where there is doubt, faith;
> Where there is despair, hope;

Where there is darkness, light; and
Where there is sadness, joy.
Oh Divine Master,
Grant that I may not so much seek
To be consoled as to console;
To be understood as to understand;
To be loved as to love;
For it is in giving that we receive;
It is in pardoning that we are pardoned;
It is in dying that we are born
to eternal life.

If another mystery of life is 'being there,' or 'luck of the draw,' or 'the right place at the right time,' then life's little more than a lottery. Everything is perchance, 'California dreaming'. The fact is, there is a much better way of running one's life. The reality that Jesus Christ is the Way, the Truth, and the Life, is the invitation one must seek to discover and accept. To realize this however, it must be presented in a more dynamic way in order to inspire the individual not only with a desire to obtain an intimate relationship with God but to see it as the greatest goal of all.

For it is in giving that we receive;
It is in pardoning that we are pardoned
It is in dying that we are born
To eternal life

***On August 12th 1977 one sunny summer morning the original free flight of the first Space Shuttle 'ENTERPRISE' took place. This event in itself was not ordinary nor was it extraordinary. The shuttle was launched from the back of a Boeing 747 in mid-flight and once released after five minutes and 21 seconds made a successful touchdown without power using the gliding technique it continued to utilize for the duration of its lengthy space career.

The event however did fire the imagination of millions worldwide and, like so many others who had witnessed the first moon landings, one awaited the ongoing developments of the NASA space programme with total excitement and admiration. Almost four years later on April 12th 1981 the reality of the dream was finally realized. The Shuttle 'COLUMBIA' was launched from Cape Kennedy to spend two days in space and return safely to Earth. For those who caught the moment in spaceflight history, the crucial-time frame of the space voyage was the 4 min. 52 secs period when 'COLUMBIA' was scheduled to effect its re-entry into the Earth's atmospheric field. During this tense period all communications between mission control and the shuttle would be temporarily cut off. The angle of re-entry had to be precise. No margin nor deviation could be possible, for until this white hot plasmatic space field was crossed, the flight controllers at the command center in Houston, Texas, could only hope and pray.

The 400 million dollar Shuttle had 32,000 hi-tech Teflon heat resistance carbon tiles designed to withstand a temperature of 2300 degrees Fahrenheit, (1510 degrees Centigrade), which would be fired up by the friction the Shuttle would generate entering the atmospheric field at 97,000 miles per hour. The necessity therefore of literally cutting a safe flight path through this space field of incredible temperatures in order to accomplish re-entry into the Earth's atmosphere was to be its only attempt. No amount of flight simulation, no models, no flight trials could guarantee the outcome of those 4.5 minutes. It was not only the NASA personnel and families who were praying, millions around the world glued to their television sets anxiously awaited for the moment radio contact with the craft would be re-established.

After four and a half agonizingly long minutes suddenly the crackling voice contact came through to rousing cheers of joy, happiness, and relief. Everyone relaxed. The whole family of man had somehow actually been there with these two astronauts. Fifty-four hours, twenty minutes and fifty two seconds after lift off, the shuttle 'COLUMBIA' touched down safely on runway 23 at Edwards Air Force Base in Southern California. Mission accomplished.

This first shuttle space flight and the first moon landing in 1969, were real frontier events; they were 'where were you when' moments, and they were ones which today seem unlikely to be equalled or surpassed. The first shuttle astronauts had ten years training for the flight. The planning, the design, the innovation, were all meticulous in detail; nothing was overlooked or omitted. The years of intense training, the time spent on each stage, the camaraderie amongst all those dedicated men and women makes one realize just what man is capable of achieving when driven by a common goal.

In fact, if one thinks in terms of the origins of the whole space programme one can discuss many aspects of it from different angles but, in the final analysis, the combination of effort and talents, dedication and desire, strength and resolve made it possible for man to achieve his sense of purpose. The photographed planet Earth as a beautiful blue orb suspended in space made everyone wonder at the glory of creation. As if for the first time Man was being introduced to Mother Earth in all her celestial beauty.***

In whatever way we may choose to throw portions of our life away, we do so for the reason that we fail to give it its rightful value, it's vital meaning, and its true importance. We fail to appreciate, to see, or to try and understand the reality we were each born to seek. This omega question that most people spend their entire lives seeking an answer to forever remains the same! Why was I born? It is without doubt the ultimate 'Why' question, and in its most simplistic format the Penny Catechism that served the Church so well for 200 years or so, supplied the answer;

> "God made us to know, love and serve Him here on Earth, and, by this means, to be happy with Him forever in Heaven."

This answer, and how each person responds to it, could be said to be the starting point of this book as one maneuvers one's life's purpose and progress in relation to seeking God through the Catholic faith. It is the assurance that life was given to each of us individually, a gift from God. We did not make our own life; only through our parents were we physically able to receive it. To grow as an infant through childhood necessitates all the help we are given, and which we in turn must receive and utilise. It is only then after puberty, adolescence and the teenage years are reached and when the maturity of young adulthood takes over that one can choose or not choose a deeper knowledge and and relationship with God. This dual omniscient relationship must be established; otherwise the lack of it distorts all other meaningful and intimate relationships. We are most likely to appreciate others as individuals only after we have first recognised them primarily as equal Sons and Daughters of God. The ideal of unification with God therefore rests within each of us; failure to achieve this realization leaves one incomplete. Life viewed in a casual careless way means the mistakes one makes eventually become so numerous that one ceases to care. For life to become self-centred and egoistic, unbridled ambition by its very nature will take control; once this occurs, the person abdicates his or her own personal spiritual integrity.

For those locked into a demanding career, a difficult marriage, experiencing a serious health problem or a poverty ghetto the appeal of escaping one way or another appears attractive. Crime, for example, for many may seem the only way out of a financial meltdown, yet all of these chances, dreams, and distortions are only illusions of lifestyles that must be recognized as totally at odds with our spiritual reality. This balance of existence between both a physical and spiritual plane is in itself hard enough to achieve, and even harder to maintain, yet it is essential for one to try. The inevitable result and consequences of not having this sense of balance is that one gets caught in a dysfunctional, inward, self-centred existence which is both harmful and dangerous and leads into all sorts of forbidden territories. Life, first and foremost, must therefore be seen and appreciated as a 'gift'. This fact is so important and essential that it cannot be overemphasized; it must be kept in a clear range of vision never to be clouded.

> "Before I formed thee in the bowels of thy mother I knew thee and before thou comest forth out of the womb, I sanctified thee, and made thee a prophet unto the nations." Jer. 1.5

The enormity of this truth is that it gives each single person a quiet confidence in believing in himself, his self-worth, and his self-value. It also places each person into a sibling relationship with one another, be that our neighbour, our colleague or our friend. In addition, it underwrites the relationship one should be seeking with God. The relationship of Father and son (or, Father and daughter) can provide us with great comfort in spite of perhaps a poor relationship with our earthly parents. The invitation of life established even before one's birth forces us to take a much more intensive high-definition view of our daily existence, and the daily contribution we make to God's plan. Travelling by train at high-speed through the countryside one is aware the whole time of covering quite a distance and even though one is not actually aware of all the houses and villages one may be passing the reality remains that the houses, people and lives one is passing by are being lived although at a different pace. Our lives are similar. We are part of communities, of work forces, of friends, of families. At whatever pace we may be moving or whatever direction we are taking, our world and our life includes all those we pass on the way.

Our view of Earth from the top of the highest mountain we know then pales in comparison to that witnessed by the astronauts Young and Crippen as they gazed at the planet Earth floating high in space above them. Similarly our meagre attempts to come to terms with and understand the magnitude of what our lives are capable of also almost totally escapes us. The sole individuality of one's life as created by God and brought into fruition through the co-operation and physical expression of one's natural parents should always be a constant in one's whole existence and the meaning we put into it. For those who may have difficulty in understanding how such a spiritual creation is possible one only has to consider the anticipation of grandparents awaiting the arrival of their first grandchild. The baby has yet to be born but the grandparent looks forward tremendously to the event as they have the experience of knowing what actually lies ahead. Whether the baby will have his father's mouth or his mother's chin, blue eyes or brown eyes are all questions yet to be answered but, inevitably, they are no more than blanks waiting to be filled in. For God every baby is an image of his creation waiting to materialize. It may well be each infant represents a vote of confidence that God has placed in mankind and the mission that that person performs is confirmation of it. The awful reality now has established that wholesale contraception is such an 'acceptable' fact in modern life, and used so frequently both within and without marriage means that the infant planned in the mind of God is not allowed to materialise. Those fortunate enough to have safely entered this world can feel most blessed from the onset to have 'made it' and are now an integral part of the family of mankind.

Comparing this view of life to that of the actual mission undertaken by an astronaut makes for a very fascinating and challenging analogy. What if, in addition to our physical journey through life, we are also undertaking in tandem a spiritual shuttle hurtling through a parallel universe? On the day of our death we will have to accomplish our own individual spiritual Re-Entry. How well prepared we may be for such an eventuality will be the apogee of our mission. To try and comprehend the reality of the mission, the planning stage can be seen as the pre-birth, the pregnancy, the launch mode, the time awaiting the infant and juvenile years. The birth itself then becomes the lift-off and the space mission one's life. The fourth quarter of life, would be the preparation for Re-Entry, death itself the actual intense heat field, and one's re-entry would be, on a successful landing, an entry into God's Eternal Kingdom.

If this analogy is sustainable than the questions asked by every young person, 'What's it all about?' and 'What difference does it make?'are not only addressed but answered now in detail, in a most understandable and unique way!

Once we begin to turn our mind into this very specific train of thought, it is not only evident to see just what is at stake, but it is also possible to see what the stakes actually are. Likewise it is necessary to make new appraisals and take stock of the situation. A firm control must be exercised and some serious living may have to be contemplated to replace what has, up to now, been a fairly slack or lax regime. Most importantly, the voyage one is currently on may have to be re-routed or a new flight plan lodged if there is going to be any degree of revamped mission successfully accomplished. Until such appraisals are made it is hard to know where one really exists and in what condition one is in. Regardless of the life one has been living until now, regardless of what has already been achieved, little matters unless the landing is successful. Should this fail to happen, losing contact with ground control on re-entry would leave the craft listed as either missing in action, or destroyed.

The mystery of life is one that has a far more profound or significant depth of meaning than its genetic ramification. The fact is as children of God we are given the moment we were formed at conception and it complements the very start of our existence, when we were each individually known to God prior to even our pre-birth stage

> "Do not be afraid – I will save you, I have called you by name – you are mine." Is 43.1

This is the gift of 'Salvation' obtained for each of us by the Life, Death and Resurrection of Our Lord, Jesus Christ. Our life was gifted to us as is our eternity regardless of whether or not we are prepared to receive it. Our lives moving within the rhythm and motion of the universe will be lived as each of us chooses in either a good state or a bad state. The doctrine of the Catholic church teaches that on passing through the door of death our life on Earth ceases and our eternal life begins. For this to happen, judgement awaits each single person. The life that has ceased gave, to those, who sought God the opportunity to follow Him up-close or from afar. Those who were indifferent or chose to ignore Him or disregarded Him will also be asked to account for their life's work.

The period of God's love and mercy freely available 24/7 while one was alive on earth after death no longer exists. Judgement now replaces it and those who have tried in even the smallest degree to do their childlike best will, be seen as such, while those who hardened their hearts into stone will realise the enormity of their transgressions and the price they now are destined to pay. This teaching, along with all the other teachings each person receiving the sacrament of baptism is obliged to seriously seek is an obligation which must not be ignored. To do so is in itself a grievous transgression to be avoided. Catholic doctrine is there for one's spiritual growth and protection. One is seriously obliged to seek out the truth it offers and having pursued it then one must try to live by it.

This lifestyle choice is the challenge one faces so that one can participate in the fulfilment and completion of one's own individual contribution to God's creation.This invitation to each of us as sons and daughters of God can only be seen once it is appreciated as such, for it has been given in love and must be returned in the same way. Our life comes to us as a 'gift' with total freedom of choice. It is unlikely that anybody in a pre-birth situation, given the opportunity to reject their opportunity to 'life,' would choose to do so. This must be assumed regardless of how horrible or terrible the life ahead maybe. Years later if the life proves to be too difficult to cope with, if all hope is crushed and if despair becomes too much to bear, it is possible that some may choose to throw back the gift of life as being totally worthless. Should this terrible, sinful act be committed, it may however be that it was the misuse rather than the use of it which was the reason. For any life to be rejected however the sadness of the act strikes God its Maker more than can ever be imagined. It is certain He will take all the mitigating circumstances into account should this be the case, yet even in human terms a gift returned or wilfully broken is usually beyond repair. Salvation on the other hand is the culmination of ultimate mutual love, and may be seen as such. How we seek to accept it is the choice each person must make and by doing so one will move closer to, or further away from God. Salvation is the invitation given to each person by God whether it is actually opened and accepted or thrown away unopened into the trash bin. This is the real choice that each person has to make. This then is also the frequently stressed 'what' in the question, 'What difference does it make?'

In space terms the significance of salvation also has a more structured or dominant role. The reason for this is that the final stage of the mission is always controlled by NASA, and the decision to end, alter, terminate, conclude, abort or extend the mission remains in the controller's province and power. It is never the pilot's and it is this one unknown single factor which the pilot must always be ready to react to. Our lives on 'lift off' give us the necessary tools, skills, and abilities to have a successful mission, but should we wander too far, get involved in negative actions or activities, behave in detrimental ways, our recall command may well catch us unawares. If that were to happen one could suddenly find oneself totally unprepared for the immediate action required and so have to risk a dangerous re-entry procedure under very adverse conditions. Our own personal lives we know end in death but when, where or how mostly remains unknown. The need to be always ready must therefore constantly be in our minds as without it one's safe re-entry may not be guaranteed and a successful touch-down or landing cannot be assured.

How can one identify with such space terminology regarding our own odyssey when one must finally admit that he/she is well and truly lost? This is the awkward question that has got to be addressed, and like many questions, many answers tend to present themselves. Picking the right one that offers the best solution is the first step to success. For sailors, airmen, experienced hill walkers, and a host of other adventurers the possibilities of losing themselves in various situations is not uncommon. For any stranger in a big city the 'where am I' experience is a common 'shock moment' which occurs in an instant. One's spiritual awareness is no different, and if we allow it to be unused then we even fail to realize that we are where we are, stranded, going totally nowhere. For a pilot to be lost in deep space, the need to acquire coordinates, to hook into a navigational system, to re-establish some form of communications with another spacecraft or command base is vital. Until this is done there is no hope of any re-alignment or possibility of plotting a course in order to get back into mission status. What must be avoided at all costs is getting lost even further, getting into deeper trouble leading into more intense danger.

As Catholics there are many strata in our lives that overlay and interlink both within ourselves, our immediate families and others. To try and get an actual 'fix' on 'where one stands' is also multi problematic. This has got to be so because one's early childhood, one's parents, one's school, one's relationships the events one chooses to highlight and even those one may try to forget are all factored into the equation. Indeed, to ascertain how one has arrived where one is, let alone where one intended going, is difficult to achieve. The early goals one had planned to reach have by now been altered so many times that the necessity to identify new goals is now a major chore. It is at this juncture one should become aware of the need for help. Once one begins to sense spiritually that unless a lifeline is secured, one may get drawn ever closer towards a Black Hole from which there may be little or indeed any chance of escape, the need to alter one's course becomes imperative. How then can one find a terrestrial compass point or coordinates that are so desperately needed? How can one re-fire an engine that has been dormant for such a long time in order to bring one's self back to the real meaning of life? This surely is the first step towards the giant leap to be made.

CHAPTER

2

For non-practising Catholics their dissatisfaction with religion can only be addressed if it can be brought into focus: a clarification of doubt, leading to an acceptable plateau for discussion that must be crossed in order to reach the far side. Unless this chasm is addressed and resolved the non-practising Catholic remains trapped in a spiritual abyss, destined to remain divorced from their church with no way of regaining the trust lost in their faith.

The need for the renewal of religion in one's life begins with identifying the very kernel of the scepticism that invaded their faith in the first place. For very many people, some proud, some arrogant, some simply foolish, the mantra 'I will not serve' is the inevitable rock on which they find themselves stranded, and from which there is no hope of escape. It is hard to talk in terms of faith, grace and sacrifice to those who not only lack knowledge, but even more so to lack any genuine interest in attempting to acquire some understanding of basic Catholic doctrine.

Over the latter half of the twentieth century, the Catholic Church allowed herself to be bullied, intimidated and misrepresented to such an extent that she ceased to ignite or inspire the hearts of those she sought most to inflame. Her post-Vatican II presentations lacked any cutting edge theologies, and without a confidence in Catholic teaching or any spiritual realism, the young people drifted away from the church in every increasing numbers.

As the hierarchy in many western countries began to water down the hard truths and doctrines of the Church with a tepid liturgy, the stream became a river until what can only be described as a major exodus took place. There is little doubt remaining that since classical Catholic theology formulated by the Magisterium of the Church was set aside, the new, revised liturgy has failed dismally to produce the awakening of the new dawn promised by Vatican II. New teaching methods and modern progressive texts introduced and fostered by forward seeking catechists has altered downward the minds and hearts of millions. The formerly solid religious knowledge accepted by the laity over many previous generations has become a thing of the past.

After the Council, a new mentality or neo mindset spread an almost totally revamped religious instruction package, loaded with opinions and formulae that were so bland they gave little, and demanded even less, in return. The effect of dispensing such lacklustre information was those who received it were neither evangelised nor fervent in their spiritual lives. In fact the religious instruction knowledge dispersed over the past few decades has been of such poor quality that the reduction in vocations was inevitable. Still little was done to diagnose the cause of the almost total collapse which has occurred in the western world. Because of this 'bury one's head in the sand' dynamic, the Catholic Church has not received the love she so badly needs from her children. The love that invigorates and motivates the pastors of quality and courage she so badly requires today in order to spread the Gospel.

During the last three or four decades of the last century countless peripheral and dubious teachers have contaminated the singular purity of Catholic faith. They failed badly in their attempts to transfer quality religious knowledge. The modern methods broadened erroneous horizons resulted in the confused mentality prevalent today among so many Catholics. This appalling and ineffective transfer of Catholic doctrine by those in authority has been responsible for so many young people rejecting, out of hand, the core beliefs of Catholicism. This indifference to the faith so much in evidence today, reflects the most juvenile level of rebellion, one which avoids accepting the more positive challenge, that of seeking for themselves and reaching spiritually upward to grasp in both hands the authority of truth.

Due to the major changes made by those in the highest authority the continuity or quality of 'deep faith' being transferred from one generation to the next is destined therefore to become almost a thing of the past. The study of apologetics, for so long a cornerstone in the fundamental teaching of Catholicism, was almost totally pushed aside, and the loss of such a serious topic spiritually endangering the lives of countless Catholics the world over.

The spiritual requirements and knowledge needed in today's world have been so badly taught and presented by those entrusted with the task, that a large percentage of the laity now appears to believe that one's social responsibilities should somehow take precedence over one's spiritual obligations. This modern identity of being a good Christian has somehow superseded the identity of being a good Catholic, thereby making the latter role somehow obsolete.

The shuttle analogy leaves one in no doubt that it is only the most comprehensive navigational space manual that will help a lost space pilot to reset or re-position his stranded shuttle, if he has any chance of survival.

So it is with today's lost Catholics and their need to know what the true 'deposit of faith' means if they are to regain their original mission status. The life they were born into was not haphazard or random. It was chosen by God to be as fully realized in their physical existence as possible. Each person was individually picked to undertake his or her particular role. It is this crucial bit of knowledge, denied to so many young people today, that could indeed enable those who have gone missing to recommence the journey that they alone were chosen to accomplish. This simple reality, unless emphasized and explained, is all too easily lost over time and the quest to secure the glory reserved for them in Heaven, is never undertaken.

The early signs of difficulties in life can easily be ignored or disregarded. Why fix anything if one can get by without doing so or if one can deny the damage exists in the first place? Without the correct administration of obedience that served the child well during his formative years, the teenager, upon reaching the rebel years, now feels entitled to identify any assertion of control as an intrusion into his or her private life. A confrontation with any authority, school, parents or family hierarchy is normally staged before any further advance is made. Few avoid the turbulent transition from these late teenage years and into the twenties, and so learning by experience instead replaces the college routine with a much more radical and individual way of managing one's life. How one handles these tempestuous years very much depends on the discipline one was exposed to at each stage of one's previous levels of life.

For far too many, the primary faith into which they were introduced was never developed into a more adult and spiritual level that would deepen the meaning of their faith as they progressed in years. The adolescent state of faith they reached was no more than that of a seed in a seed tray which fails to germinate and reach its continuous growth pattern. For many young adults, the Sunday ritual of going to Mass is all too often motivated by a sense of compliance rather than a sense of conviction and gratitude for the privilege of being called upon to attend.

Unlike the pilot in charge of his Shuttle, the need for the young person to conference call or link in with his Commander under whose patronage he is obliged to serve, is neither appreciated nor understood. Upon reaching a higher altitude or some other training standard away from familiar surroundings, the Sunday ritual becomes more and more meaningless until it ceases altogether to fulfil its spiritual purpose. At this stage of independence, of flying free, the 'break away' from mission control becomes almost total; and although it appears as a sense of total freedom, there remains an in-built safety system or encrypted chip designed to protect the pilot. This fail-safe device activates and becomes operational when the morality of conscience is over-ridden by actions, thoughts and deeds which are detrimental to one's soul, and one's immediate society.

The pursuit of pleasure is a path of illusion, just as the road to fame, riches and fortune, tantalizing as it may appear, reflects nothing more than a deceitful mirage of an oasis in the mists of a barren hot desert landscape. The great desires of youth, so potent and powerful, are comparable to such an illusion yet seldom are they recognized as such, let alone, for what they actually are. The preoccupation with and the pursuit of temporal pleasures are only achieved at the expense of ignoring the early warning system and built-in interior voice of conscience that was designed to save one from serious spiritual danger. Once the red light begins to glow in the cockpit the control systems activate and hard decisions must be made. It would be a tremendous design flaw if one were able to override an entire back-up safety system by putting it on hold or ignoring it completely. In order to become more and more involved with materialism and one's own self, one has to commit to a degree of selfishness that will only lead further and further into a mean and cruel lifestyle.

This shallow or shadow existence is the opposite of a Christian life, yet for many it is now the accepted or preferred choice. To develop the spiritual capacity, one needs to share, one needs to love, one needs to belong and one needs to become for others a refuge of hope. Otherwise the self takes control and puts more and more distance between it and others until such vast amounts of space and time exist and the very idea of a Catholic life is almost obliterated. This space canyon of immense magnitude must be re-crossed eventually before one can hope to be re-commissioned. Until one finally acknowledges this basic truth one is truly lost and these futile wanderings continue.

It is only after an intense search to find where a point of light crystallizes that the realisation one can begin to hope again can be established. This realization does not come easy. Those who sense immediate danger may find that awareness will bring them into line:- to those who choose to pause once the red lights go on in the cockpit, will find their flight plan revised or updated: but those who freely choose to take the alternate or negative action will enter into a new arena, a galaxy of both unknown and unfathomable dimensions, in which they may certainly experience the real meaning of pain.

The choice of materialism over spiritualism is of course never quite appreciated for what it is:- a lifelong maze of choices manifesting itself in a lifestyle of meetings and junctions that in turn lead into fruitless and endless intersections. How could it be otherwise, given the perpetual lack of awareness in the spiritual lives of today's young Catholics? The concept of a most close and intimate personal mission is vague at best as one's spiritual life is far too often treated as an enigma.

The distortion today by some Church leaders of ecumenism has prompted the most naive and foolish to accept it as a blanket, a quilt that covers all churches making them somehow equal. The most acceptable or perhaps palatable package by which ecumenism can be promoted or presented as acceptable to most Sunday Mass going Catholics is for them to believe that it's best and right and good that all Christians should agree on the commonly held beliefs and 'park' any items or truths which are not agreeable.

This overall customizing, this uniformity through diversity sadly does not nor cannot work unless truths are exchanged for half truths and concessions are made contrary to some of the very core beliefs of Catholicism. Hopefully this will never be the case as it is only where truth exists that all can be one. Just as it is true that in faithfulness we flourish. To trade genuine truth for quasi truth makes no sense, regardless of how well marketed the reproduction is. The inevitable outcome of such trading can only lead to a disingenuous, distorted group of articles not based on faith at all but on a fabrication of truth and an aberration of the original content.

In the overall attractiveness of a false ecumenism, the believer chooses to see a totality of everything good overcoming everything bad. All will become equal and ultimately true in itself, as God is love and so all must be saved. This God of Love becomes the God of Man, and the God of Mercy and Justice becomes obsolete. For Catholics who not only recite the Nicene Creed, but understand and embrace it, such can never be the case. The Creed can leave no Catholic in any doubt that 'He will come again in glory to judge both the living and the dead, and His Kingdom will have no end'. What more faith than that need one have?

Accepting or promoting an indifference to the faith, lacking in love, and through a life of on- going carelessness, one can sideline and exclude God from more and more of one's life until one's spiritual mission is eventually just abandoned. When this juncture is reached, one has decided, consciously or not to focus only on the temporal pleasures life has to offer. This choice of a comfort-driven Catholicity where chequebook participation is preferred to actual real participation is now almost entirely centred on a 'gated global community' mentality in which the inhabitant believes the security badged personnel are there to act as well paid friends and supporters.

One may very well live one's entire adult life on such a temporal level unless one is blessed enough to be rescued by someone who cares enough to save them. Also, one needs to understand what is at stake when choosing to live in this material world taking whatever pleasures one can. Should one follow such a route, it then leaves one totally removed from the protection of one's command structure and eventually must almost checkmate one into a frozen state of compliance. The person who has led the life of total self-satisfaction eventually is trapped within it, jaded and bored but unable to escape. There is nothing new to experience: all the pleasures of life have been savoured to their limit and with no intimate family or friends a fear of the nothingness that lies ahead begins to grow.

It is this age-old process of hanging out, of losing one's self in an ever-revolving circular doorway serving as both entrance and exit as the speed increases, it seems to entice one to push harder all the time, going around faster and faster, where paradoxically one is going absolutely nowhere at all.

There are moments and moods in life when the sun suddenly disappears behind the clouds and one doubts that it will reappear again. No matter how hard one tries it always appears impossible to imagine it ever re-emerging. Should friends give assurances that it is only a passing phase, the effort to believe it will return requires a degree of faith. In the major Greek, Celtic and Shakespearean tragedies, the broken heart, the unrequited love, the forced separation allows the lover to eulogize the pain of parting, the division, the loneliness and the total uncertainty of what lies ahead. These mirrored reflections all mask deep hidden truths. Our spiritual identity, gained at Baptism, is also similarly affected. Once a soul breaks away from God there is a different consciousness, a void left behind causing it to move further and further away from Him. This lingering anti-consciousness or sense of rejection lessens over a period until eventually the original sense of loss is creating for itself a land forever overshadowed by cloud without even the memory of a bright and brilliant sun.

Arriving at this stage one may be beyond spiritual awareness experiencing a reverse spiritual metamorphosis that produces a deadly blemish rather than a nourishing bloom. The blemish then becomes a growth causing as much danger to the soul as an HIV infection does to a healthy body. This spiritual wasteland that the soul now inhabits when the umbilical spiritual cord is severed is impossible to fathom and remains the destination of those whose missions are in serious jeopardy.

In order to find oneself, the Gospel teaches that one must first lose oneself. On the surface this simple sounding instruction seems hard to understand, let alone accept. To come to terms with the concept one must recognize that one is always more or less complete as one person. Over time one may have picked up appendages or add-ons that cause one to be untrue to oneself; these aberrations must be discarded if one is to return to one's core self. Likewise, if one has become a lesser person for many reasons than that person must also be relinquished. In a functioning sense the feeling of incompleteness registers in one's consciousness. It is difficult, if not impossible, to remember an answer once the question has been forgotten, yet that is exactly what happens at some poignant or deep moment when one is quietly overcome with emotion. Happiness at a wedding, the deep sorrow expressed at a funeral, the tremendous joy of a christening or at the simple arrival of a friend at the airport, enables the sun to suddenly burst forth once more, as if from nowhere, instantaneously spreading light, warmth and joy. This flash feeling of finding oneself somehow alive again, without knowing how or why, just happens, and by casting off the negative alter ego, the moment can without doubt be life changing.

In response to the intellect's demand for answers many rational and intellectual driven reasons can be considered, yet without the acknowledgement of these questions, gaps, doubts and a sense of remote dissatisfaction often remains. This is because one is beginning in a most vague way to suspect there must be a truth somewhere, and even when it is still somewhat hidden or distant the need or urge to discover the sense of its existence remains. This quest for knowledge may be triggered in many different ways. It demands attention, yet only through the efforts of prayer, fasting and a genuine longing to seek God can one hope for such guidance and strength to resuscitate the lost or wandering soul. This discipline however harsh is the discipline required to set aside one's false self and find one's true self. As the Gospel explains, the loving grace of God can and will enter into the most dehydrated and worn out souls.

Grace is the central 'Key' to Catholic, universal faith. It is the central truth of Catholicism, the mystery of all spiritual life. Grace is the sacredness of the Holy Spirit given to each follower of Christ through prayer and the sacraments. Our spiritual desire and need for grace can be no more adequately described than that of one's need for water. How great can one's thirst be for a crystal clear well? There can be few who having witnessed a great hardship at close quarters have not murmured beneath their breath, 'There but for the grace of God, go I'. Whether it is by instinct or intuition that one murmurs this prayer, it is instinctively made for having been spared some terrible misfortune and so is said automatically. What is more important to realize is that it is always said in thankfulness that one is not facing the severe test confronting another. Known or unknown, it is only the grace of God that sustains every person in their greatest crisis.

To identify grace as the key, it is necessary to understand what it is. To condense the writings on grace into a simple definition, one would have to see grace as a means of being able to perform goodness in its actual realization, and then witness the wonderful result in what has been realized. The stabilization of a morphine laden injection that is shot into a vein of a person close to death by a paramedic at a crash site is the physical equivalent. For a parent to pray that their son or daughter will not end up on the wrong side of town late at night and commit grievous sin is that cry for grace. Once heard and freely given the young person may meet by 'sheer chance' another acquaintance and go off in a different harmless direction.

Simplified, the more one can access grace through prayer the greater one's contribution to God's kingdom can be. Once one begins to understand the implications this message has the more one can seriously thirst for grace as it is only by its power that one is able to seek and play an active positive role doing God's loving will. This longing for grace must be with a passion, as it is given, on demand, to those who seek it most. Once obtained, it will then be for the person to make as much use of it as they can, sharing it with others as one delves deeper and deeper into the beauty and meaning of truth. To begin a search for grace there is no better way than by asking for the grace to 'believe in grace'.

The Athanasian Creed, The Apostles Creed and The Nicene Creed are three 'declarations of Faith' which reveal the Trinity of God. These creeds as factual and beautiful prayers recited daily in many monasteries worldwide and are the true declaration of one's faith and what one hopes to enjoy in 'the life of the world to come'. It is this universal and singular central belief system on which the Holy Roman Catholic Church was founded and entrusted to Peter, the first Pope. By this commission given by Christ the individual Pope takes command of the Catholic Church and exercises his full spiritual authority. Just as there can only be one true God, there can only be one true Church and one true doctrine which teaches that to achieve eternal salvation it is necessary for man to reach God through His Church. The Creed outlines the Faith, the Sacraments deliver the Grace.

The need for grace is as vital for the soul as fuel is for the space vehicle, for without it one can go nowhere except drift aimlessly along only to be drawn into whatever sphere or field of gravity one may happen to enter. Once one begins to fuel up one's rockets, one can begin to feel what it is like to once more know where one is going. This advent or renewal period that for so long may have seemed impossible to experience, gives one time to make preparations: the opportunity to check all items are on-board to ensure that re-igniting procedure will be successful and a perfect re-launch will take place. Most important of all is the need to apply for and obtain a new flight plan from mission control with whom for so long one has been posted as 'missing'.

The grace one is now seeking is so powerful it exudes through the person radiating a glow or spiritual power seldom visible to others. How this in itself is possible is not relevant yet 'grace' primarily does 'occupy' oneself. It gives one hope, it makes one dispense charity, and above all it allows one, in some peculiar way, to reflect in a minute sense the power of God's love. It is this hidden quality of holiness which others experience that surrounds such persons making them somehow different. This difference, this saint-like quality or potential is in each person yet few ever discover it. To achieve this level of spirituality is remarkable and rare, but It can also be accepted as a further challenge facing those returning to the church, newly baptised converts and all seeking to act according to God's will. It is only in possessing it does one open and expand one's spiritual antennae ever wider reflecting more and more of God's love. In seeking to attain such a high level of devotion through prayer and fasting, the desire to incorporate one's individual will with that of God's grows continuously.

When such a will becomes perfectly pure and sanctified in union with God, it achieves sainthood while still on earth. This sought after intimacy and one's efforts to reach out further, are therefore both loved and reciprocated by God. Just as a child beside the father pushes against an open door, we also in the smallest of ways, get to be united in God's plan for mankind. It is this harmony, this unity within unity, however minuscule, that one can almost sense when filled with sanctifying grace. It is here that the soul momentarily reposes as part of the kingdom, and part of the kingdom in return rests within the soul. It is a mystery of infinite meditation how this kernel of faith can be contemplated, yet it can only make sense in so far as we are a millionth part of the most beautiful garden ever brought into existence.

In this sense, just as the tiniest petal on the smallest flower is somehow part of the whole, so also each of us is part of God's kingdom. If one could imagine oneself each day working in God's garden, forever tending, cultivating, sowing, planting, adding more and more beauty to its creation, one would still be far short of a meaningful metaphor, yet the image is one of comfort. It is in a quiet corner in the garden of one's soul that one can always find God's grace and peace.

Understanding then that grace is vital for one's spiritual existence and life mission, the priority one places on it cannot be over-exaggerated. One of the many valleys of life however is the gap between knowledge and wisdom. Knowledge may give one the answer one seeks, but unless one has the wisdom to put it to good use, it must remain under- utilised. Saint Augustine of Hippo is reputed to have prayed,

"O God, grant me grace to persevere, but not just yet."

Knowledge then or the fear of knowledge, which is indeed referred to in the Gospel as 'the beginning of all wisdom' is the reference point from which one must begin to begin.

Once we accept the analogy of the drifting spacecraft lost in space, the need for it to obtain some signals can be compared to that of the lost soul in need of grace. As the spacecraft drifts aimlessly in the vastness of space so also does the soul hover in trepidation knowing that it is lost, and seriously lost. Space in its multitude of emptiness defies what the mind can comprehend. It is vital that some communication, even the very faintest flicker of a radio signal, reaches the stranded spacecraft, yet in spiritual terms how greater and more urgent is the need for the grace of God to reach the lost soul.

To look for a deeper understanding of grace, what it means, and how it can be obtained must be of more intense significance than one can fully understand. Saints undoubtedly achieve not just the knowledge of grace, but also the desire, determination and unceasing passion to grow within it.

For them it is no different than the oxygen their bodies require. The lost traveller in the precarious position of being barely alive, yet emitting no more than the minutest signal, is similar to that of the candle flame in the darkest vault, attracting the all-embracing attention of God's love. Its existence alone no darkness can quench and, no matter how hard it is for the lost person fighting the darkness, grace forever proves the reality of life and confirms the belief in hope.

How then can the beleaguered pilot and the seriousness of his stalled mission be spiritually addressed? On reflection, one must first admit that in addition to being lost, in need of fuel and life supporting supplies, no contact with ground control or the Supreme Commander, one could hardly be in a more precarious position. This realization without any reservation and sense of loss promotes a deep unease but it is still an unease that is manageable and not one yet moving into the realm of terror. The need to find some meaning is now crucial but one is left with a sense of, where can one actually look to find it?

As in all earthly matters temporal and spiritual, one has to evaluate, decide and implement whatever decisions are made. Old ways, bad habits, false friends and all other danger areas must be identified and set aside. Choices must be made and decisions have to be taken. The availability of grace is clearly flagged. All that is required is a cry for help but the decision to do so must be made. For some this simple message maybe clear for others complicated, yet for all who seek it, prayers will be answered.

This is the true beginning, realizing one is devoid of grace and the desire to seek it as a vital priority must be undertaken. This truth, however painful is a tremendous truth as once it is understood it opens up a whole new pathway, completely blocked off uptil now. As a truth it cannot be rejected and sent back, like any knowledge acquired it is almost impossible to un-acquire it. In the spiritual realm there is no middle path, no neutral ground. No viewing stand exists from which one can take an overview or academic interest in God's creation. Those who are not committed to the service of God are dictated by their own choice and freewill to working against Him. The saying that "all roads lead to Rome" was for very many centuries an extremely accurate adage as Rome was indeed the center of the civilized world and all roads did lead there. In God's creation a similar adage exists for one is forever travelling towards God or else moving away further and further away.

Just as the love and grace of God brings warmth to and comfort to those who are moving towards Him, the opposite is also true. Where warmth fosters love, coldness signifies hatred.

The coldness and the hatred of the fallen archangel Lucifer known as Satan brings nothing but abject shame, misery and pain to all who travel in his domain. This is the terrible decision which at some stage in one's life which one must inevitably make. Whether it is taken with an informed or misinformed mind, in the fullness of day or the darkest of nights, it is one that cannot be avoided. It is a decision far too often made by those who are completely unaware of what they are committing to and will remain with them not just for their earthly life but for all eternity.

When the words, message, fuel, grace, signal, knowledge finally occur, the overlapping confusion and likelihood of misinterpretation is not only possible but indeed almost inevitable. Words are like components, or infants coloured building blocks insofar as they are only of use if placed in the right order. In the wrong sequence or context they are almost meaningless.

In the case of the lost spaceship it is of some help to focus on the image of the temporal life as that of the spacecraft. The pilot in charge of the vehicle has got both physical and spiritual elements within him and combined they are vital for survival. Without unification the ability to pray is limited and so is access to clean fuel. Once this is realized the natural course is to do the utmost to keep open communication at all times.

This is the reason God's response to our prayers is dispensed, bestowed and channelled through the seven sacraments, Baptism, Confirmation, Holy Eucharist, Penance, Extreme Unction, Holy Orders, and Matrimony. Offered constantly throughout one's life mission this is the open invitation for one to put aside material concerns and focus instead on following God. It is through His Bride, His Catholic Church that the way exists, yet currently it is for so many the road less travelled. Today many claim that they know God and are on the best possible terms with Him, while at the same time ignoring and bad-mouthing His bride. How this can make sense or in any way be reconcilable with a genuine love of God makes no sense. If prayer is not presented or offered by active members of the church then the sacraments are inaccessible, and so God's love also remains inaccessible.

The Italian priest saint, St Padre Pio, simplified the message in stark and vivid terms:

> "Who prays much is saved
> Who prays little is in danger
> Who does not pray at all, is damned."

The need for fuel therefore is not optional. For people who seek to perform their mission claiming all fuels are the same is ridiculous and so for those who do not care enough to examine what they are using the results may be disastrous. If this is the case and one seeks to be fuelled from an unknown source they must be prepared to accept the consequences. It is one's own choice, freely made, but a choice with dire results, and made without even discovering the price of the alternative fuel. The depth of knowledge or understanding one receives by taking on fuel or grace from one's own command structure gives one on-going unification with one's own space fleet comprising a host of other pilots each on different missions for the same supreme commander giving great solidarity to the overall master plan.

In contrast the information or indoctrination that one receives from accepting fuel from the alternative source places one in a totally different position under the control of another structure whose commander's energy is based on pure evil. This disgraced archangel or commander known as Satan thereby gains another pilot who from that moment on is chained to an acceptance and a contract to carry out orders as part payment for the fuel. Only the search for the right signal will lead one into pure spiritual grace, essential truths and realities. This is the grace that must first be realised and obtained to enable one to meet one's crucial needs and for the mission that lies ahead.

To use another metaphor that of the man dying of thirst who somehow manages with a final effort to stumble to a well, it is crucial he only begins to drink in small quantities. The desire and need for grace is as urgent for the soul as water is for the body. Grace, the supernatural gift from God, forever given freely to those who seek it enables those who receive it to achieve salvation. Both its sanctifying and actual forms are essential because without them as fuel for the soul, the mission cannot be completed.

It is also essential that the vehicle itself is ready to receive and retain fuel as there is little reason in having it pumped on-board if conditions could cause it to leak, evaporate, or burn off. To prevent this from happening, it is again necessary to make certain that the fuel tanks can absorb the tremendous pressure as the fuel is pumped on-board and the gauge rises. After one has been given the all clear, and sufficient fuel is loaded, only then does one get the order to lift-off. It is the amalgamation of both the fuel and orders the pilot receives that allows him to proceed again and re-establish the spacecraft's true course.

Knowing where one is destined for tends to reveal the 'reality of meaning,' and brings the pilot back into a fully operational mode. Most pilots receive instructions and for those seeking to be re-commissioned as active participating members of the Church it is no different. Once one fulfils the necessary application to have one's orders re-issued and updated the call-up will be issued and the horror of being left stranded in space will be over.

Trying to know God today is the same as trying to know God as 'infinite', He must, being God surpass our intellect in every way, direction, and from every angle. The route and only route map we have been given to follow Him is contained in the Gospel, the path and life of Christ. It is only through the imitation of the Life and Love of Christ that one can hope to begin to get to know, love and serve Him. Only in this way in the fullness of time can one grow nearer to God to love Him. For one cannot love what one does not know, and the mission one undertakes is forever a mission grounded in love. At this level of spiritual realization it becomes clear that the knowledge of God and the love of God must be one and the same thing.

To know God must, as already stated, come first. Since time immemorial this is the most essential point, easy enough for even a child to seek and accept yet for far too many today it is almost incomprehensible and way beyond their reach. How this can be is in itself a mystery as it was this good news, this Gospel, that was lived and drawn up by the Church for all followers of Christ to share. First we must get to know God, secondly we must begin to love God and thirdly we must start to serve God.

Christ as God the Son, made Man, by his Life, Passion, Death and Resurrection is presented to us through the Catholic Church, as the Way, the Truth and the Life. It is this gift of faith one receives at Baptism that allows us the incredible privilege of being granted the individual right to have an intimacy with God. This sacrament enrolls and entitles us to be as 'Children of God' and as such from that moment bestows on each baptized person all the advantages of family within which one is entitled to grow and be nourished, loved and fulfilled in the Grace of God.

Once we have been instructed and are prepared to fulfill our own personal role, we are than given the sacrament of Confirmation. This in turn leads us onto our commission, our invitation to shoulder our load, accept our duty and perform it to the best of our abilities. This commissioning is for each one of us no more than the role the single pebble plays on the seashore beside a vast ocean. A role of almost nothingness while at the same time greatness individually adding our humble efforts to God's majestic overall plan of galactic proportions covering the entire universe. The part one plays is played by each one of us and is ours alone, God's gift to you was life, your life to do with as you alone must choose. The freedom of choice remains with you. It is this discovery and depth of knowledge that gives you the realization of why your salvation and the salvation of all those lives you touch is so central and vital to your mission. The challenge is to live the faith now that only you have been given.

Before moving forward into this field of thought a word of warning must prevail, and that word is caution. To know what is right may be common knowledge but to accomplish right by actually converting thoughts into action can be tremendously difficult. The temptation to resist doing good can be presented by Satan in such an attractive manner that the visit to a nursing home to see someone special is forever delayed or put on hold. The job advertisement that may appear in some newspaper but is never passed on to the person who could use it, is never done, the moment to say to someone that one has truly hurt, 'I am so sorry' is suppressed and lost forever, are all examples which clearly indicate the inherent weakness and sinfulness that somehow inhabits the heart of man.

The one part of the equation which is missing, lost or disregarded in what earlier was referred to as the collection of building blocks in different shapes and sizes is, 'grace' and it is only grace which gives one the courage needed to convert the desire to do good into the reality of doing good. The quest then turns as to how and where one may obtain this wonderful and marvellous gift of grace from God.

In trying to come to terms with grace, it is necessary to quantify the urge felt by those who seek it. There are numerous well-documented accounts regarding the conversion of atheists and agnostics who found their salvation in the Roman Catholic Church. Starting with Saul on the road to Damascus through to Augustine of Hippo, and followed by a whole litany from every spectrum of society, the Path to Rome was and is still sought and found by many. One of the most interesting and intellectual groups attracted to the Catholic Church early in the last century was a generation or two of English university graduates referred to as The Oxford Movement. These artistic and literary young people had the urge to strive hard to seek the Catholic faith, but once found were more than able ambassadors and promoted the faith throughout England. What prompted them is what still prompts people today: the search for a deeper understanding of spiritual awareness that will challenge them all the way and meet the deep void longing to be filled.

For the inquiring mind born into a misdirected religious community or a family that places little or no emphasis on any form of religion or faith path eventually the need or curiosity to seek the truth will assert itself. Converts to Catholicism from other denominations all express the urge they felt that there had to be a deeper truth which they found only in Roman Catholicism.

Much today is written on the need for a greater ecumenism and for different religions to join together, yet one wonders how such a demand can be validated? Surely the opposite must be the case as there can only be one God, it follows that there can only be one religion. The Catholic Church teaches that it was founded by Jesus Christ, the Son of God then should this be true, it must follow that the Catholic Church is the one true Church, and there is no authenticity in any other. This logical path led many holy men and women to search and find God in the Catholic faith as represented by his Church on Earth. The stories of their lives and what they were prepared to endure in order to secure and embrace the Faith renders most demands for various forms of ecumenism virtually meaningless.

Today, however, a new entirely different world order exists in which not only is ecumenism encouraged but radical movements exist that promote the inclusion and repatriation of churches founded on almost anti-Catholic doctrinal disputes. This peculiar state of affairs has led many Catholics to fall away from their faith as it becomes less and less relevant in their lives. It could be argued that today only the most progressive type of Catholicism is acceptable in some hierarchical circles, and this modern faith is almost reminiscent of the pot smoking, flower power era of the 1960s in which the leaders claimed they were more popular than Jesus Christ. Should today's church be seeking to win converts by being the most popular of churches with the most-popular leaders and the biggest youth get-togethers, then it is far removed from what Christ asked His disciples and His followers, in the most simplest of terms do:

"Deny themselves, take up their cross and follow Him"

For many Catholics today it is becoming more clear that a new church founded on practical needs and social dimensions is evolving, and is greatly preferred by many clerics and laity to what the church founded by Christ was intended to be. This divisive modern attitude between doctrine and practice continues to grow in acceptance and until this chasm is addressed only more and more disharmony will be perpetuated. How the Holy Father intends dealing with the miscreant and those who refuse to submit bishops remains to be seen yet again until this is done much progress will continue to be stymied.

There are only two causes that can be responsible for the Church today to be undergoing the most major metamorphosis it has experienced in many centuries. The first is that the Gospel known and taught for almost 2,000 years is now deemed somewhat irrelevant and must be altered to conform to present day requirements and secondly, the teachers themselves, those responsible for passing on the faith have altered it so dramatically that it has become almost meaningless in the lives of those who hear it.

These people are the hapless, the disbelievers and desolate people who have become the 'New' non-practicing Catholics. For some reason they have by their willfulness or neglect decided to abandon their faith. Faith as a gift easily attained through baptism at birth is all too often seldom really appreciated or understood. This errant dissatisfaction of cradle Catholic as opposed to the convert who had to fight hard to seek the faith is a clear distinction that is obvious in far too many young Catholics. It appears as if the baptised Catholic has to be baptised once more by a genuine desire before their Faith can be re-ignited. The root cause of the personal dissatisfaction must be clearly identified before any meaningful dialogue can happen. Until this is done, the disconnected Catholic remains in a spiritual vacuum. Young Catholics who appear to accept their loss of faith as if it is some form or rite of passage upon reaching a certain age must be challenged.

Their defence in spite of variations always contains some mitigating circumstances. Some of these are perhaps valid while others are definitely not, yet all must be considered on their merits. Just as, in the normal course of events ignorance is not accepted as a genuine form of defence in the eyes of the law, the official view of the Catholic Church is comparable. Sadly this knowledge is seldom if ever preached to young Catholic adults today; however, the Church teaches;

> "It is a mortal sin for a Catholic to be ignorant of these things, if it be through one's own willfulness or neglect."

CHAPTER

3

S ailors lost at sea without a compass point or chart reference are forced to seek directions or look for some celestial sign such as the North Star before they can have any hope of redeeming their whereabouts. Lost space travellers are even more susceptible in relation to their position in the cosmos. Not being multi-latitudinal or longitudinal in a space sector, 'sense' their existence becomes gradually less and less viable, until it eventually means they will either burn up or disintegrate.

To look for signs or some form of references in order to move away from a negative lifestyle can also equate to such a situation. There are a million scenarios woven each week by people dreaming of a starting a new life, the most obvious being, winning the lotto. The odds on such a million-to-one happening are ridiculously remote and so the dream continues to be no more than that. For others, for whom reality is much closer to hand, they are prepared to ask and seek directions. Once they have gathered enough information they will then start to work their way out of the difficult situation by setting a new course.

They will then continue to plan an alternative route or journey, all the time giving themselves an even greater chance of success. It can only be accepted, that, whereas some people genuinely find themselves well and truly lost, due to some form of accident or calamity, others by their own actions, risks, short cuts and foolish behavior keep straying into more and more danger zones, until eventually they end up in seriously hazardous conditions. From such a position there is little more than the very least possibility of navigating to safety. It is only after making some frantic 'May-Day' calls and sending out distress signals that there can be any hope of rescue.

A further percentage of travellers on any long journey will again decide by choice to take rather than contribute, to control rather than conform, to intimidate rather than to co-operate and all the while reach out to possess what is not theirs. Their use of others to further their own particular interests is always quite ruthless, callous and destructive. These are the people who will never serve but always seek to be served. Their purpose in life means they will never declare for Christ. After they have reached a certain point they will knowingly, or more likely unknowingly, declare for Satan. For them having arrived at a certain point there is no turning back as their ambition is now in control, and the grip of pride is securely fastened.

In order to try and decipher where one should begin to find oneself it is vital to attempt to establish some location or 'Now' position which will at least provide a new alpha point from which one can believe he or she can start again. This 'Now' point may be little more than a temporary resting spot, but it will make one realise what one's last position was the last time things were "good" and what must now be done to begin again to repatriate oneself in the right direction.

Some of the most harrowing moments in Space take place when a sequential series or an operational system is disrupted and thrown into some hibernation mode or glitch. This can be caused by some computer software overriding another program or indeed a technical malfunction which in itself causes a shut-down to automatically come into effect. The emergency systems then move into a back-up situation and an immediate diagnostic prognosis recommends whatever remedial action is necessary. This activation is undertaken with the maximum care and the minimum delay.

'Lost man' however is not quite this simple. Man, as trinity, of body, spirit and soul, is far more complex than a joining up of some super computer bits and pieces. Man has a kernel of eternity in his soul, and in the deepest recesses of his spirit, he is aware somehow or other of this single grain of infinity. This is what forces him to question the heavens in the night sky of ten million stars, when he is falteringly forced to ask, "Why am I here? What am I here? Where am I going? What am I doing? What am I meant to be doing?" To re-emphasize these questions reflects the pauses in one's mind and the occasions in one's life as they intermittently interfere like an old ailment or complaint and keep reminding one of one's own immortality

These are the questions which at some stage must reach the lips of every person ever born. Overcome by the beauty of the sunrise or its setting at dusk, man feels the raw need to know the answers. This need can only be met within the realm of God's creation for it is the only place the answers exist. Put in its simplest form, 'life' is the search for the answers. Life is the search for God. It is possible the great mystical writer Cecil Day Lewis uncovered the mystery when he wrote,

"You don't have a soul, You are a soul, You have a body."

How the ownership, authority, and harmony are divided (or united) between the spiritual and the physical is also a great mystery, but one has a full mission in which to solve it. Perhaps, to set forth to find God is the beginning of the beginning, to start to know God is the beginning of the journey, to begin to love God is the beginning of the mystery, and to desire nothing more than to serve God is the homecoming.

To start again is never possible in space parlance. After a defunct standard Shuttle launch there are several abort modes built into the launch, the first being less than seven minutes into the flight over the ocean. This time frame allows for an abort procedure to happen if one of the main engines fail and the craft has to go for an emergency landing in Europe or North Africa. The next option is an 'abort once around', and a third option an 'abort to orbit' mode which again would curtail the projected flight in order to save the mission. Should any of these abortions be activated, the rescue is effected and the mission ends. In the life analogy the baby would be still-born for natural reasons or aborted for un-natural reasons. In the normal birth mode we call life, one's only exit is the death one must endure on re-entry. To further embellish the soul's progress as it makes its arduous journey through its life mission it must always move in harmony with the plans of its commander. These are forever to be constantly thwarted by the forces of his enemy. The more destruction Satan can inflict on God's creation, the more pain and suffering he can unleash on mankind. For Satan therefore to take advantage of those in dire distress is his most basic plan of action. By stopping or crippling the launch of so many missions before, during, or immediately after a shuttle goes into orbit, gives him the greatest satisfaction of all, knowing what goodness on God's behalf such pilots could have accomplished throughout their mission, will now probably never take place.

To achieve a successful birth today is now the first actual accomplishment of the soul and must happen in order for the very mission of life to begin. This primary gift of life given freely by God was safe while considered sacred by all men but somehow Satan managed to avoid life's value through the introduction and acceptance of contraception. It was through this gateway that the subsequent introduction of abortion was made readily available. Initially contraception was introduced as a much hyped and needed health benefit and basic 'right' or 'freedom' demanded by the supposedly sophisticated women in the western world. This ensured its acceptance and so the global appeal was then spread to less well educated women in developing countries who were taught that the control of their fertility was a fundamental health-care priority, and like the women of the developed world their own "personal right to control".

To lodge a more comprehensive demand for the right to terminate a pregnancy was only a short number of steps away. From the medical clinics of Los Angeles, London and Paris, the abortion industry was established as a woman's 'Right to chose.' This "right" over the past 50 years has led to the present laws of abortion that have been enacted as a beneficial social necessity, demanded and legislated for in one country after another, and sought after by all radical and secular societies. In Denmark today abortions are available well into the third trimester. Over the past five or six decades more than 60 million Americans have failed to achieve even a momentary birth that may have given them Baptism and what was possible for all, prior to 1974, is today reduced to a grotesque mathematical equation.

Where God intends life to be given to 10 babies, man now determines only eight are to survive; two examples of what should have been God's love are destined for termination. This life mission, launched to perfection in an image given to it by God and the natural act of love by its parents, is today under the ever increasing threat of Satan. For those for whom the normal act of sacramental love is nothing more than the physical satisfaction of a primal sexual urge, the hand of God which shaped the infant is maybe the only hand the child ever knew. For those parents who desire with love the baby's safe arrival, their concerns embellished in prayer, seeks to see their baby develop according to its Creator's plan, provided by them both in their baby's surroundings and its education. Only as much as these parental supports are in place is the infant's future firmly secured.

This scenario however in today's world is becoming less and less assured and further and further removed from the truth. The reality is that of the number of infants fortunate enough to achieve a healthy birth, only a very modest majority of every 100 born can expect to experience a 'normal' two-parent natural family structure in which they will live up to their eighteenth birthday. The ravages of today's lifestyles on the stable family unit, living in a post-Christian society means that half of today's children are now very unlikely to reach full maturity without experiencing some serious personal damage inflicted upon them as they grow through their formative, adolescent and teenage years. Sadly one must realise that today's parents, who, through their own selfishness and negligence fail in their parental responsibilities, thereby further compound their failure by condoning the institutions of the state taking over the control and welfare of their children.

In addition to the daily needs of the children, their immediate surroundings and environment, the whole shape and selection of education has changed radically over the past three or four decades. Up to the middle of the last century society was founded primarily on a triple educational dependency which was common to all. These were the laws of God, the moral laws and the laws of the land.

Today for very many, the laws of God and the moral laws are no longer considered binding or really relevant, and a form of civics is very much preferred. The advanced post-Christian secular society also means that for many the most basic simple educational standards have also changed dramatically. No longer are literary studies, history and geography the primary subjects they once were, as they have long been replaced by business acumen, economics and a host of other correct, politically correct, gender friendly, humanistic, alternative lifestyle variables portrayed as the modern progressive paradigms more relevant to today's highest values.

For those who seek to practise a Catholic driven lifestyle based on the discipline necessary to live according to the Ten Commandments, the challenge to remain faithful to them is quite clear. Living within such a religious commitment one would hope to be guaranteed an integrity which would automatically embrace all the moral and civil laws of the state but today that does not necessarily mean that one is automatically a law abiding citizen. Where the laws of man infringe upon the laws of God, a faithful Catholic is obliged to honor God's law first, regardless of the consequences he or she maybe forced to suffer.

It is easy enough to proclaim as an unassailable fact that a man is the total sum of his thoughts, deeds, words and actions. What he is taught therefore, he should make every effort to learn and remember. If he fails to do this then, he cannot know. Once he disregards his education he ends up with a major knowledge deficit, and he cannot really participate fully in society or function in a social sense of the word. Indeed, he finds himself isolated in an ignorance or a loneliness that can only lead to the most negative of feelings, doubts and misgivings progressing onwards into the most marginalized and unfulfilled lives.

The problem therefore, when viewed objectively, is that without education the possibilities of a worthwhile and meaningful life are severely restricted and almost totally curtailed. On the other hand, another scenario presents itself which is even harder to come to terms with. If an environment or social climate exists which presents and promotes a sophisticated set of erroneous values which in turn are fed into the educational system then the whole meaning or value that society is based upon will be disjointed, distorted and fundamentally flawed. In the totalitarian and fascist movements of the last century it was obvious to the educated sections of society that some governments and rulers only retained power because of their grip on the educational systems and the forces of authority under their control.

To outsiders such countries and their methods of government were obviously wrong, and yet the hope was that given enough time such blots on humanity such as the Berlin Wall would inevitably collapse taking the cruel system with it. Now, however, the opposite is beginning to happen. Demands and changes thought of as unimaginable several decades ago are now being made; all the government has to do is adapt to the role of giving to the people what, they claim, the people are demanding. In common language, it is the bottom up theory now, rather than the trickle down one which appears to be playing directly into the hands of the federal government and its local departments. An alleged overpopulation of the planet is a prime example where world governments are quite determined to fully exploit this myth to their own national advantage, when, in fact, the projected world population catastrophe has never been proven let alone internationally ratified by any United Nations body.

The climate of acceptable sterilization, stem cell research, birth control, abortion and euthanasia laws in some countries today would perhaps never have been given the protection in law they enjoy currently, had both the Church and the vast laity mounted a more dynamic and vigorous opposition. The almost global war on homophobia, (a non-existent term 30 years ago) the demand for same-sex partnerships, marriage and adoption rights for the Lesbian, Bisexual, Gay, and Transsexual relationships are all areas at variance with the teachings and laws of the Catholic Church. The demands being made by all these divergent groups are being met one after another in country after country.

It is perhaps here the discarded obsolescence of the moral code is most evident. The absence of a strong religious education amongst young people in particular is also much in evidence in the acceptance of such diverse lifestyles. In contrast and almost without acknowledgement the Church upholds the rights of the individual from conception till death, it seeks to protect the rights of the family, and it invites all men and women of goodwill to adhere to and become members of the Catholic faith. The church must ask itself, if what we are offering is so good and wholesome, why are we not attracting more people who would like to belong to such a church? Such is today's society that the laws demanded by people are now in so many cases and pursuits, at variance with the teachings of the Catholic Church. The rights of the individual are only allotted at birth. For infants existing in a pre-birth nine-month gestation period no protection is given or formally recognized in any UN charter.

It may well be that for the agnostic, atheist or well educated adult, The Universal Declaration of Human Rights, as established by the UN in 1948, epitomizes the apogee of man's care for man but, for well educated Catholics who practice their faith and are concerned for their fellow man, this seemingly well-promoted declaration does not even begin to offer any degree of comfort, other than a set of minimal regulations. These in themselves are suspect as the best guarantee they appear to offer the individual, is that a person is allowed to exist without fear of persecution and harassment provided.

'he obeys the laws of the country in which he lives'.

This incredible weak and almost meaningless 'guarantee' is perhaps the lowest point of all declarations which have been issued by the United Nations since its formation.

The one Holy Catholic Church however offers more, much more, as it is entrusted to present and offer the love of God to all mankind regardless of ethnicity, class, color or creed. It has the full and complete message of eternal salvation which is offered individually to each person in the hope that they will acknowledge and choose freely to respond to God's love which reaches out to them through the bride of His Son, the one holy Catholic and Apostolic Church. For the new arrival, the seeker of truth, the convert, the fallen by the wayside, the penitent wishing to return home, the welcome is there for each and every one. How then does one begin?

The 'Now' position for every person is vitally important. Its major significance should never be far from our consciousness especially when rising each morning to begin yet again. For like the sand in an hour glass, the life of every man finally reaches its last 100 days, and even then, these days can be spent in the pursuit of little or nothing until finally his/her life's last day on earth arrives unannounced and unknown as they leave their house or apartment for work that morning never to return.

To know where we were when we last checked in on our position is therefore always important to remember. It may indeed be possible to choose or pick a point in time which one can relate to and then work forward from that point. If one was to decide that upon leaving school one deliberately chose to ignore one's religious education and start a new life free of any interference, then that would be a genuine and good 'Now' position from which to start. There are so many 'Now' positions: the death of a parent, a major emotional crisis, a drug dependency problem, a particular traumatic relationship, a career crash or whatever, all allow one to say that up to some fixed moment in time, their personal faith and their Catholic religion meant something to them in their life.

It was only after a particular incident took place or was experienced that the acceptance, practice and loyalty to their faith began to diminish, as something or some part of themselves started to find it too difficult, too demanding or, worst of all, too boring to live with. What is needed therefore for most young adults today who are searching, wondering or worse, still in deep despair of ever finding some meaning to their lives, is a form of spiritual 'system restore' command which will give the lost soul a new restoration point from which to start again. If no such point exists, then accept this book as an invitation and start from here!

Why one deviates, why one alters one's course, why one makes changes, usually on account of a foolish nature, are questions which are usually asked only with the benefit of hindsight. To avoid such recriminations it is vital to think ahead. Everybody is well aware that a course alteration of five or 10 degrees at sea is of great significance, yet in space terms even one-tenth of half of one half a degree, over so many hundreds of thousands of space miles, is an error of incalculable magnitude, leading one into sectors of millions of space-miles far from the original mission flight plan. In trying to understand a similar spiritual simile once applied to one's life's journey, the very same consequences apply. Just as a spaceship can be in great danger, one's spiritual life must also face the terrifying danger of straying into some form of black hole, never comprehensible until one is within, and then realizing too late that from that moment everything is destined to become deleted and unknown.

The Shuttle communications systems of which maybe two are constantly on-line, carrying voice, data or digitized encrypted code seldom fail in their umbilical role. A third system also exists which is 'wireless' in every sense yet forever remains plugged in. The soul of man also maintains such communications with God in many various different ways. It Is common to the role of a Cistercian monk, living the contemplative life, to try and achieve a most constant union with God whereas the missionary in the third world or the ordinary lay worker in some downtown office, have different levels of communication entirely. The essential need to keep in spiritual touch is as vital for the soul as the need for the body to breath in oxygen. This formal command structure of accepting directions, the individual face-to-face relationships one may have with priests and the last and most hidden golden thread concept of direct conscience are all methods of remaining in contact. Whatever form it takes however it is our life in prayer that keeps sustaining us and insofar as we can offer a purity of prayer our union with our Supreme Commander is reciprocated. The graces we receive daily in return enable us to proceed with our mission. The in-flight transfer of resources, fuel, supplies and spares between vehicles in space now tend to be taken for granted, yet, to take oxygen as the prime example, without fresh supplies being transferred to the International Space Station after a certain period in Space this unique space complex would be totally uninhabitable.

The necessity to receive new supplies constantly during one's mission is statutory, and regardless of whether they are once off or frequent, they are only provided by our mother Church in the form of Seven Sacraments. Without the legitimate and worthy reception of these spiritually life-sustaining sacraments, one is constantly going to be at risk of travelling off course into unknown danger or ultimately failing in one's mission. The sacraments therefore must be understood for what they are and appreciated by the penitent seeking to effect that 'system renewal'. This ignition, this spark of faith is enough to allow for a re-commencement of full engine burn and a re-opening of communications with Mission Control.

To repeat the list as previously outlined, The Seven Sacraments of the Church are:

Baptism, Confirmation, Eucharist, Penance, Extreme Unction, Holy Orders and Matrimony.

These Sacraments, worthily received, provide particular graces which are conferred to sustain, strengthen and encourage the recipient. A person who chooses to dedicate his or her life to the imitation of Christ, must by the nature of such an act, be both able and worthy to receive and contain the grace necessary to sustain it. Once received, they are then put fully into the use for which they were intended and can never become stagnated. Their dispersement is in their fulfilment. The same fundamental principle applies to all the sacraments in that they must be entered into with a clear mind seeking to unite with God's will. If not then the abundance of grace cannot be received and, if anything, the emptiness instead is increased. To equate this with our space parlance further, unless all efforts to dock with the mother ship or space station are made to receive necessary vital supplies successfully, then the whole operation is put into grave danger.

The Catechism of the Catholic Church devotes and outlines the Celebration of the Christian Mystery as one of its four parts. Over 600 pages compiled in great detail, piece by piece, builds into a wall of knowledge, giving whoever is seeking the truth so much to meditate upon. Contained in its 2,885 paragraphs are the windows into the Catholic religion, clear for all to look through and examine. For the more in-depth scholars the knowledge and wisdom of the earlier traditional catechisms such as The Baltimore and the Council of Trent catechisms can be researched. Today's Catechism of the Catholic Church is considered the standard basic reader.

An abbreviated Compendium was introduced in 2005 by Pope Benedict XVI during the first year of his pontificate and he described it as "a faithful and sure synthesis of the Catechism of the Catholic Church". This shortened version of the Catechism allows the discerning mind to view briefly what the Catechism in its full beauty contains. For the most reticent person who hesitates taking the first step, the easiest guide book may be the introductory compendium YOUCAT published in 2011. This catechism, or 'unusual book,' as it was called by Pope Benedict XI was introduced as a stepping stone for the youth of today, and must be seen as an introductory or gateway book leading on to the Catechism of the Catholic Church.

To begin examining the Sacraments the obvious first choice must always be Baptism. In fact for most non-believers the sacraments of Baptism and Confirmation are the most familiar and easily understood sacraments. Like Holy Orders they can only be received once, and so are forever. The Eucharist, God's greatest gift of Himself, spiritually feeds one's soul throughout one's life's mission, and sustains the sanctifying grace within which one must remain within in order to be spiritually alive, conscious and free. This is the only true freedom that means one is not bound by entrapment, enslavement or encroachment of sin.

Extreme Unction is the sacrament of arriving. It is the last and final guidance instruction in order to bring one safely home. This sacrament administered by a priest, conveys the final blessing, the whisper of advice into the pilot's ear in order to assist him safely down executing a perfect landing.

In a Shuttle scenario the final manoeuvres are made as one's craft prepares to re-enter the earth's atmosphere, and make ready for landing. The comparative details of how important the re-alignment is, the flight checks and the last minute landing instructions are carried out to the last exacting detail. The sacrament of Extreme Unction reflects the very same procedure as it has the full power and ability to bring even the most damaged craft and pilot safely down. That is what this sacrament entails; the worthy reception of it therefore conveys a beauty so wonderful that the impact of death has no more discomfort or disruption than the most smooth landing by the spacecraft as it glides to the softest halt on the runway of Edwards AFB, in the Mojave Desert of Southern California.

CHAPTER

4

The Old Testament portrays Moses as handing down the law of God given to him on Mount Sinai. It had become necessary to impose it on the tribes as they had become wayward, lawless and decadent. Moses knew its imposition was necessary if they were to be brought back safely to God. Today the Ten Commandments remain central to the practice of Catholicism and even though they may no longer be superimposed with an unbending rule of authority, adherence to them is still fully expected by the Catholic Church. Unless one lives the Law and remains as faithful as possible to the Commandments one cannot consider oneself a true follower of Christ.

Today's phenomenon is that so many different interpretations of the commandments and the truths as expressed in the gospel have become so commonplace, they have allowed a climate of ambiguity and irrational thought to have developed, which have not only rendered the commandments less meaningful, but have to a large extent degraded their primary function as 'actual spiritual law'. The interpretation of the Commandments as outlined in the Catechism of the Catholic Church (Paragraphs 2052 /2550, all 462 of them, stresses clearly the importance placed on them) yet even here the formulae presented is not that of an interpretation designed to make one conform through fear, but rather it is to perpetuate a unification of love with God and one's fellow man, without fear of judgement.

This benign relaxed Catechism therefore differs from most of its predecessors which clearly emphasised the great divide between fear of hell and desire of heaven. Prior to the Second Vatican Council it was clearly taught that once the Commandments were transgressed the law was broken. Either venially or seriously the penitent who broke the law was seen as 'being in the wrong' and held spiritually accountable. For minor transgressions sorrow for one's sins could well be expressed through an Act of Contrition. For the more grievous sins the sinner was obliged to receive the Sacrament of Penance before he/she was entitled to once more receive Holy Communion. Today it is more necessary than ever before that such clarity of content, containing much of the Church's teachings be reinstated, emphasising both God's Divine mercy and His infinite judgement.

Now, more than ever before the Commandments are needed by society, and it is only the adherence to them by practising Catholics that will return to them their validity. Having such a loyalty to them, both practiced and enforced, will help identify Catholics as true Christians living their faith as Christ intended. Such devotion to the Commandments leads Catholics to once more participate fully in the sacrament of Penance which for far too long many families appear to have set aside, giving much cause for concern. In most normal Catholic families the children are told they must participate in the sacrament of reconciliation on a regular basis. This term 'reconciliation', however well-intended by the liturgists, was a dilution of the actual meaning of the word 'penance' and the obligation of the penitent in expressing sorrow and apology was somehow reduced. The Catholic Family in the true sense of the word should try to go together as 'family' to receive this Sacrament as many times as possible during the year. The children or teenagers could then witness their parents seeking forgiveness before they in turn would make their own Confession. In this way the parents would practise humility and lead their children by example. Such occasions together with the celebrations of Easter and Christmas would give tremendous strength to the family's faith and solidarity. It is this communal practice which enables Catholic families to realize we are all God's children, and it is as children we must come together to seek and accept God's loving pardon.

What family or families would not benefit from such a joint expression of love, forgiveness and happiness? By experiencing this sacrament today on a regular basis its powerful grace and intercession instills a sense of rejuvenation and renewal direct from the representative of Christ. It not only reconciles the soul to God it also strengthens one's fortitude for the many temptations that lie ahead. What can never be overlooked is that whereas a natural father may, through anger, pride or despair, refuse to forgive a son or a daughter for some act of foolishness or omission, God will always forgive unconditionally and it is in this unconditionality the true magnitude of the Sacrament resides. It is God's omniscient expression as Father of true love and forgiveness that we as children can forever seek out His divine mercy. It is hard to comprehend how the domestic church, the parish church of the family, can expect to flourish without this sacrament being more central and more availed of constantly throughout the entire year.

In the opening address of Vatican II on October 11th 1962, St Pope John Paul XXIII stated:

> "The great problem confronting the world after almost 2,000 years remains unchanged. Christ is ever the centre of history and of life. Men are either with Him and His Church and then they enjoy light, goodness, order and peace. Or else they are without Him or against Him and deliberately opposed to His Church, and give rise to confusion, to bitterness in human relations, and to the constant danger of fratricidal wars."

This was quite an overwhelming statement and made by any ordinary person would perhaps have been considered an incredible exaggeration. Made by such an extraordinary man however it must, even now in hindsight, be treated with a great degree of deference. Fifty years have passed since it was first uttered and looking at today's world the accuracy of its content has only grown with the passage of time. It may be too much to hope for that as Man moves from one level of technical achievement to another, his relationship with God would somehow fluctuate from one plane of consciousness to another, sometimes fervent, sometimes casual but always upward. However this theory seems difficult to advance and instead the reality appears to be that both paths lead to very different destinations. With the Catechism of the Catholic Church it is possible for any thinking person, who is seeking the truth to understand why Catholicism was, is and will remain the One True Church from which so many offshoots have sprung.

Reading back over so many centuries it is possible to see also how the human frailties and vices of so many individuals distorted and pillaged the truth thereby creating chaos. Nevertheless allowing for so many Papal upheavals and cruel injunctions there can be no doubt Rome still remained the Seat of Peter and the home of the one true Church. It was for this reason the great convert English Cardinals, Manning and Newman, took the road to Rome as indeed did so many of their fellow countrymen and women in the early part of the last century. These scholars, intellectuals, writers and poets did not take this path without great courage, and it is quite enlightening to read just how many of them in their earlier lives had fought so hard to reject what they eventually were forced to acknowledge was God's truth.

One reads of many conversions like that of the Washington lawyer Jason Workmaster an Evangelical Christian and his wife Nicki, who, with their family finally found the road to Rome and the welcome that awaited them. Like so many others the descriptions of how and why the journey was almost inevitable are stories that resonate with all who know the truth exists but cannot locate it. This hunger in the soul to make contact with its creator is the force which drives people to keep on searching up to the very end of their lives. This possibility of finding God is as open as the invitation extended in the open arms of Christ the King on the summit of the Sugar Loaf overlooking Rio de Janeiro. It is as it has always been and forever will be.

"Behold, I stand at the gate, and knock. If any man shall
hear my voice, and open to me the door, I will come in
to him, and will sup with him, and he with me."

Apoc. 3.20

This message is again constantly extended to anybody so they
maybe able to find their own personal Jesus Christ who gave His life
for them. The great sadness for those actively seeking the truth today
is that it is becoming more and more difficult to ascertain in more and
more regions of the world. In up-to maybe 200 countries which harbour
some degree of antagonism or hatred towards the Catholic Church it
is almost impossible to access the Catholic faith, and even where some
governments claim it is available, the opposite is too often the case. In
the meantime it can only be hoped and prayed for that eventually a
change of heart will take place in the leaders of these desolate countries,
which will allow them to realise the true meaning of the universal
Catholic Church and the love of its saviour, Our Lord Jesus Christ.

Ironically, in some Christian countries individuals receiving the
Sacrament of Baptism at birth do so with almost a minimal degree of piety.
It sometimes appears that the easier the Sacrament is received at birth the
less value is placed on it in life and, rather than embrace and cherish it, the
opposite happens as it becomes discarded and unacceptable. Whether this
is because over the past 50 years so many unwarranted changes have taken
place, making it less and less compatible with modern living or whether the
lure and attractions of the technical secular world are becoming too difficult
to overcome, the decline and indifference to the Catholic Church and the
Sacraments is increasing at an alarming rate. There also can be little doubt
that over recent years the scandals emanating from deep within the Catholic
Clergy were so repulsive that the fall-out of their actions drove countless
thousands away from the Church. It is clear, however, from history that
whenever obstacles, no matter how hard, were placed in the way of the laity,
they were always prepared to overcome their reticence and cling more firmly
to their faith. The converts and the pilgrims who find Rome today do so
with a more sincere and deeper realization of the faith than those baptized
at birth who seldom tend to it, or want to delve into its glory.

As mentioned previously, according to the Catechism of the Catholic Church the search for the faith is not optional. Once Baptized and Confirmed, the obligation to nourish and grow one's faith must continue. At some point, for one reason or another, one may desist or depart from the church and its teachings but the obligation to remain loyal to one's faith is still there. For those born into other Christian communities or religions the obligation to seek the truth also applies, perhaps for them as a yearning. The reason being that God demands we seek to know him. The effort therefore must be made and whereas for some it may be difficult and for others almost impossible, it is by our efforts to find God each one will be judged.

This demand born out of God's unselfish sacrifice is a demand made for us to seek unification with Him. One must do this in order to become whole. Equally it is always possible for any Catholic, who is out of communication, out of practice, or out of love, to look for the help needed in the rekindling one's faith. The mystery behind the Sacrament of Penance is one designed not just to forgive the penitent the sins committed but, even more, to re-ignite the desire to seek again God's love. Once one begins to neglect the obligation to go to Confession on a regular basis this rekindling of spiritual desire is dimmed and dimmed again until eventually it is extinguished altogether. The greatest understanding of the Sacrament is for it to be seen in the light of a new Baptism, of being truly alive again in Christ, a new explosion of life, a born-again Christian.

In the fifth and sixth centuries the harshness of the early church bore down on the penitents with a regime of strict demands on the sinner before he was allowed to be accepted back within the church. The writings of the early church fathers such as St Augustine made it clear that the need was not just for sorrow and contrition but also for a visible degree of public retribution for one's sins. It was not until the seventh century that Irish monks sought to introduce into mainland Europe the concept or opportunity of private penitential confessions. This was to allow the sinner to make his petition or plea for forgiveness through the priest privately, thereby avoiding much public shame. This practice became formalized and eventually passed into Canon law, except in exceptional circumstances. The minimal requirement today to receive this Sacrament is once per church year at Easter and failure to do so is in itself a grievous sin. Today however the need to confess one's sins through a priest appears to have become negated as more and more individuals claim their relationship with God is strong enough for them to approach Him directly. Such spiritual arrogance is almost beyond belief and the ultimate degree of sinful presumption. It insinuates that the sacrifice made by Christ as God's only Son was not necessary. When Christ commissioned Peter by giving him authority to forgive sins on earth He Himself not only established the Sacrament but also the method by which it would be provided. Without absolution being administered by a priest acting as God's agent one cannot receive this sacrament. This growth in modern individualism in which each person claims the right to promote their own singular form of contrition was one which Pope Pius XII warned against very clearly concerning the misuse of the Sacrament of Penance when he said that it was

> "Contrary to the mind of Christ and very disastrous for the mystical body of the Saviour".

To see the Sacrament of Penance in a different light one need not look any further than the omnipotent role of Father. The loving Father referred to so many times throughout the Gospel.

> "And which of you, if he ask his Father for bread, will He give him a stone? Or a fish, will he give him a serpent? Or if he shall ask an egg, will he reach him a scorpion? If you then, being evil, know how to give good gifts to your children, how much more will your Father from heaven give the good Spirit to them that ask him?" Lk 11:11-13

For many young people the word Father does not always represent love, support, affection and encouragement; indeed for far too often it may well mean the exact opposite, rejection, disapproval, indifference and even hostility. Why this should be can best be attributed to a myriad of mental disorders all of which are perhaps too deeply rooted in both psychological and physiological patterns to be dissected here. Going to such a Father in serious need or in trouble would certainly gain for the child no understanding or relief. Consider instead the reaction to the ever-listening, ever-caring, ever-loving priest confessor, who can not only offer comfort and solace but, even more, can offer the penitent in despair God's total love and forgiveness.

In today's world and in today's church, a church saddened by so many fallen priests and flawed bishops, it is perhaps no great wonder that so many young people are discouraged from making their Confessions on a regular basis. Today's priests, unable to administer this Sacrament as they were ordained to do, become disheartened and disillusioned while at the same time the young faithful are alienated from those who are there to help them most by providing them directly with God's love and forgiveness. It is a situation that cannot be allowed to worsen and must be resolved as one of the Church's top priorities in order that young people may find their spiritual way again, rather than wither on the vine.

In this spiritually confused environment is it any wonder so many young people are in such a state of isolation with their religion and disenchantment with their clergy? They now inhabit a world in which a great number of their leaders deserve little merit and less respect. The planet on which we all have to live is itself under threat and it is their personal futures which are insecure.

In a world therefore of instant gratification where rap music and coke lines are as normal as newspapers and coffee, can people wonder why so many young people opt out? Having at best been given a very mediocre, casual level of religious knowledge or at worse, a totally superficial or meaningless degree of spiritual junk, by the time the young person reaches their late teenage years, the actual ability to make the journey through life successfully is now under serious threat, and what was originally a somewhat difficult journey has now become considerably more hazardous.

Astronauts on the other hand leave nothing to chance. Every item, every bit of knowledge, every tiny instruction that can assist them in their mission is passed on by ground control. Their preparation and awareness is second to none and unless an emergency or unforeseen incident take place their mission will be successful. They achieve their launch instructions and countdowns only after they have acquired all the necessary knowledge, skills and training. It may not be possible to duplicate such a rigorous routine for Catholics to acquire nevertheless if, instead of the life skills which appear to be so popular today, a serious attempt was made to teach Catholic doctrine in great detail then it is possible to envisage a far more capable, compassionate and confident young people contributing to the overall welfare of their families, neighbours and society. Until this type of format takes place the senselessness of drugs, violence, social and domestic breakdown, overflowing courts and futureless appalling lifestyles will continue to be the way forward for so many today who are denied such a spiritual awareness.

In the meantime, what is happening is that there are insufficient search-and-rescue teams trying to reach those who are already stranded without such fuel, without direction and, most of all, without love. These are the lost sons and daughters, brothers and sisters who are so far adrift in spiritual space that they seldom can be reached before they drift further and deeper into the void of oblivion, the place which has now become almost laughable and unspoken of when referred to by its original title, Hell.

It is often said a journey of a thousand miles begins with a single step, so equally it may be said that the reflection of the Sun's rays require only the minutest fraction of a mirror. The Hubble Telescope launched in 1990 was such a precise and scientifically unique instrument. Its lifespan over the past few decades has been dedicated to capturing and relaying images covering aeons of time and space. God's rays are millions of times more far-reaching and pulsating yet the slightest cry for help or the softest spoken prayer will never go unheard. Who seeks God will never need to find him, for by their prayer He has already found them. The prayer that is heard is the one that is needed to be heard, in order to secure grace which in turn leads to faith, and in the fullness of time, to love. Unlike human love that one can desire for over a complete lifetime and never find, the opposite is true for God. His love is guaranteed and unconditional, it is real, it is for eternity and all we need to do is to seek it with an open heart and devoted mind.

Man has always been his own worst enemy; the day when he makes the grade, secures the job or gets the promotion is the very day he is most likely to succumb to temptation. On the day he actually reaches the summit he falls prey to the world and its material pleasures; he has finally reached the top and feels entitled to all the world has to offer. On such a triumphant day of success the devil likes to claim the benefits and inserts the deadliest of sins, pride into the unsuspecting victim. More often than not the price that is demanded is greater than the success achieved and all the more difficult to pay.

As one rises more and more to some higher pinnacle of power the desire or need to acknowledge one's religious obligations and obey its laws lessens greatly. The routine of attending Mass on a constant basis, of receiving the Sacrament of Penance, all begin to fade until finally the day arrives when one turns one's back on God's love. On this day pride, conquers all, and one chooses consciously or unconsciously to believe, they no longer have any need of God's love.

The mirror turns away from the Sun just as man now chooses to live in the shade rather than the sunlight. How one makes such a decision is no mystery; the life-paths each person must choose, different though they may-be have all their own signposts and warnings. Once one leaves their given path or flight plan and decides to make one's own way, one very soon experiences dense undergrowth, deep ravines and rock faces all of which present considerable difficulties and danger.

It is the road less travelled and so dangerous one is almost certain to lose one's way, and once lost to continue to remain so in hostile regions. For the individual to go it alone, to be independent, is the great attraction of pride which may eventually lead to his/her downfall. Without God's grace just how much of a person's life can go leading all the while into even greater dangers is impossible to calculate. What one can be certain of however is that the unknown hardships and misery that awaits the lost traveller will increase rather than lessen over time. In modern warfare jargon the motto is 'Who dares wins' in the war against the principalities of evil the opposite is more often the case 'Who dares loses'.

To return again to the Sacrament of Penance, forgiveness and reconciliation, one must see it in the light of a sacred mystery that can never be ever fully analysed or realized. Regardless of how deep one tries to understand this gift founded on God's divine mercy the enormity of grace it bestows on us touches one with a total sense of awe. The magnitude of turning darkness into light is about as close as one can get to any meaningful or recognisable analogy.

One of the most loved parables of the gospel is that of the Prodigal Son, in which God's mercy is beautifully illustrated. The moving account tells of the return of the son who has, grievously offended his father yet finally returns to offer his genuine repentance. The young man in question is embraced and overwhelmed by the Father's welcome, whose rejoicing is without limit, providing him with the finest robe, the valuable ring and the wonderful banquet. The Church teaches that this welcome is not unique; rather we are all encouraged to identify with the wayward son in seeking God's unlimited forgiveness. The great beauty of the parable is that the welcome today's lost son or daughter receives will be no less on their return, and for them too, the welcoming banquet will also be prepared.

The new life of being pure, made worthy to be once more called 'son/daughter' awaits every penitent who seeks forgiveness. Penance then must be looked on in relation to our understanding of sin, for just as the darkest night cannot withstand the dawn, penance like the midday sun banishes all shadow and all shame. The adage one must always remember is, God's greatest mercy is reserved for those in the greatest need.

To talk in terms of our understanding of sin, the need to describe it in image form does little more than introduce it. If we try to form an image of our soul as being represented by a tiny mirror and God represented by an enormous Sun then as we bask we reflect the light, warmth and knowledge of creation. On the other hand as we rotate our axis more and more away from Him eventually the mirror must pivot fully until finally it is facing away from the Sun, reflecting absolutely nothing. The movement and available surface of reflection is fully ours to control.

By aligning ourselves with God the light is forever contained between us and our Creator. Should we choose to move fractionally in and out of synch we cease to be static, so there is constant need for cleaning, for care and for attention as these obligations are always our responsibility. This mirror image thereby tries to convey in a most basic way our never ending need for the Sacrament of Penance, in which all our stains, sins and wrongdoings will be totally wiped away.

To explore the image of the mirror forever rotating on its edge, a cosmic coin spinning very slowly on a plain surface is easy enough to visualize. As the face of the mirror loses more and more contact with the Sun, finally at the last moment of contact, the final minute reflection of light disappears, it is gone.

Sin, likewise, turns the soul partially in only fractions of degrees away from God until eventually by indulging in an ongoing dependence on sin the split second occurs when one becomes doomed and spiritually eclipsed. Turned from the light with no maintenance possible, the cleaning of the mirror stops, and what was once a spotless dish now becomes caked with dirt and grime. Now turned from the Sun's rays it ceases to function and does nothing more than remain an inert immovable object suspended in space gathering more and more dirt.

For the soul which does not receive God's rays or graces freely available through the Sacraments, the movement into darkness begins slowly to take place. As the voice of the spirit, one's conscience, becomes almost silent, other distractions begin to exert their influence until finally, over time, their influence dominates and their control is copper-fastened. Sin in any one form allows other sins to gain entry into one's sphere or space. One's sexual desires increases one's fall as one's anger, pride, jealousy and other sins now begin to move in to take control.

For one who has arrived at this sad state of serious sin any actions performed now, of however meagre value, carry no merit whatsoever. The motivation for any such acts being driven by sinful motivation rather than any other desire makes them worthless and of no value to the one who is performing them. The Catholic Church which over centuries promoted this doctrine and was prepared to defend it is now seldom heard and like many other doctrines rarely preached. Why such a clear spiritual truth is today consigned to some out of reach shelf adds to the confusion that fills so many young adults today.

This teaching for many progressive and contemporary driven Catholics is just too difficult to both accept and appreciate as it leaves little room for prognostication or discussion. The Gospel makes clear that, the deeper one strives and prays for more wisdom the deeper the vision will become. To continuously seek, one will find, to continuously knock, means, the door will be opened. The Gospel states quite frankly :-

> Seek ye first the Kingdom of God and His justice and
> all these things shall be given onto you. Luke 12:31

In so many very ways the fact that today's generation's' spirituality is the result of such a huge deficit of religious knowledge one must wonder how such an inadequacy will be finally judged. The temptation to believe that the mitigating circumstances are sufficient enough to warrant only a slight punishment is temptingly close to hand. The Gospel however does not entertain such a presumption and more than once goes into some harsh detail to dispel this point of view:-

> "Much is required from the person to whom much is
> given much more is required from the person to whom
> much more is given. Lk 12:47-48

St Luke is always the evangelist who tells it like it is. His is the stark, no frills version of what took place. To keep such a powerful message in one's consciousness at all times helps greatly in the decisions one must sometimes make in everyday living. Large or small is of little matter as seen in the light of St Luke's clear instruction: and our obligations are clear. We are responsible to our brother or sister and by ignoring them we will be firmly judged. Without having such a reference point on which to secure our beliefs one's rate of spiritual descent is almost impossible to quantify.

Sadly, as is so often the case, a descent however slow at the beginning by its very nature gathers momentum and unless checked gathers more and more speed. For some it may be possible to measure but for others nearly impossible. The fact remains that, 'there are none so blind as those who cannot see' except perhaps those who plainly refuse to see, and this establishes the reality which takes place once the soul is severed from God through serious sin. The son or daughter of the rightful owner who had been given so much is now spiritually dead. Only the sacrament of Penance can fully restore him or her to life. The sinner without any graces whatsoever cannot prefer justice to injustice, truth to falsehood, purity to impurity, mercy to cruelty or perfection to imperfection as all these vices in which he or she is trapped are opposed to God's love.

Sin today therefore is rarely seen for what it is. The Commandments are seldom presented for what they are. The Sacraments and the graces they bestow are unappreciated, and God's love for mankind is far too often taken for granted through the most successful sin of presumption. For God's love to be sought after, desired and welcomed one must feel the need and look in some detail to see the reason, need and desire for it.

In the great mystery of salvation, Christ redeemed mankind and welcomed each individual back into a new life, a life totally unique into which one could be born again. This life designed and created by God starts for many after nine months preparation for birth. For Catholics it is through the Sacrament of Baptism that one is spiritually born. For others less fortunate a strong desire to know of Jesus Christ, his life and his teachings is enough to enable the individual access the graces he or she will need for their journey.

This Baptism of desire is legitimised when the Sacrament is actually received. In addition and in order that each life could continuously be renewed when contaminated by sin, the Sacrament of Penance was initiated. Just as water drawn from a well is needed continuously to wash so also is this Sacrament available in order to keep one's soul constantly and spotlessly clean. The references to repent, to seek forgiveness and to make reconciliation in the gospel are many. It is evident and key to the very central core of the gospel that sin once repented is forever forgiven. The resolution of God to sacrifice his Son was made in reparation for Man's original sin. Being saved was only gained by Christ for man through his sacrifice and resurrection. In one of the few parables in which God's anger manifests itself, the Unforgiving Servant, Matt 18: 21-35 it is through own actions he is unforgivable: Jesus explains the compassion of the king in forgiving his debtor the debt he owes him. The debtor on receiving his lord's forgiveness refuses to extend any similar compassion to a lesser servant who owes him money and instead has him committed to prison. Upon hearing of this cruel act the king revokes his clemency and seeks the original amount repaid in full without any mercy.

The tone of this parable on forgiveness differs from most of the others in that there are two elements which are not usually apparent. One is the petition brought by the whole body of servants which brings the dastardly act of the debtor to the king's attention. Not only is he prepared to listen to what they have to say and pay heed to it, he demonstrates how one must learn from it and act accordingly. God does not share his mercy with us if we deny mercy to others. To do so puts one immediately into the very path of God's judgement from which a full and final settlement will have to be paid.

From the parable it is necessary to understand that all goodness and everything one possesses comes as gifts from God. Wealth, status, power, influence may be all material, temporal and social possessions and attributed to one's own efforts but they should be seen even more as gifts from God. How we appreciate them, how we share them reflects our capacity to love. The more we can give of ourselves to others the more we in turn will receive.

The well of God's love is bottomless; we need to have the courage to draw from it. God's love is total. It cannot be anything less as it is Divine. By experiencing such love and forgiveness through the Sacrament of Penance one must then fully attempt to offer one's own personal forgiveness to those who have hurt us. The path for those seeking God is beautifully highlighted in the mystical work of St Thomas a Kempis in his, 'Imitation of Christ' which has encouraged and accompanied so many people over the centuries who have striven to do everything in their power to live their lives in imitation of Christ.

CHAPTER

5

After an initial introduction to the sacraments and gaining an understanding of the graces which are bestowed upon one through them, it becomes clear that the more one prays and seeks to understand the more one's comprehension will develop and deepen. By being aware of the spiritual forces the Sacraments contain it is possible to learn with greater and greater intensity the power of God's love. Through this 'growth of love' one's union with God becomes more and more intimate until everything becomes more real in both a natural and supernatural way.

It is quite impossible to deeply appreciate the sacraments without living the Law of God and keeping His commandments. To live the Law of God one can do so at a simple or at a more advanced level. The aspirant who chooses the simpler path is by no means seeking the easier one, the one who chooses the more advanced level only does so as a lifestyle choice, foregoing the joy of marriage to choose instead the Sacrament of Holy Orders. It is in loving the Law of God that loving God becomes more joy centred and a true reality for the individual who remains single or the married spouse or the religious man or woman seeking such a close intimate relationship with God. Loving God, loving his law and loving Him through loving one's neighbor becomes all the more consuming. This is not the love of Eros but rather the love demonstrated by St Maximilian Kolbe, the Polish Franciscan priest who freely sacrificed his life for that of another, a father of four, in the Auschwitz Concentration Camp in 1941. This degree of self-mortifying love is likewise shown by the most destitute parent who sacrifices everything for the well-being of their child.

It is this highest form of love that one must try to realize one is called upon to give witness to. The invitation of Christ was simple and straightforward to the young man who asked him what his final step must be. He had kept all the Commandments, he had paid all his dues but he knew instinctively there had to be, something else, something more, and so when he asked Jesus what it was that he had to do, in order to secure his place in the Kingdom, gently Jesus told him,

> "Dispose of all your worldly possessions, give the proceeds to the poor, and follow Me." Mt 19 – 21

For the young man it was too much. It was the final step he could not make and so he departed, downcast, lacking the courage to begin what would have been the start of his eternity, on earth.

Penance then keeps one alive in hope. Just as mortal sin destroys one's charity and begins one's fall, penance will continue to release one from the shame of sin and lift one back up again within God's glory. Who, one must ask oneself, is better able to see, those affected by blindness or those free of blindness? It is often said that, 'in the valley of the blind men, the one-eyed man is king', maybe it should also be said that whoever is most free of sin, can see it better than all others. It is a good man who knows when he has committed a sin, and to what extent he has offended God. The better a person he or she is the more they can understand the depth of their sin. A sinner on the other hand who chooses to remain in mortal sin is not able or even prepared to acknowledge the evil his actions have caused. He is not able, for the simple reason, that he has been blinded by them. His pride, arrogance and vanity will keep him in total darkness until the ultimate sin of no repentance, for one reason or another, is committed, destroying for ever his chance of eternal salvation. For this reason, if for no other, it is of the utmost importance for every Catholic to receive the Sacrament of Penance at least once a year.

It is inconceivable that any person can go a full liturgical year without committing even a minor or venial sin. For even such a slight transgression, an apology, is still necessary. For a more grievous sin, so much greater is the need to offer repentance, and seek forgiveness. In either case however failure to meet this obligation of receiving this Sacrament once a year constitutes a further serious sin, for which repentance, at some future date will also be required.

The Sacrament of Penance is the Sacrament of God's on-going, constant, eternally available love. It is only available direct from God, through the priest who administers it, as His agent. The penitent in the confessional is direct to God, and God is direct to the penitent. No person can forgive themselves; their conscience refuses to allow, condone or accept it. No matter how hard one tries, it is an attempt at self-deception which always fails, leaving one in even greater despair as, one's sin burns itself deeper and deeper into one's soul. In the sacred mystery of Penance, the moment of truth becomes manifest when the remorse is genuinely expressed, and the priest on behalf of God utters the omnipotent words of absolution, breathing new life back into the dormant soul. Instantaneously midnight becomes midday.

A sincere and contrite heart is the prerequisite for seeking forgiveness. It is only with full sincerity and a contrite heart that one can present oneself to confess one's sins.

The astronaut who is trying to redeem his mission does not mention seven faults appearing on his console and conceal two others, from ground control, as it would make his report meaningless.

In the same way the more perfect one's confession the more abundant the graces one receives. God's divine mercy is limitless, unlike human mercy which is so often limited and conditional. In the solitude of the confessional the penitent's declaration of one's sins secures God's mercy through the words of absolution the priest has been given authority to murmur, freeing the sinner with tears of joy from his abject sorrow. Whatever reparation one can then make to atone for the harm or pain the sins have caused, remains.

One is of course always obliged to try and make good through practical help, wherever possible, whatever damage was caused. The cycle of repentance, forgiveness, renewal and return to the Father, all foster and nurture our life's mission in order that we may grow in God's love. Our human frailties, our sinfulness and our selfishness must never be able to deceive us. At least one must always be able to recognize and admit the reality that each one, every person, individually is a sinner, and by so doing, turn back again and again to seek forgiveness. Penance must always be recognized as the moment in which one can actually experience momentarily, the love of Christ in this life.

This realization in turn we are obliged to extend to our neighbour, for just as we have been forgiven, we must also forgive those who have injured us. Once one fails to avail of and appreciate the Sacrament one ceases to receive the special graces it bestows and so becomes less and less inclined to forgive others. Penance one can never do without; the more one receives the more one needs to feel the desire to share God's forgiveness with others. The renewal of this sacrament brings one who is spiritually dead back to the satisfaction and joy of eternal life, imbued with the three great virtues: Faith, Hope and Charity.

For the graces needed to nourish faith there must be a link-up, a channel of communication, a means whereby one can continuously experience the love of God. Through the endorsement of faith the Sacraments gives us it is this channel that is sustained and strengthened. Without this conduit one can become dissuaded and disheartened. Impossible as it may appear it is through carelessness or indeed a major distraction, one can lose oneself in such a way that the loss takes place in almost an unconscious or insidious manner. In the rough and tumble of life few, if any, have not experienced the allure of the dangerous companion, the person who for one reason or another is fascinating or attractive or just always in the fast lane looking good. Knowing such a person and wanting to know a lot more about them, can be a relationship that will blow many people off course as they put their regular friends, companions and lifestyle on hold, to follow this other man/woman. Without paying much attention to our spiritual needs and obligations, our antenna is now pointed in a far different direction and one is not sure in even what direction one is heading. Penance for the moment is being put on the very long finger.

In space terms, as one spirals or rotates one's reflective mirror away from one's own mission control, seeking other sources to investigate because one has allowed oneself to be seduced into believing that perhaps other signals offer more promise and titillation with their false intrigue. This option to go where one should not go, is governed by our freewill, and one exercises it foolishly by believing such communications are there to be checked out, and one's need for grace is somehow less important than it really is and can be taken care of later without too much concern. This confusion of priorities or allowing one's intellect to be overruled by one's curiosity is a dangerous no-go area, that more often than not, will appeal to the most intelligent just as easily as to the foolhardy and foolish.

In believing what we want to believe, one can set aside the knowledge, information, guidance, advice and whatever else we choose in order to satisfy our own stupid desires. What we cannot set aside is faith. The depth, the bedrock, the strength of our faith is what must be secured if one is going to be able to remain in communication with one's Supreme Commander and through one's mission control. The effect of space storms, minuscule meteorites and the particles of space-matter, which can endanger any spacecraft, vehicle or station are constantly being monitored in as much detail as possible, so that the maximum warning can be given.

To disregard the Law of God, to cease to fulfil one's religious obligations, to choose not to participate in the life of our Mother Church, only leaves us totally open and exposed to all the temptations of sin. This situation renders one defenceless and makes one totally susceptible in allowing sin into our lives, although initially in perhaps the smallest of ways. Over an extended period however its influence increases until, like a cloud crossing the sky, it becomes the dominant storm force in our lives, depriving us of the blazing sunshine representing the divine love of God.

Sin is always the choice of the sinner. It is a choice which he exercises freely and one from which he seldom escapes. A sinner, once he has embraced his favourite sin is seldom without it either in thought, word or deed and so faced with God's goodness he is unable to choose or accept it. He may as well be on the far bank of a river looking at the other side. By his lifestyle the unrepentant sinner cannot choose goodness any more than a blind man can choose to see or a deaf man choose to hear. Being outside the state of grace, or rather inside the state of sin, determines the sinner's choice for sin as 99% certain. For those who would claim to be spiritually uncommitted this is an untenable position motivated only by pride.

To consciously commit or condone any thought, word or deed contrary to God's Law must also, to whatever degree it warrants, be recognized as a 'sin'. The raw awareness of what the difference is between the state of grace and the state of sin and what this entails is what one's own spiritual strength should always be conscious of. One can only truly function if one is aware or conscious of one's Catholic role or mission and is doing one's utmost to live in accordance with it. This commission which was individually chosen for each son or daughter was given the moment the Sacrament of Baptism was bestowed upon them. For some the mission may be one they may have to learn to come to terms with, for others their struggle may not be as difficult as it seems, while for others their rejection may have been like Satan's: 'I will not serve,' The young man in the parable who felt he had to ask, received the the same response, as does anyone who seeks to know. In its quintessential form it is "Follow Me".

For the space pilot in control of his ship the on-going protection he seeks for his mission has both internal and external dimensions. The internal operational modes must be set and maintained whilst the external functions of the vehicle have to be secured in other different ways. The high temperature surface insulation tiles which protect the belly of the Shuttle from incredible heat degrees of over 1510˚C/2300˚F must constantly be monitored to make sure they are in excellent condition, as it is on their integrity the safety of the space vehicle depends on re-entering the Earth's atmosphere.

The Commandments should have enabled the Israelites to achieve their rightful place as God's chosen people. Sadly this was not to be. The New Testament was likewise created in order to allow mankind to achieve the salvation redeemed for us by Christ's Passion, Death and Resurrection. Sadly this Gospel in the care of His Church is no longer fully appreciated or preached as Our Lord intended and so as is often the case, it is not reaching the hearts of men. That God's Son Christ died for all mankind collectively and for each person individually is official Catholic doctrine. It is the same doctrine which teaches that it does not mean that all persons will be saved. Just as one who has been given the key to a door can somehow mislay or lose it, so also each of us can put it to one side as we too become careless and corrupt through the seduction of Satan and fail to retrieve it as we had planned.

Our mother Church, our religion and the Catechism of the Catholic Church all combine in great detail to utilize the Bible story of God's creation. For many Catholics today who choose to prefer the theory of evolution, or for those who reject the biblical account and instead prefer the Big Bang or some other alpha origin theory the choice is theirs. As in many similar situations there are those who are eager to learn, those who want to know and always those others for whom the journey back will be a great deal longer. The fall of Satan, and the eventual fall of Man, makes the Catholic religion a religion of finality redeemed through the Life, Death and Resurrection of Christ. The key to salvation redeemed by Christ, and presented to each of us at our Baptism is the key each one of us receives and with which we will have to insert in the Door of Death before we stand before the Throne of Judgement. As St Augustine so clearly puts it:

"It is only when facing death the true nature of the man
is known."

This Door of Death then is the apogee of reality and the one to which every person moves closer each moment of each day. This is the awesome challenge of time we choose to ignore, and prefer to hope it will be many years before we must face our last day on earth. For some it will be easy and a wonderful arrival into Heaven, for others an instantaneous revelation of horror, staring at the terrifying vista of Hell.

In today's world of high definition technology, multimedia, super interconnected highways and global internet web-cams the spiritual universe may seem irrelevant, meaningless and very inconsequential. This is the core opposite of reality. Whilst mankind remained in his agrarian, rural, and pre-industrial periods his development was limited to local regional and national horizons.

Today in this new millennium, a far more widespread and frightening situation exists: satellite footprints overshadow vast areas beaming culture, morals and media messages, subtle and degenerative in both blatant and subliminal modes to vast numbers of people most of whom are in no way capable of understanding the reality of what is happening. The spiritual forces of darkness are so enforced by the power generated through the vast quantities of sin being committed that the love of God and the intrinsic beauty of Mother Church are being overshadowed, ignored and rejected by millions who prefer to think, talk and promote a totally secular world.

Sin today is no longer recognized for what it is and no longer acknowledged for what it does. The teaching about its threatening power is set aside, and the consequences of its destruction on families, societies and communities is so appalling that, rather than try to combat it, countries have altered their constitutions and legislative systems to accommodate sin within the framework of their own legal and judicial systems. The effects of some such horrific decisions are obvious in the havoc being caused by such legislation on all classes of society. It must be re-emphasized that of all the Christian churches claiming to follow and preach the teachings of Christ today, only the Holy Roman Catholic Church stands firm in its claims to present, promote and protect the dignity of man and the sacredness of all life from pre-born through to death.

This message of individual respect, love and eternal life redeemed through the Passion, Death and Resurrection of Jesus Christ is today being savagely attacked and disregarded globally as never before. The eternal love of God which redeems those who choose the message of salvation is opposed by the architect of all sin, Satan, who uses his power to corrupt and enslave man with a myriad of choices, temptations and opportunities. In his power, sin is freely dispersed and made easily accessible for those who have not prepared any astute defence or protection against it. The onslaught of Satan is directed against each and every baptized, confirmed and practising Catholic. It is essential from Satan's viewpoint that anyone who seeks to protect the 'True Faith' must be compromised and destroyed.

On another plateau the clerical members of Mother Church who have received the Sacrament of Holy Orders are even more constantly being subjected to vicious attacks. The overall level of acceptance enjoyed by the state of sin today through such global evils as pornography, unjust wars, famine, planet pollution, contraception, abortion and divorce were introduced and made law by those in power and global authorities who were collectively able to claim they are acting on behalf of the 'common good'. The destruction of our Mother Church is foremost in the mind of Satan as it always has been since his own cataclysmic fall took place.

That the Catholic Church will suffer, that it will be shamed, and that it may well face persecution in the future appears almost inevitable but the assurance of Christ to His Church was that it will never be destroyed. For this reason it is necessary for all of today's Catholics to realize the full extent of the onslaught that is currently being orchestrated by Satan. With a far greater awareness of this spiritual combat taking place across the world it will be every Catholic's own personal commitment which will be brought into direct focus.

To pray for one's own spiritual strengths and loyalty to our Church has never been so important as it is today yet seldom is this singular prayer called for. It is difficult to make a case that God, His Church or Our Blessed Mother will save us from all peril and woe whilst we ourselves do very little. It is in loving God, loving our family, loving our neighbour, loving one's self that we are serving God as He intended, and the time is rapidly approaching when we will all be expected to strengthen and develop our prayer life and take on a great many more responsibilities.

Cardinal F George of Chicago (1936 / 2014) speaking to seminarians in 2010 made the observation;

> "I expect to die in bed, my successor will die in prison and his successor will die a martyr in the public square. His successor will pick up the shards of a ruined society and slowly help rebuild civilization, as the church has so often done in human history"

Should Cardinal George's words prove to be accurate, it would appear the world as we know it is indeed heading into some extremely difficult times and the Church will again need to call on her sons and daughters to come to her aid.

In controlling one's own mission, preparations are also needed and must be undertaken for what lies ahead. Enough quantities of grace must be accessible as there is no way one can function without it. Confidence in our free will is so often misplaced because we have not taken sufficient care to acquaint ourselves fully with our religion. We take silly risks at our peril, as we are over dependent sometimes on our religion for strength and protection. Unless, however, the limitation of our protection is understood our own pride keeps us very vulnerable and liable to fall. It is our own deposit of faith which empowers us in our mission.

One's basic need therefore is to gain a sufficient amount of spiritual strength to be able to withstand a sinful onslaught through one temptation or another by turning to prayer in time to gain the necessary strength. Unless we have mastered this defence we will fail to develop a sufficient spiritual integrity, thereby allowing all sorts of spiritual doubts and concerns to take control, where assurance and rebuttal should be the automatic response. We recklessly assume what little instructions or knowledge we have accumulated will be adequate, and we commence our mission almost totally unaware that the very sin of presumption itself is almost sufficient to contaminate and corrupt our chances of success.

If one can love the Sacraments, and keep the Commandments, one is well within God's love and protection. Nevertheless this is never as easy as it sounds as temptations are seldom far away and sin is never more than a step behind them. As so many saints have demonstrated over the centuries it is difficult, but not impossible, to conquer sin. It certainly becomes easier if one knows what one may be called upon to face. Then one can begin to believe why the need for grace is so great and the Gospel reinforces the message:

'To whom much has been given, more will be given'

in order to strengthen one's religion one has been given the faith and as it grows stronger, one will also be given the grace to combat the greater temptations which continue to attack in one form or another, throughout one's entire life. Sin in all its deceptions and enticements must be exposed to the light of truth and recognized for what it is, a deadly spiritual danger that can kill. Today the vast majority of people in the secular world prefer to describe sin in a rather erroneous or esoteric way insofar that it really is something totally vague which need not be taken too seriously, if at all.

It is possible to experience the love of God through prayer, fasting, the Sacraments and the gospel. Through this we are all invited to live in God's Love. The message of the love of God is encapsulated in the divine truths. The law of God is given to us through Moses in The Commandments and highlighted in the gospel which we are clearly instructed to follow. Sin is diametrically opposed to God's love and through it Satan entices the individual to break away from the Commandments tempting one to believe foolishly that by doing so one is achieving freedom. At the same time Satan is making one sin in particular so attractive as to exploit the individual's prime weakness. Satan's power is inflicted through hatred of God, and designed and devised to corrupt mankind collectively while individually harming God's creation through as many sons and daughters who allowed themselves to be swayed.

Should we break a Commandment in a venial or serious way we know we have done wrong. We know if for no other reason than our conscience, the voice of our soul, clearly tells us so. Our level of religious knowledge, the accumulative instructions we have been given over our early and formative years also guides us. Having such a broad understanding, it is strange to witness so many people upon reaching maturity allow their attitude to sin to be both obscure and obtuse.

It is apparent that the clear and categorized list of lesser sins identified by our Mother Church appears to have little if any direct overriding influence on the way we live today. This should not even be conceivable but it is the subtle seduction of Satan, forever at work, which has furthered this popular misconception and or indifference to sin that has somehow made sin obsolete. In the scale of sins today is it conceivable that the theft of a 10 dollar bill does not matter, whereas the theft of 10,000 dollars does? For this to be the case then of course a rationale for any sin is conceivable but this can never be the case.

Somehow or other sin today lacks a spiritual cutting edge. What was once thought of as serious sin is now considered somewhat less and God's love is so magnanimous that one is now automatically forgiven. Such views formulated by the dissident monk Luther were responsible for originating and igniting this ever-popular heresy, and such was its enormous appeal that its acceptance was widespread amongst great numbers of German Catholics who choose to move over to the dark side of the mirror.

Today among many Catholics such liberal and progressive thinking is not seen as an obstacle to their faith, and it is such false teaching and thinking that has almost brought the Church to her knees. For those who prefer to believe such deceptions it is a prime example of what one can be led into through common consensus, rather than what is the real actual truth as clearly explained by Church doctrine on a one-on-one basis or by a formal course of studies.

In essence the Catholic Church teaches that there are seven deadly sins: pride, covetousness, lust, anger, gluttony, envy and sloth. These are the vices through which sin will manifest itself in order to try to seduce and ensnare every man, woman and child who possesses free will. Remarkable as it seems, the vast majority of people assume they are spiritually strong enough to withstand such entreatments and temptations. The Catholic Church teaches the opposite. Without sanctifying grace one has little hope of withstanding Satan's onslaught. A man of pride will become more proud, a man of anger will become more angry, a man of envy will become more, envious, as sin is always an ongoing lifestyle or state. Once the grip of sin takes over, like an appetite it must be constantly fed and satisfied. In the ancient Bardic world of poetry Satan responds to the questioning Saint as to how gleefully he entices the poor ordinary common Man into believing his lies.

'What bait do you use,' said the Saint to the Devil,
'When you fish where the souls of men abound?'
'Well, for special tastes,' said the King of Evil,

'Gold and fame are the best I've found.'
'But for common use?' asked the Saint, 'Ah then,'
Said the Devil, 'I angle for Man, not men,
And a thing I hate
Is to change my bait,
So I fish with a woman the whole year round.'

Indeed the sin of covetousness may be so incredibly difficult to resist that the Church's teaching on it, as on other sins, has somehow been placed a little to one side in some form of abeyance. One is unlikely to hear a sermon based on the above poem at Mass next Sunday whilst the likely positive side of Catholic social justice such as tolerance, understanding and peace may all be highlighted. The fact that such noble attributes can be claimed by very many religions and organisations seems to be always overlooked, as the Church expands on her social role at perhaps some cost to her spiritual one. The most significant fact still remains however and that is only those who are faithful and possess sanctifying grace can hope to defeat the temptations of Satan, and in so doing then spread the Gospel of God's love and forgiveness. It is for this very reason that Christ invites each one of us to be a follower in spreading the good news. Those who are fallen and remain so, forfeit all graces and privileges, contaminated as they are within a permanent state of sin.

The people, the places, the friends and those who surround us will usually reflect to some extent what state of lifestyle we choose to adopt. In today's world it has never been easier to disregard sin partially or altogether, and so set it aside. The pitfall by taking sole total control over one's own personal life and value system without any reference or contact with God is that one risks getting totally and horribly lost. Sin mutates just as the AIDS virus mutates. For one person sin will always be seen as the act of a good person committing evil. For another, sin will be the lack of action a person could have taken in order to help another. Sin in its deception is always removed and seen only in the distance as the action or lack of action, unless of course it is a private or hidden secret sin.

In general terms one is reticent to accept or recognize one's personal sins. Even if one is humble or courageous enough to acknowledge one's past sins, one still has to fight off the temptation to claim them as venial rather than grievous. The acceptance of a personal or temporal spiritual punishment due in relation to the sins one commits during one's life has also, over the past half century or so, become more and more refined, to the extent that if this is the case then it must be fashioned in a benevolent way.

The severe places referred to in Catholic teaching as Purgatory and Hell which for hundreds of years were presented as true dimensions of pain and suffering are seldom thought of today in such terms. Purgatory in its true sense of being a place of purification where each person will experience various degrees of suffering before being able to sustain the presence of God's eternal glory is rarely explained, yet it is an article of faith. Hell is a doctrine of faith. These are not debatable points, yet their presentation and interpretation has rendered them almost irrelevant in their insignificance. If anything it is the modern presentation of Purgatory and Hell which has created the new mindset within the Church to proclaim that both of these spiritual realms no longer contain the intense pain and suffering elements that the Church taught and preached before the 2nd Vatican Council (1962-1965). This present darkness of sin thus allows for minimal punishments, if at all.

The popular and current Christian belief on dying is that of an almost painless transition with immediate access to Heaven. This being the maxim for today of course makes it a far more preferable and attractive concept to accept. Today, with only a minimal fear of God, man by his actions has proved he is capable of committing the most appalling crimes against humanity, the scale of which a hundred years or so ago would have been totally unimaginable to most societies yet, in the present day appear almost normal.

The world as a dangerous place is now an acceptable reality and even though man appears to want to talk more and more about God he really only wants to talk about Him on his own human terms. Man seems quite unable to comprehend that no matter what public claims may be made today, such as the promotion of a just and equitable global society, without God's love, Man's cruel and exploitative nature is incapable of promoting and sustaining a genuine and just global society.

Sin today world-wide is not only tolerated and accepted, it is openly promoted. Truth today is misrepresented and misreported. Once the power of Satan conquers a territory it moves further on. There may-be isolated pockets of resistance, there may be some good people suppressed and living under great pressure attempting to survive the adversity. These can, and will, be re-visited and destroyed later, at Satan's leisure. The numerous churches which claim to represent Christ may like to do so in a sense of goodwill, yet their doctrines and services fall far short of what Jesus Christ taught and what He continues to promote in the Catholic Church.

It is primarily for this reason that the Catholic Church is more under constant attack today than ever before and portrayed by the media in the most unforgiving and alien way possible. This picture painted by so many secular journalists around the world today is a further demonstration of Satan's power and influence. Were the details of the Church's charitable streams, foundations of Catholic benefits, overseas Catholic relief agencies and aid money of one kind or another totalled up globally there would be no other governmental or non-governmental body on earth to equal or surpass its financial, food and aid support to those most in need.

The Catholic ethos of giving for living seldom if ever adds any terms and conditions to its aid programs. God's love is universal, His church is universal, and His love for all mankind is also proclaimed in its truth and light. The fact that it is a message so many sinister governments and countries hostile to Catholicism alter and prohibit reaching their people means that a greater understanding of God's love never reaches much of mankind. South Korea is a wonderful testament to a country where the love of God was freely introduced and today shines brightly on its people due to the warmth of the welcome Our Lord Jesus Christ received in this faithful Catholic country.

Even in the most secular of countries it is not unknown for Muslims to choose Catholic education for their children in preference to state schools. This is commendable as most intelligent parents would prefer to choose an educational system based on Catholic virtues of faith, truth and fairness.

However where the Catholic Church or its educational system is not accepted a different type of society can and is being forged. Rather than addressing the needs of others of lesser importance, the needs of the State, the needs of the politicians and the needs of all public servants come first. The previous Russian federation, the dreaded USSR, tried for more than half a century through its brutal Communist apparatchik to stamp out Christianity and failed to do so. The Hammer and Sickle only altered its stance once it had reached some discreet arrangement with the Vatican who would cease to denounce Communism. This decision was taken by Pope John XXIII on the condition the Russian Communist Government would allow the Russian Orthodox Church to send its own observers to the 2nd Vatican Council (1962-1965).

In today's world where spin is used to enhance political gain where government policies are enacted to restrain rather than to promote the common good, there is little doubt that the world must suffer from such corruption, and war and poverty must both prevail. The Catholic Church however refuses to let go of mankind. It continues to proclaim the good news and claims the right to identify itself as the one 'True' Church. This Universal Roman Church presents, preaches and teaches the entire message of Christ in clear unequivocal terms, making it popular with few while at the same time making it unpopular with many. It continues to teach that contraception is wrong, divorce is sinful, re-marriage is unacceptable and abortion is the world's most heinous crime.

This last crime of immense global proportions is particularly evil in that it is condoned by some of the world's foremost and fortunate Christian countries. Not only do these Judaic-Christian countries enjoy considerable wealth and power, it is their own nominated aid agencies which fund and provide facilities to further this appalling global holocaust in the most underdeveloped countries. For such pronouncements the Catholic Church continues to be attacked relentlessly from both without and within so that its conductive power to transmit God's love to mankind via the Sacraments is constantly under threat. It is likely to be given to them regardless as if some other form of distribution or shared authority would make them better Catholics. It is painful to witness such demands being made by those who seem intent on continuously questioning authority, those who seek to promote a new order and who forever wish to debate fundamental church doctrine. To equate the deterioration of the planet's natural resources with the deterioration of the understanding and acceptance of Catholic doctrine is not very difficult. The phenomenon of change taking place within the Catholic Church today is both mammoth and radical. How the most senior cardinals in the Church can discuss the variance between the interpretations of doctrinal and pastoral doctrine as if they were some modern problems seeking modern solutions is quite extraordinary.

Where today's Bishop of Rome seeks to lead the church remains to be seen, however what is certain is that Christ's bride will prevail. Over recent decades it must be acknowledged that there have been many clerics who have chosen to follow Satan and continue to do so. For selfish reasons the cover-ups, the sex scandals and the overall clerical corruption are engineered and controlled by those who are entrusted with the power and privilege to protect our Mother Church yet instead have wilfully chosen to harm her.

To delve even deeper into the realm of sin which is controlled by the power of Satan, it is again necessary to consider the situation of the lost space station drifting aimlessly in deep space. Being isolated without any communications or vital supplies, its on-board monitors signal an alert in the early warning fault activation system. Whilst it may be unclear whether this is a fault which can be contained by one of the on-board computers or is a problem of a much more serious nature, it is obvious that a swift response is needed to offset serious potential consequences.

Unless this happens the result is inevitable. Sin, the approach of sin, the temptation, the occasion, all indicate an early warning of unknown degree approaching. Such a series of alerts for many young Catholics no longer appears to convey the real sense of impending spiritual disaster that lies directly ahead.

As the danger approaches sin will mutate. It will not remain static. It will never take part control; it will never be a half full or half empty vessel. It must be up to the very brim, every thought, every word and every action. Satan does not do half measures. It may be an ongoing process, it may be a chain reaction, it may be a fell swoop, it may even be a sudden melt-down but unless sin is vanquished at the onset it will destroy. The overwhelming conundrum of sin is that it is twofold. It presents itself as so powerful one really can be tempted into believing that its power is too great to resist, and no real attempt is made to fight it. On the other hand the temptation is also there to see just how close one can get without being caught. Its' intrigue is in its web and to explore more, to look closer, to touch just once, to caress fractionally more intimately is fatal, as suddenly, it is no longer temptation, but now a real full-on red raw active raging sin. Such a tremendous sinful force spiralling totally outside of one's control is utterly impossible to escape from until it is fully satisfied and one's inevitable fall, follows.

The initial spiritual gifts bestowed on one at Baptism through sanctifying grace are the three divine virtues. These are given to each infant until they are ready to receive the Sacraments of Penance and Eucharist. These are as presents a father would give his son or daughter and form the trinity of Faith, Hope and Charity. Until one makes one's First Holy Communion these three virtues are there to guide the child who upon reaching the age commonly referred to as 'the use of reason' is then expected to make their First Confession. This prerequisite for preparation in turn allows them to then make their First Holy Communion, their first meeting with their Saviour. From this date the actual law as passed down by Moses in the form of The Commandments must now become their rule and their law which they henceforth will be expected to adhere to. The further seven gifts of wisdom, understanding, counsel, fortitude, knowledge, piety and a fear of the Lord, will be added later to their spiritual strength through the Sacrament of Confirmation in encouraging the young person to enter into the adult world seeking the mission entrusted to him or her by their own personal Creator.

In the growth of faith it is essential that one's awareness and love of God is consummated within the trinity of Faith, Hope and Charity. The new born baby, infant and young child should be well nourished in the code of rights and wrongs up to the time he or she is both ready and prepared for the reception of their First Sacrament of Penance/Reconciliation and their First Holy Communion. After these Sacraments have been administered the Law of God, encapsulated in the Ten Commandments already outlined, becomes the formal criteria one is commanded to live by. Should one fail to develop one's appreciation and harmony with the trinity of virtues one originally received at Baptism, then one is immediately faced with the Law or the Commandments which are then seen in a more stern context and rigour of the law.

The Commandments viewed in this way can seldom be enshrined, only feared, and so where love should have taken root, fear now dwells. This is a further clever deception, and one Satan never fails to exploit to the full for there becomes a state of mind which could be entitled 'The Fear of God.' It is through this seed of fear planted by Satan that he seeks to directly control, dominate, and utilize his plan for the destruction of one's individual's hope of salvation.

Fear in the heart or mind of any man can lead to despair, and despair is Satan's most bitter cup which is always sinful. One's acceptance of despair is contrary to the very first commandment in that it is the refusal to trust in God for the graces necessary for salvation. By succumbing to despair one ceases to have faith in God and one looks elsewhere, one listens to others, and one rejects what was given to them at Baptism. In refusing to believe that God will supply the graces needed to gain salvation one decides knowingly or unknowingly to believe in the power of Satan. If one looks around at the amount of despair on a local, national or global level, it is impossible not to realize the vastness of the state of sin. Despair through the pain of failure, of poverty, of loneliness, of drug addiction, of marital breakdown and of infidelity, is remorseless.

Unless seen for what it is, and isolated, despair becomes all-consuming, doing irreparable damage until finally it can only lead to the final travesty of self-destruction. Today in the harshness of reality, such phrases as 'I wish I were dead!' and 'I did not ask to be born!' are all too common. The number of people, young and old, who commit suicide each year is increasing yet the enormity of the deed and its spiritual consequences are the two aspects of suicide which are seldom if ever discussed. The epidemic, the illness, the mental health, the mitigating circumstances are all topics which are presented at seminars to try and prove that this sin is never actually wilfully committed.

Interestingly it is the priest, or in today's church, the celebrant who insists at the funeral Mass that the deceased is, being made welcome and escorted into the new and holy city, the new Jerusalem, that causes the appalling confusion. How he can possibly make such a statement is quite amazing and the ongoing effect such an assurance makes others present somewhat more at ease with the sin. The teaching of the Catholic Church is clear. The act is in itself intrinsically evil, and like all other grievous sins unless it is repented must have terrible consequences. Such teaching today is seldom heard let alone emphasized. At all masses for such recently deceased persons young and old it should be obligatory for the priest to invite all present to plead with him for Divine mercy for the soul of the remains now facing the altar. The celebrant should also emphasize it is the lack of love shown to the deceased in this world, which has led to the despair, culminating in this act. Sadly today the sin of despair is a sin which has almost vanished from the spiritual radar and again as seldom preached on its depth and deadliness remains hidden until yet another funeral Mass is sacrificed.

The more one succumbs to the sin of despair the more it grinds one down in choosing to believe that God has deserted us, rather than we have deserted Him. In this cruel description of despair it is also likely for one to begin to believe that this sin is far removed and reserved mainly for those in some sector or social level of society, where temporal hardships are widespread and material comforts minimal. That being the case, if one were fortunate enough to be modestly affluent then there would be little need to be concerned about it. Though this may be the opinion many people choose to believe in it is sadly not the case. In fact it could not be further from the truth. Regardless of class or affluence, job profile or marital situation, despair can never be very far away. Despair cuts across all social and economic classes. It is extremely foolish to think there is a spiritual imbalance which favours one level of society whilst another is summarily crushed. Despair destroys faith in one way, presumption does so in an even more invasive fashion. To comprehend presumption as sin it is necessary to believe that Christ's Life, Passion, Death and Resurrection were meaningless and may as well have never taken place. This is the enormity of presumption.

In the evaluation of the purposeful or meaningful life the anchorage of faith is one which gives some stability and some strength against the tremendous tides and currents which are destined to blow through one's life. For the baptised Catholic unless one tries to live fully within one's faith there is always the risk of yielding to temptation and falling into the state of serious sin. It is at such junctions the support and massive input of grace that is readily available through the sacrament of Penance that must be called upon. Unless this happens than it is almost impossible to live as a follower of Christ, as one is indeed lost. Despair driven by Satan takes control and rather than seek God's infinite mercy, the sinner continues to live in sin by choosing to believe he or she cannot be forgiven.

Presumption on the other hand convinces us that God's sacrifice on earth was enough not only to guarantee us salvation but to relieve us of any need through prayers and good works to actually contribute to our own salvation. This blind faith frees us from our own obligations, allows us to ignore our spiritual responsibilities and totally disregard our life's mission. So much so that no one has any need to worry or fret as one is already assured of eternity. Here it must be evident that God accepted Christ's sacrifice on behalf of those who would love and follow Him. For them the kingdom of eternal salvation has been prepared as their just reward, it awaits those who complete their mission and claim it. For those who choose not to accept Christ's sacrifice or attempt to fulfill their mission God's kingdom will remain forever closed. So even though Christ died for each and every person that they may be saved, His sacrifice in no way guarantees it. First one must seek and find God in order to secure one's place in the kingdom.

Presumption is the sin that encourages all, even the most contemptible sinner, to believe that heaven also awaits him at death, regardless of the misery, suffering pain, and hardship he may have caused so many others whilst on Earth. Presumption may not have the trappings of despair but it is certainly no less destructive. If anything presumption, which is fantasy, is even more difficult to resist, and harder to avoid, for just as reality hides nothing, fantasy hides everything, and for that reason is extremely difficult to detect.

By our thoughts, actions and words we are known. Our lifestyles our families our careers all indicate the type of person we are and the lives we appear to live. For Catholics one's life centered on being a follower of Christ is the real challenge. One is expected not only to know the gospel but to actually seek to live it and embrace it. The great conundrum: if one were arrested and thrown into prison accused of being a Catholic, would sufficient evidence be found to find one 'guilty'? To try and gain a continuous understanding of what one's role is and what one's mission really means should never be more than a thought away from one's mind or one's prayers. It is only through constant prayer and fasting that the meaning of faith, hope and charity will ever become evident. This need to keep updating these virtues enables us to understand how one must live, purified, like children, seeking always the Kingdom of Heaven.

In the situation of a burn-out or whatever reason an automatic main engine shut-down occurs, the space vehicle now locked in a hibernation mode drifts helplessly, it has no ability to function in its primary role, and can only exist suspended in space for a finite period of time. In this state it is at the mercy of whatever space elements may influence it or force it to move in whatever direction the prevailing cosmic forces drive it. Sin is even more ruthless, not only does it seek to capture and destroy, but having succeeded it will then use its captive as a ways and means host through which it will seek to ensnare and destroy as many other space vehicles and their crews as possible.

In its essence sin destroys charity and alienates love. Once serious mortal sin has been committed, the divine virtue of charity is totally removed from one's soul as one's primary task to remain in union with God is broken. The ability to continue in sanctifying grace is gone, By one's own action love can no longer exist, and no works done whilst in this state can be of any sanctifying merit. Once the individual is committed to the state of sin it is sin which that person will then promote. No genuine love or charity exists, as Satan now controls one's mission. Whatever sinful thoughts or actions one commits are automatically added to and further consolidates the new regime of which he is now a part.

The principles of compound interest apply more to sin than even to finance. The virtues of hope and faith are not instantly removed, as is charity from one's soul. To some greater or lesser extent they remain with the heart of the sinner trapped as he/she now is and knowing instinctively the actual loss of charity his soul is suffering. The person may still wish to believe and may still somehow attempt to hope yet for how long, and how strong must eventually depend on whether or not their faith and their memory of God's mercy will prevail. The possibility that somehow some significant spiritual rescue will take place to save him or her from the despotic commander he now serves, slight though it maybe, can never be ruled out.

Having outlined in some detail the reality of sin and the state of sin, it is possible that one is tempted to believe that the choice one makes is perhaps still somewhat outside one's own control. This is not so. By choosing to follow Christ as an active disciple seeking his grace and love, our desire to remain within the state of grace is evident. By choosing to treat our Mother Church in a dismissive fashion and involve oneself more in the affairs of the world is without doubt a lazy ill- conceived choice, freely made, and one that will only lead into greater and greater danger.

Today the disenchantment within the Catholic Church is expressed by Her own members, both clerical and laity who appear disunited and fractured, unsure of where they are being led. For centuries the onslaughts against the Church were orchestrated and controlled by its powerful enemies on the outside. Today the threat comes from within. Sadly unlike the world's greatest football clubs whose directors, managers, coaches and players have sometimes let their club down, the support of the fans for the club itself has always remained loyal and true, never wavering.

The club itself is beyond reproach; only its officers and agents are found wanting. In today's Church this is not the case. If anything, the complete reversal applies. It is the very senior administrators and the fans who are demanding that it is the most sweeping changes that must be made. Ironically the architects for change are more often than not those with a hidden hostility to the Church who even though they continue to inflict damage, still appear to hold positions of high rank and are held by many in the highest esteem.

The fact that so much dissension and dissatisfaction resonates within our Mother Church today only adds to the turmoil. Now, more than ever before one's relationship with God needs to be increased and strengthened. The need for individual commitment to steadfastness and strength has never been greater. In one's private and public life, today's

Catholic must be an example of both courage and determination to stand up for both the love and the law of God.

It is in this role, as a follower of Christ that the Law of God in the form of the Ten Commandments must now become more fully woven into one's life. The Gospel makes clear that, in order for one to gain salvation, one's life must be led in accordance with the commandments. To speak therefore of sin, the vices which lead to sin, the occasions where one knows one will be in danger of sin are all extraneous. It is only when one is actually living the Gospel, resisting temptation, falling time and time again only to pick oneself up that the way, the truth and the life begins to have real meaning. It is all important that one learns not just to know and understand what the Commandments mean but in knowing the Law one can then understand in depth their necessity if one is to grow fully into dedicated fortitude and loving obedience.

'The just man has the Law of the Lord written on his heart.'

It is difficult to describe sin and the depth of pain and suffering, inflicted on oneself and on others through leading a sinful life, yet many great saints and scholars in retrospect have attempted to do so, if for no other reason than to dissuade others from taking this path. One way in which to attain a degree of awareness of sin is maybe to examine its origins. A sin of deep premeditation differs greatly from one emanating from instinct or impulse. The former is committed with no excuse, the latter by its nature deserves some degree of mitigation. A sin of the moment has some sense of madness, a planned sin has none.

From the moment we begin to employ our 'use of reason' as our moral guidance, our free will allows us to take control of our mission. What was given to us at Baptism, Penance and Holy Communion must now begin to blossom and show signs of spiritual growth. The faith of a child is, a faith of love, and the supernatural love of God for the child is given reality through as many channels as possible. Naturally in the normal sense of the word the parents are the most immediate providers of all love and joy to the infant. These parents united themselves in the Sacrament of Marriage and seeing the creation of their baby as a gift from God, readily and willingly supply God's love with their own love. As the child grows and experiences the growth of love, the first experiences of good and bad, joy and sadness, pain and pleasure, all must be learned and childishly understood at the mother's knee.

It is the beginnings of awareness of the natural world which in turn prepare the young 'faithful' person to start their awareness of the supernatural world and understand that with the spiritual voice of their soul to guide them they must begin, not only to walk in the love of God, but also to understand the Laws of God, Faith therefore in God, in the world around them, both seen and unseen, is central to their existence, their life and their mission, and the understanding of God's Law is like everything else emanating from God.

The flight deck consoles on the NASA Space Shuttle while complex and detailed in appearance are totally familiar to the pilot whose training over a long period of time has given him an intimate knowledge of what purpose each row of dials activates and what functions the banks of switches are designed to perform. In one's life mission as Catholics the situation is no different. After one's birth, one's successful launch, on receiving the Sacrament of Baptism, one is under the guidance of one's parents. It is only after we have received the Sacraments of Penance, Eucharist and Confirmation that we are free in some high altitude orbit to act independently of our mission control. This period however is still being observed by our parents and others who may wish to advise and provide some additional information.

This intermediate period is crucial to one's subsequent ability to successfully complete one's mission. Unless one accumulates and understands the knowledge, the awareness and prowess needed to accomplish the mission, one may still need further instructions and training. The interim young adulthood period is the life-graduating one in which the final adjustments must be made and refined just as in moving from a close earth orbit into the realms of deeper space, a whole new voyage is about to begin. This final thrust from Earth's gravitational influence finally puts the control of the craft into the hands of the pilot and, with the help of ground control, he must now be the one to take and make the life-saving decisions over the full course of his forthcoming mission.

The Ten Commandments are the fundamental rules for all men and women to live by. In addition they are to the forefront in particular for Roman Catholic Christians who seek to complete their life's mission in the most exemplary way they can. If one follows them they are assured of success, and can have every confidence they will return to their Father on their Re-Entry. For practising Catholics there can never be the slightest doubt in accepting them as they are essential for one's spiritual strength and survival. For the lapsed or dissident Catholic who chooses to ignore, alter or reformat these laws they do so only at enormous risk. To choose to wilfully ignore, disregard or continuously break them is inviting disaster leading nowhere but spiritual suicide.

These Commandments were originally kept, maintained and upheld by the Jews as part of their faith until the birth of Jesus. Once Jesus established the New Covenant the Law remained central to the New Church and so it has continued, enshrined in the Catholic faith. These Commandments are mandatory not just for all Catholics and Christians who claim to accept them but also for all mankind, who choose to work in earnest for the love of one's neighbour and the coming of God's kingdom.

To understand and live God's Law through the practice of one's faith makes life an ongoing pilgrimage from which any deviation if at all possible must be avoided. The path is not an easy one, and for the majority it becomes more difficult rather than easier as time goes by. This spiritual paradox is one with which even some of the greatest saints themselves had to contend. To overcome this barrier is in a way a final challenge. It is only within the Law of God itself where one must start to take control of one's life and honour God through one's committed allegiance.

To a certain extent it is only as one grows in grace and understanding that the Commandments become more recognisable and somehow more demanding, as the urge for sainthood continues to grow. For children or in one's youth stealing may be a grave temptation but as one gets older the attractiveness of impurity may take over and indeed one may have to become somewhat elderly before the sin of choice is gluttony and so the struggle continues.

The Gospel makes very clear that the Ten Commandments are the compass rose with clear pointers which will allow one to plot their way forward through life. What must always be remembered, however, is where the route leads us is very much of one's own making and choice, and depends on how one freely lives them in accordance with one's life in a fully positive and loving manner.

By the time one receives the Sacrament of Confirmation the actual quality of religious knowledge and the depth of instruction one has received, is of the greatest importance as is the realization of God's Law. The Gospel story which has been projected and dissected in detail so very many times, has already made one well aware of God's Love and Incarnation. It is this knowledge of faith that makes the reception of the Commandments a most obvious and welcomed choice. Should one receive them with little or minimal faith foundation or depth of meaning, they may well appear to be a disconnected and repressive set of rules. Satan seeks to use this initial juvenile reaction as a reason to reject the Commandments from the onset, and by this means he successfully tempts many badly educated Catholics into believing that the Commandments are not for them.

Of all the vices which entice Man, pride is the number one in the list as being the sin that Man's ego finds almost impossible to resist and defeat. For Satan to convince the proud person, who has achieved a great deal of material wealth, that they are not in need of the Commandments, or they can take their forgiveness direct from God with little effort on their part, is sometimes all that is needed, and Satan's conquest is both easy and assured.

How then must one try to understand and meditate on these Commandments given by God to meet man's great need of them? A need perhaps as great now as when Moses brought the original tablets down from Mt Sinai. Without them today Man returns once more to the worship of the Golden Calf and tempts God to deliver the terrible chastisement. These Commandments then must be concentrated upon and made central in one's life, along with the divine virtues as sentinels or bulwarks of one's faith. It is necessary to appreciate the Commandments as a gift from God by which Man is encouraged to live by, without any great temporal or spiritual fear. They are being obeyed and constantly renewed through the Sacrament of Penance which is received as a way of being refreshed with God's divine mercy.

It is interesting to consider them as if for the first time, written in the following manner:

THE TEN COMMANDMENTS

I   I AM THE LORD YOUR GOD YOU SHALT NOT HAVE ANY OTHER GOD BEFORE ME

II   YOU WILL NOT MISUSE MY NAME

III   YOU WILL KEEP MY DAY HOLY

IV   YOU WILL HONOUR YOUR FATHER AND YOUR MOTHER

V   YOU WILL NOT KILL

VI   YOU WILL NOT COMMIT ADULTERY

VII   YOU WILL NOT STEAL

VIII   YOU WILL NOT LIE

IX   YOU WILL NOT DESIRE YOUR NEIGHBOUR'S WIFE

X   YOU WILL NOT DESIRE YOUR NEIGHBOUR'S GOODS

In the fullness of light these commandments cannot be more direct or crystal clear, and yet in the shade, shadow or darkest of nights they are somehow made almost obstructive and obsolete. How this can be seems quite impossible to comprehend yet, the more closely one examines the situation, the more one begins to realize how sensitive and fragile the life of the soul really is. In fact the necessity or the need to surround the soul, like the most fragile flower, with the maximum protection makes the actual living of the Law a great deal easier to appreciate and understand.

In a spacecraft or space station the on-board bank of computers processing data of various digitized and encrypted forms are all programmed and maintained by various forms of protocol and best practice. Whatever minor faults or glitches occur, the backup protective code will identify and isolate the problem while the automatic corrective procedures lock into action. Major problems requiring interim shut down are far more serious, yet must be overcome for the mission to proceed.

The Commandments, which are our spiritual defence parameters, are both vital and essential for the success of one's life mission. To alter, interfere, distract or neutralize the meaning or interpretation of the Commandments renders them disingenuous to the extent that having been breached they must eventually become more and more meaningless. Finally the protection they were designed to offer loses the support and effectiveness they were intended to provide.

Taking a closer look at God's Law and the totality of its meaning, it encapsulates an entirety, or a unity stating man's responsibilities to his God first and then to his fellow man. It is within this entirety which we, as fragile human beings are contained, yet vulnerable to attacks from the temptations of sin launched by Satan constantly to penetrate the defences. This collective human entity can be attacked through any of the 10 portals, each of which needs to be securely defended. Each stronghold therefore must be fully maintained for if one is overrun or worse still, seriously breached, then the other nine remaining defensive shields are also compromised to varying degrees. The effectiveness of the Commandments therefore, is that they must be seen and appreciated as a complete system.

One missing heat-resisting tile may be sufficient to cause catastrophic damage to a Shuttle and so it is that once any part of one's weakness is exposed then the frailty of one's craft becomes crucial and the mission is in imminent danger.

For this reason our knowledge and acceptance of God's Law must be central to our thinking, as only in living the Commandments as best we can, will we be enabled one to remain fully in control of our life's mission.

Had man ever been able to achieve true love of God there would never have been any need for the Commandments. Adam on behalf of man fell and Satan corrupted not only our original parents, but also corrupted each and every individual ever born, through the inheritance they received of 'Original Sin'. The sole exception in all humanity ever born, being Our Blessed Mother, Mary, Mother of all mankind. Satan the fallen archangel who succeeded in corrupting our first parents was thus assured that the existence of sin would always expose Man's 'original' weakness. The instruction of our Saviour was emphasized more than once in the Gospel when he told his disciples;

> "If you keep My Commandments you shall abide in my love" John 15:10

In the world of genetic science, the isolation and identification of genes is standard routine practice; in a spiritual sense the smear of original sin is no different. It was, is, and will be passed to every person born on Earth, and the mystery of the Incarnation was, and is, the spiritual antidote. Today man's need for the Commandments has never been greater or paradoxically his indifference to them more apparent. For the holy ones the living saints it may well be that, as they concentrate on the two Commandments, love of God and love of Neighbour, acts such as cheating, coveting and killing, are not even relevant.

However, for the ordinary person struggling daily with many foolish and subtle temptations the need to inspect our souls for damage, inflicted both by our thoughts and actions and the actions and thoughts of others, is of vital importance. How else can we salve our injuries, bandage our wounds and seek help from our supreme Commander, unless we develop a close awareness of sin. Such awareness through our understanding of the commandments, our faith in the Sacraments and our confidence in our Faith is where we find our temporal refuge here on Earth. When we experience this trinity of faith we can spiritually sense the fragility of our soul. In this spiritual realm, as in the material one, the pain of ignorance is only assuaged by the joy and confidence of knowledge. This spiritual knowledge gives one that cleaner sharper image of the mission which one has been entrusted with, and that image allows us to live our lives only through a true love of God in carrying out His Will.

CHAPTER

6

How then must the Ten Commandments be absorbed? Relating to God, the first three must be acknowledged and accepted as predominant in that they glorify God. The remainder are subsequent and beneficial in that their compliance guarantees man's harmony. The first three account for one's Love of God, the remaining seven combined, account for one's Love of Neighbour. The Commandments given to all God's chosen people are the same, yet their reception by each generation both by men of goodwill and men of cruel indifference means that the leaders and teachers of the Church bear a tremendous responsibility in passing on the faith.

If St Pope John Paul II is to be remembered for any single practical act of his Pontificate, his commissioning of the Catechism of the Catholic Church was maybe his most beneficial legacy. In so far as to how well it was accepted and taught in Catholic schools and colleges after its introduction is another matter entirely. Of the 2,856 paragraphs which formulate this Catechism almost a quarter of them, pps 2052/2550, are dedicated to explaining The Commandments in great detail, both in their depth, and truth.

ONE

Looking closely at the love of God, it is clear to see that from the very first Commandment this love is to be both freely given and reciprocated forever uniting in harmony. The beautiful passage in the Book of Corinthians says it all:

> "I will walk among you, and will be your God, and you shall be my people."
>
> Corinthians 6:16

There can be little doubt that nothing is to come between God and His people. God wanted man to know that they had not been forgotten or abandoned; He was indeed their God, real and forever, and not the golden idol or image the children of Moses had fashioned. To demonstrate His love, He sent His only Son Jesus to sacrifice His life for all mankind collectively, and for each person individually, in order that they may be saved. This covenant He made to repatriate man within His Kingdom which was to be restored by the Word being made Flesh. Man for his part would be once again, re-fashioned and re-born, be saved from sin and given the freedom to choose Christ as his Messiah.

TWO

Do not abuse the name of God. This Commandment is too often disregarded and diluted by those who adopt the casual act of swearing or cursing and even blaspheming the sacred name, by the use of vile lecherous language. Such foul-mouthedness and anti-reverence should never take place, even in the most heated of moments. The most grievous sins of false oaths and perjuries are too terrible to contemplate, as they are committing God to underwrite a sin, or guarantee a lie. Having given us His name, we must take every care of it as, by the lives we live, we either reverence or misuse it. Just as any family is shamed or disgraced by the actions of one of its members so also by our abuse of God's name, we shame not only ourselves, but Him. Having been given the right at Baptism to call ourselves Children of God, by blaspheming His name we disconnect ourselves completely from Him and from our brothers and sisters.

THREE

There are so many reasons why the Sabbath should remain holy and be recognized exclusively as the Lord's Day. It is the one day of the week during which we are formally obliged to acknowledge God, recognizing Him as the Sovereign Lord of all Creation. By such a recognition it allows us to meet with Him in a special way, on a day free from work and, other demands, on our time. The obligation for practising Catholics to attend Sunday (or if necessary the Saturday vigil) Mass is that they can witness regularly on a weekly basis Christ's ultimate sacrifice made on their behalf.

On what other day in the week can we truly say, today I will be with You God and I am happy to spend as much time as possible with You. The Sabbath therefore encourages us to talk with God, to walk with God and to work with God. Just as a child eagerly seeks to try to help his Father so we should also seek to help Our Father working with Him, perhaps helping others, we are invited to share this intimacy. Maybe it is with our own family or those who need us in their lives, or the community in general but in whatever way we perform some good works, we are doing so according to His will in fulfilling this need. By engaging in such actions we are keeping holy the Sabbath day.

FOUR

The Commandments tell us in many ways what we must not do, for example we must not steal, we must not kill, we must not commit adultery. It is only the fourth Commandment which actually commands us as to what we must do "Honour one's father and mother." Why should this Commandment be so precise? That God chose to make it so directly, placing it in such a premier position, forces one to give it a special reverence. For young people in particular, it appears very easy to somehow degrade, diminish or disregard this fourth Commandment. After three commandments binding us as children to honour God, it is not surprising that God now binds us to honour our own parents. In the Catechism there is a most significant difference drawn between the gravity of violence towards one's parents and the gravity of violence towards strangers.

Today any acknowledgement or realization by adult children that this commandment, seriously infringed, leads them into grievous sin is practically unheard of. Nevertheless in the national press daily accounts appear of adult children bullying and intimidating their elderly parents over money, property or even pension rights. Christ throughout his life sanctified the family and within the gospel this sanctification is evident. It tells us everything we need to know.

The collapse of the family in the secular western world heralds the collapse of modern man and society. If this should happen and a new order evolve, based on a different family cornerstone, society will be without its greatest bulwark. Social anarchy and chaos will become all that much closer, allowing for the ominous role of the strongest, at the expense of the weakest, until only the law of the jungle remains.

The family takes each new life at birth directly from God's hands and nourishes it carefully through infancy. Such primary teaching and caring is undertaken by the parents, until the child's own use of reason asserts itself, and it is only later still after reaching the 'use of reason' that the young adult begins to fly free and gets ready to start his/her own mission. For all this period, the family is the central core unit and the safe refuge within which all the other younger members of the family are taught and protected.

In the first period the need to obey, must be firmly established. In the second and third periods the obligation to honour one's parents must be chosen as mandatory. Later as one takes over responsibility for one's life mission, this obligation to honour one's parents remains and children who leave home to start their own families, are still expected to fulfil it. Indeed even after death it is expected that adult children would continue to pray for their parents' eternal reward. As each generation therefore passes into eternity those they have left behind will in turn pray for 'the faithful departed.'

The choice to love one's parents however is a choice which can never be made based on the normal human and emotional factors of childhood. The genetic factors, the formative years, the infant family experiences are all to be somehow or other absorbed and by the time the older teenager reaches their formative years their opinion of their parents may indeed be somewhat less than positive. That this 'opinion' of course is still little more than 'an opinion in progress yet to be completed' is often no more than a passing one. The fourth Commandment therefore does not order one to love one's parents, it is rather an instruction to honour them, and regardless of whatever differences there maybe, as best possible the children are expected to comply. The forces of Satan forever seeking corruption have, seemingly been able to divide families down the center by the downplaying that has been made of this Commandment and the meaningless role and interpretation given it by so many of today's incompetent teachers. A family that exists only in name is no family, and unless it can function in a true sense, it cannot give the care, attention and love its individual members need. Family prayer, family solidarity and family love have all been weakened, and the messages of self-actualization and self-realization are now promoted as the norm in the majority of far too many Catholic schools, families and households. Such teachings are naturally contrary to the fourth Commandment, as they promote the ideal of self-centredness which inevitably leads one into sin. Clearly, to substitute such a modern altruistic goal of self, rather than prefer to see one's self as part of a whole, puts the individual ahead of family, even though one may be living as a member of a family. An everyday couple married in the eyes of God, living a good life may have a family of one, two or more children. As such a unit they would then be designated the normal as the day-by-day basis and develop as such. The antithesis of marriage where two men or two women choose to have some civil partnership not only enshrined in law but also given total moral acceptance illustrates the amount of damage already caused to the the continuous christian family. The Secretary of State at the Vatican, Cardinal Pietro Parolin, described the legalisation of the original 'Same Sex Irish Marriage Act Ireland 2015,' as, "a defeat for humanity".

The concept of a partnership couple with two career lifestyles, two bank accounts and two high performance cars, now also appears to establish their right to be determined as a modern nuclear family. Such units of non-faith committed people living together as man and wife without the protection of the graces the Sacrament of Marriage provide are most vulnerable and prone to the dangers that entice the weakest into the realms and regions that a Catholic lifestyle would automatically protect them from.

The forces of evil never miss an opportunity to introduce other groups or cult type structures into the guise of "family." The most obvious one being that of gang-like crime which makes the word family somehow attractive yet mysterious, pretending to represent 'a cohesive family life,' while at the same time only furthering the cause of evil.

The concept of honour in such crime 'families' is of course mandatory but it is to evil rather than to good that the degree of honour is pledged. Within this web the family are all the while trying to become more widespread, seeking new recruits to extend their boundaries. The loyalty to evil, in the guise of money, prestige and power, provide material outward signs of reward, yet are only masking the corruption, contamination and destruction that their "family crime" unleashes on society. The recent decree by the Archbishop of Montreale, Sicilia, Archbishop Michele Pennisi prohibiting members of the Mafiosi to stand as godparents is maybe little more than a candle in the dark, but it is a very well lit candle.

In the vivid and almost realistic world of the media, the false portrayal of power, wealth and success influences countless numbers of young people, who no longer equate the word family with love of parents and siblings, they prefer to identify instead to part of the corrupt and decadent society in which they now choose to live.

FIVE

The fifth Commandment, You Shall not Kill, cannot be clearer. because to kill is to destroy what God has created, in whatever stage, form, or precise moment of existence it is in, is a grievous sin. By choosing to kill, man is therefore trying to manipulate God's sole authority over life. Death is beyond life and it is only God's providence to decide the moments of life and death, for each individual. Alone, or in some natural disaster affecting thousands, the choice is God's. For countless centuries death was commonplace and administered through wars, calamities, disputes and authoritarian power often proclaimed in God's name.

If it were possible today to see a world where widespread inflicted death is a thing of the past, one could honestly say there is hope for mankind, but if anything the very opposite is the case. The fact that martyrdom is once more being inflicted on Christians in the Middle East, and elsewhere, is an appalling situation and every educated and civilized Muslim has a duty to acknowledge that it is contrary to God's law. Any Muslim who is not prepared to acknowledge this fact is, de facto automatically identifiable as a hard line fundamentalist and a potential terrorist,

Today a different world exists, yet unnecessary death is now more widely spread than ever before. As well as the numerous regional wars taking place, additional killing comes in many other forms. To kill with cruelty, to kill with indifference, to kill with economic power, to kill with inadequate support, to kill with deprivation, are all ways and means of destroying what God has created. Whether one functions within corporate, community or family circles, a long-term death sentence can be passed in so many ways to kill a person or group of people, who no longer fit in, or conform in such a way as to make them acceptable.

Today in some countries death via abortion, euthanasia and suicide are spoken of in medical terms, as 'rights of patients' or choices, which each individual must be allowed or entitled to make freely.

As previously stated, the availability of abortion and its promotion as a 'right' in allowing one human being deny another human being their right to life, makes euthanasia, mercy killing and suicide all the more reasonable. That so many countries now allow such heinous acts under the protection of their civil laws, makes the acceptance of sin, the very source of Satan's power, a factual practicing reality.

To deny the actual living existence of a pre-born infant from reaching its own birth is mankind's most evil pact with Satan to date and never likely to be surpassed. In the past five decades approximately 60 plus million pre-born Americans have been exterminated. A word never heard in the pro abortion lobby but one which does describe the vileness of this terrible sin.This internal federal or national holocaust, makes the Jewish, Armenian and all previous holocausts throughout history pale by comparison. What God-fearing nation that allows such an ongoing genocide or industry be promoted as 'normal' can expect any blessed future beggars belief.

Euthanasia is now the latest evil gaining acceptance in some of the more advanced societies such as Australia, Switzerland, Sweden and Holland and who knows how rapid its progress will be as it gains acceptance in two or three states in America. In Holland a recent case gained great notoriety after a woman had been euthanased against her wishes. The documents and paperwork were all in order but the woman had reservations and against her will she was held down and given the lethal injection. The subsequent hearing found that the decision to terminate her was correct as it was felt her mind was not able to calculate when would be the correct time to end her life. This being the case the responsibility to make the choice was left with her family and once they said, now is the time, the doctors only acted as they were instructed. That such barbaric behaviour could be carried out by medical professionals and later found to be in correct compliance with the law of the land would have to make one truly appalled at how inhuman the legalities of a country's laws can be.

The awareness of suicide as a further enormous phenomenon is again quite amazing, as it is in essence the act of a person determined to superimpose their will over God's. To die by one's own hand even under the most mitigating circumstances, is still the taking of a life, one's very own life, which makes it all the more horrible, as it is still self murder and can only ever be seen as such.

God is totally aware of the plight of the person considering this action and the motivation behind it. What that person may or may not have accomplished over the future years is now foiled, as it is the person her/himself who chooses to finish the life given to him. To self destruct his mission will have severe consequences, as without its completion, the re-entry that should have taken place will now never even be attempted.

SIX

The sin of adultery is presumably a sin without confusion or ambiguity and its meaning is quite stark. If one enters into the sacrament of marriage and subsequently chooses to put aside one's wife or husband and live with another man or woman is contrary to the will of God and must be considered a grievous sin. Today in most western countries, couples in second relationships not only seek to have their first union set aside as invalid they further wish to have their second union recognized as legitimate. If this is not given and the Church refuses to oblige them with an all-embracing blessing then it is seen as being out of touch and unreasonable. The campaign to liberalise marriage is becoming the new 'cause' of the 'new catholics' within both the ranks of the clergy and the laity. The fact that it is the Pope himself, Francis I who almost appears to be leading the campaign, with the publication of his encyclical Amoris Laetitia is somehow breathtaking.

In today's secular world the romantic marriage on the beach, the concert hall, or even the natural history museum, all have their allure and their attractiveness but these are not taking place in a church or a holy place dedicated to the worship of God where sacramental weddings and expected to take place. They do not invite God to attend nor do they enhance the civil ceremony with a beautiful Mass or have His ordained minister, a priest, officiate and give his blessing. Such civil marriages may be good, bad or indifferent and as they are performed without God's Blessing they are dissolvable via a civil divorce. A Catholic marriage contracted by a loving couple and administered by a priest, has no such option. Marriage before a priest administering the Sacrament of Marriage, is for life and cannot be broken. Divorce for Catholics is not an option and the commitment given in expressing their vows is taken as total.

In all pre marriage courses the priest must outline this one solemn truth to both parties without any hesitation, as it is the essential foundation their future will rest on and must only be accepted with confidence and love. What priest can add one iota to the destruction of the first marriage by blessing in God's name some form of second union which is being substituted in its place? The sixth commandment therefore condemns sexual intercourse outside of marriage as a sin of unfaithfulness and infidelity to one's spouse. It is a sin with immense consequences both within the family unit in particular and, society in general.

For this reason the sixth commandment condemns all offences against the dignity of marriage, against same sex unions demanding parity with marriage, and sins of an unnatural or bestial nature. These sins are all seen in one form or another, as sins against the sacredness and sanctity of the individual in a human form created in God's likeness, 'to go forth and multiply' in which the full spirituality of God's love for mankind, can be physically lived and only as He fully intended. Sins presented through acts of pornography, sins of sado-masochism and self abuse such as masturbation, are clearly identified as salacious and seen as sins against chastity.

SEVEN

The seventh commandment in the most simplistic of terms can be presented as the one which forbids children from taking other children's toys and sneaking up to the candy counter shop-lifting but it is not as simple as that. In its adult form the sin becomes far more grievous. To take an item, to take money, to take what does not belong to one is contrary to the seventh Commandment, which prohibits any sort of stealing. In the Catechism of the Catholic Church the parameters of the Commandment are laid out in great detail. In the Compendium of the Social Doctrine of the Church the whole areas of social justice, economic growth, political awareness and all matters that affect man's external relationships within society become so relevant.

The moral obligations and social responsibilities that one encounters throughout one's overall working career, are highlighted in both a personal and external sense. To steal a person's thoughts or plans, to rob a person of their ambitions, to duplicate a project thereby denying another person or community their rightful advantage, is a serious sin and should always be recognised as such. In today's world there now appears a business culture which not only condones such behaviour but actually encourages it, as if promoting evil over good.

That such highly unethical practices may be part of a greater global mindset, does not in any way justify how many such global commercial transactions are undertaken today. The awareness or control by corporate compliance directors and government regulatory officials are those tasked to monitor and control the behaviour of commercial society. For Catholics who respect this seventh Commandment as one gets older the acceptance and lifestyle one lives becomes more ordered and as such more free from many temptations. By starting to realize and understand the vastness of this sin's footprint one begins to develop a set of spiritual skills which will help combat it in whatever way one can.

EIGHT

To lie is the opposite of speaking the truth and it is in this Commandment we are told not to bear false witness against our neighbour. By such lies it is easy to inflict much damage, if not sometimes destroy, and it is the very opposite of what we are asked to do. Over some small difference or conflict it is always possible to have some difference with one's neighbour but such a conflict should not escalate as it then tends to puts one automatically in conflict with God. Our Christian responsibilities instruct and expect us to love our neighbour, not to deceive or lie about them. If they are dangerous or knowingly bad people, they should at best be avoided. Insofar as we are obliged to help them we can only to do this as long as it does not place us in harm's way.

This Commandment covers in essence the areas of privacy, slander, flattery and adulation in a whole series of situations, all of which allow people to wander in and out of so many grey zones. For example how many people would admit to spreading gossip, whereas very few would ever even consider themselves as being guilty of slander? The extent of the damage done or the misery caused by this sin, can be of a minor or major magnitude.

It is also necessary to do all that one can in restoring the good name and character of one we may have damaged To claim one was at work when one was in a gym or bar is a lie masking one's hidden interests. To claim one was working while engaged in some sports or training is just selfish. To claim one was out having a drink with friends while being unfaithful to one's husband or wife is a far more grievous sin and as with all deception, compounded in its magnitude by the lie.

NINE

The ninth Commandment is all encompassing to our spiritual integrity. To covet one's neighbour's spouse is sinful and an act of spiritual deception. One's neighbour has no idea, the neighbour's wife has no idea, the perpetrator's wife, if he has one, has no idea, indeed his (or her) very own spousal act of love in itself becomes an act of treachery as this sin of covetousness becomes incorporated into one's own physical act. To covet one's neighbour's daughter is even more despicable. It appears an ever increasing appetite as more and more members of both sexes stimulate the instincts of the other, through the behavioural, dress and speech. Today's society via the constant media, TV and advertising makes the desire for multiple sexual encounters almost an acceptable norm and indeed a constant invitation to sin. Such desires are always destructive to the fidelity of marriage and the vows taken by both parties to one another. The Gospel makes clear that the act of adultery takes place first in the mind and its physical consummation is then seen as the endorsement of the act, already spiritually committed. To covet one's neighbour's spouse, or indeed any spouse or woman at random is equally appalling in its overall dimensions as it allows one to randomly rape, whoever one chooses to at will.

In today's moral environment, where sexuality is almost totally physical, and centred on the actual act itself, the whole area of covetousness, lust and sexual perversion is gaining more control over men's and women's minds. The widespread use, acceptance and availability of online pornography makes the challenge of keeping the ninth commandment extremely difficult, nevertheless, this is the obligation one must fully understand and maintain if one is to live the Gospel with all the necessary courage, will power and hope required by all faithful practising Catholics.

TEN

All natural desires exist from infancy. To know, to love, to belong are all within even the tiniest baby's instincts. It is the direction in which they are fostered and encouraged to grow that matters greatly. The whole purpose of life which Catholics are taught is

> "To know, love and serve God, and, by this means,
> to be happy with Him forever in Heaven".

The parents of infants are expected to sow the seeds of such faith, knowing if the life of their child is directed in this way the child is entering the age of reason, with the solid foundation of the faith, childlike it maybe, nevertheless well established.

Sadly this is not always the case and the unhappiness of young children today who have been brought up in the very opposite regime is providing them with little hope of ever experiencing 'real life' happiness. From a very young age they are almost totally spiritually impoverished. As they grow older their dissatisfaction and feelings of disadvantage only become more acute and frustrating. The age of materialism, of marketing, of advertising, of sales, of banking, of consumerism has copper fastened intro every young western person the habit of turning a "want" into a "need." This trait is what fuels consumerization and once established knows no bounds. When any appetite gets out of control there can only be trouble ahead. Satan, for his part is quite happy to inflict the desire and the greed to individuals, at exhibitions, seminars and wherever the world of materialism exists. He does not care once a person convinces themselves that what they have is a need. As soon as the person is hooked then that person's wants, needs or desires become their priorities. One's priorities or one's passions, always have to be fed and regardless of any feelings of right or wrong the the excessive greed, masking most sins takes control.

One's ability to establish good relationships with one's neighbour also becomes more and more difficult the greater one allows one's needs to predominate. The more our neighbour maybe has, the more resentment is inclined to grow and this applies not only to one's friends but spreads to any individual who appears to have a better lifestyle. This covetousness of such lifestyles or the possessions of the celebrities, the sports personalities, the corporate leaders, ferments nothing but destructive attitudes and fruitless negative desires. In such a consumer materialistic world the collective mind and thinking of young people especially, become embittered and contaminated, until most of what one wants appearing on a screen becomes all one cannot have, as in truth it perhaps does not even exist, yet still the damage is done.

These ten 'Commandments' are portals for our spiritual protection and the growth of our souls, it is essential that their effectiveness and maintenance is never overlooked or disregarded. Through the practice of prayer, fasting and the constant Sacrament of Penance it is possible not only to protect our individual selves but, in so doing, to share our protection and strength with those around us, in our family and our acquaintances.

Having dwelt on the sacraments as the divine sources from which all graces flow into our souls, the necessity to fast and pray have over the past years become somewhat less and less appreciated. There may still be desire and enthusiasm for liturgy, there may be a strong community with whom one may wish to share the Gospel, but until the realization that prayer and fasting are also understood then many of the well-intentioned discussion groups, parish councils and community projects are unable to fully benefit from the blessings and intercessions available.

For these reasons it is therefore necessary for parishioners to come together to pray as a community in order that their prayers are answered, not only individually, but also collectively. The practice of fasting even on a symbolic level, such as eating no meat on friday, gives witness and strength to one's faith. Where like minded people are gathered together to pray the total community benefits by being blessed with an overall collective state of grace, the development of true Christian families and the spiritual growth of the community. Sadly where this does not happen the opposite is often the case, or a different type community begins to take control.

The sight of near empty and deserted churches are becoming more and more frequent within many towns and cities. On the other hand the Church of the suburbs which is 90% under the control of the finance committee is seen as 'doing OK' and quite acceptable. This however is not always the case and an even more subtle danger may develop there. As in any parish the word of God is what must be preached vigorously and truthfully. What is now happening in so many churches is that it is not the living Gospel which is preached each Sunday by the priest. As the chosen representative of Christ, it is his responsibility to make clear the meaning of the Gospel yet now this duty is getting more and more eroded by the congregation demanding what they want the church and the liturgy to be. In other words the church of the people has replaced the church of Christ whose representative as shepherd is no longer seen as the sole head. Just as the Bishop of Rome is seen today as, one amongst many, by the bishops of France, Germany and America who claim collegiality with him gives them en masse an equal parity with the pope without the obligation of subservience or obedience. Nothing could be further from the truth and just as the occupant of the Chair of Peter is absolute ruler of the church, so also is the pastor the sole shepherd in charge of his parish, and answerable only to his bishop. To revive the real order of the Gospel, if it is to be revealed in the fulness and in truth as it was for centuries past, it must again be preached by the pastor as the true Gospel of Christ.

The Church Militant, the congregation of the faithful comprising all the families, the single people, the pensioners the lone parents, the prisoners, there exists many individuals, who believe they were most hard done by, by clerical figures in their past. Their resentment of the church is a cul de sac situation from which there is only one way out. To rediscover the church, find the right pastor and be prepared to listen to him, as he tries to relate the meaning of Christ back into their life and so restart again from a new beginning. It is a beginning of hope and one which those who are now suffering are entitled to experience. For those fortunate enough to be comfortable and confident in their faith it is their responsibility to invite those less fortunate to the banquet so they also can once more feel the warmth of God's love. The need for 'serving priests' to open their own churches has never been greater than today, and it is for them to regain their role of shepherds. If only one weary person per day were to seek and find comfort, solace and encouragement from that priest then he would indeed be wonderfully fulfilling a great mission.

On the other hand if the house of God is being run primarily as an administrative centre concerned with social and economic affairs, and the pastor or his assistants are seldom to be found there then, how is that parish ever going to be served? Should the pastor be made quasi redundant or overtaken by some group of well-meaning parishioners, every genuine effort must be made to bring him back to 'the mark.' By reinstating him in his leadership role his performance level is restored to where it was meant to be and he can regain his overall responsibilities in serving his flock and leading them to God.

The Bar-B-Q's, the functions, the festivities and the whole holiday fiestas are all fine and dandy, but they must always be considered secondary. As social functions more and more replace spiritual ones the misconception grows that everything is just wonderful; whereas in truth maybe here is yet another parish which is slowly disengaging itself from its Mother-ship. The lack of vocations and the present workloads of priests only serve to perpetuate this lay trend, where the cause is wilfully ignored and the wrongful remedy is applied. So evident has this lay involvement become that some congregations now appear to gather to worship themselves as community per se, rather than to worship God.

To seek God's love, to ask our Blessed Mother to intercede on one's behalf, to invoke the help of the Saints all are components of an active prayer life. One's soul yearns to pray to reach out spiritually meeting the needs of each person, whose need for prayer is as great as a dying man's need for a priest. Prayer is like poetry: the purer it is the better it gets. As the ancient rhyme has it:

> My prayers go up
> My thoughts remain below
> Prayers without thoughts
> Never to heaven go...

And so even the avid daily Mass-goer who attends constantly without prayer in their heart is no more in communion with God then the arrogant Pharisee whose only prayer was self-edification, regardless of his fellow men, for whom he had nothing but contempt.

His Holiness Paul VI stated: "Unless a person prays, he cannot call himself a Christian."

In many poor countries where the evil of affluence has not yet become the predominant yardstick or material meter, spiritual awareness is still expressed very much through a simple lifestyle. In some of the poorer regions of the Developing World, for example the rural population will always endeavour to dress in clean clothes for Mass on Sunday. To participate in the Eucharist in working clothes or even casual clothes would be unthinkable and considered most disrespectful. Likewise the appreciation to fast from food or drink for a minimum of three hours before receiving the Eucharist, is long forgotten or ignored by the "Westerner." It is however easily understood by the spiritually conscious manual labourer. Fasting sharpens the spiritual appetite, increases awareness, and allows one to offer a small sacrifice in advance of the prayer one wishes to make and seeks to be heard.

In this manner most formal traditional pilgrimages have always promoted fasting as an intrinsic and meaningful part of the event. Like so many of the adopted Christian practises strictly observed by practising Muslims, fasting is central to their prayer life. An entire month each year is given over to fasting. Known as Ramadan this fast is both harsh and severe, it lasts from dawn till dusk each day for 30 consecutive days, bringing the followers of the Prophet closer to Abraham.

In today's world the enclosed monastic contemplative orders of Mother Church still practise fasting as a central part of their rule. In order to enhance and add value to the prayers they will recite over each 24 hour cycle. Their community prayer is already of such a pure and high quality, fasting only adds to its value tenfold. Today when serious, rigorous fasting is no longer obligatory, the practice of fasting or self-denial is one which rests individually within one's self. To choose two days a week to fast is an option one can always exercise: by-passing a meal, dessert tray or mid-morning coffee is an exercise which rewards one enormously. Whichever way one chooses, the offering of such small physical sacrifices followed by prayer, encourages one to reach higher and higher as one presents one's prayers to God with a far greater awareness of how much we always need to repay Him.

In the age of instant gratification the great lie of today's consumer society is usually designed to hamper and block all spiritual devotion and growth. Satan the Deceptor can orchestrate any scenario privately or publicly to meet any level of required sin. For the individual that is consumed by lust a torrid physical encounter is possible. For a community which seeks to host a major outdoor music jamboree regardless of the drink, drug or spiritual damage it may well cause, it is possible for Satan to orchestrate the event and make sure it happens. Should society demand a law that allows for some restrictions be relaxed to allow for a more liberal divorce procedure to take place then of course Satan is there, working on the legislators to make it happen. Satan never rests his attacks on the Church and he never ceases to provide all the opportunities he can, for people to sin.

Where God has been rejected and Satan, or his agent, has been accepted either by an individual or by a community, it is extremely difficult to get rid of him as little if any 'Graces' now get dispersed through lack of prayer. In so many cities, towns and parishes now churches are being closed, orders are moving out, vocations are drying up and people are complaining about the quality of their lives. The Satanic presence is all around the neighbourhood and nobody wants to even try and understand what is taking place or what is going on. The withdrawal of priests and the Sacraments seldom appears to create any major concerns and the sales of parcels of land to speculators and developers sometimes actually appears to activate the greed of some religious orders themselves, into making some very advantageous financial gains.

Such may well be the power of Satan. The new liturgies and parish consolidations are presented to the people as the way forward, yet suicides and drug abuse appear to be making more and more inroads into society, as the progress into this brave new world proceeds unabated. For people to talk in terms of prayer the realization and meaningfulness of what the purpose of what prayer can actually achieve are seldom really understood. The purpose of prayer is to raise the mind and heart always higher and always closer to God. The Saints never stopped striving to reach such heights and their need and desire for prayer could never be satisfied, growing always further into God's love.

It was by never ceasing in their every day efforts and their need for continuous prayer that even the most humble and self effacing penitents became saints. In trying to unite one's own thoughts with God, our prayers are the most simple and basic means we have. The more we pray the more we become in tune with Him. Without prayer one cannot live spiritually, and one's soul starves to death. A prayer less community likewise cannot be considered Christian. Inevitably, one must then address the question where does a prayer less nation stand in relation to its moral code, its legal system and the welfare it provides its most needful members of society?

Prayer in its beauty, form and function has evolved since man first looked at the sunrise in amazement and felt the need to kneel and pray to relieve his rapturous emotions. These single and silent moments in life when one is momentarily fully open to the living beauty of the universe are no more than fleeting glimpses. When they happen, for that one single inspired instant the urge to pray, to acknowledge, to give thanks to God is overwhelming. This feeling however is sadly one which is impossible to duplicate or recall at will and after a moment or so it disappears like winter snow.

Only the mystics and people of great holiness appear able to immerse themselves so much in such intense prayer that they can somehow achieve this awareness and reach a level of ecstasy holding them spellbound. For the ordinary, rather than the extraordinary person, living their life as best they can, the role of prayer is often seen as too hard to concentrate and improve upon. For the everyday normal person going about their everyday lives it can be said they pray to live, whereas for the mystic, the celibate, the hermit they live to pray. It is seldom the pastor at Mass on Sunday preaches on the need for prayer in any great depth, and sadly the brief bidding prayers appear no more than requests for needed items as if on a shopping list waiting to be filled.

Prayer gives each person three great opportunities to reach out to God: It gives one the chance to adore, bowing down in submission to God's greatness and formally acknowledging His overall kingship of the universe; It gives one the ability to thank God in his greatness for all he has done for them individually and collectively; and it enables one to petition, to seek, to ask God for further graces and blessings. So often today the prayer format is shortened to the final stage or at best the two primary aspects are dispensed with rapidly to make way for the needs and the wants. What makes man come together with is not just his soul or his spirit, it is first and foremost his relationship; the feeling of wanting to share simple things fiirst with someone and as times goes on wanting to share more and more the bigger things.

As one of the Trappist monks in Xavier Beauvois' wonderful Cannes Grand Prix winning film, "Of Gods and Men" said when asked directly by the teenage girl,

> "Were you ever in love Father?" to which he duly replied,
> "But, of course my child, 'I was, until I discovered a much greater love."

Indeed St Augustine recounting his own conversion in his Confessions, 1600 hundred years earlier, when he wrote:

> Late have I loved Thee,
> O Beauty so ancient and so new,
> Late have I loved Thee.

God being the Supreme Spirit, the very essence of 'love' encourages all our attempts and supplications not just as a loving Father welcomes his children's efforts, but as we wish and want Him to receive us. In our everyday lives, at work or on the playing fields we sometimes refer to our best buddy as 'having our back' God can be seen in a similar light as, not only has He got our back, He has our soul.

God is constant and in all things He remains in place. It is man that moves and prevaricates, who changes with the moods and the tides, who advances and retreats, who blows hot and cold. As man today is less and less in harmony with nature and his appreciation of the planet, he must by definition be also out of harmony with God, the author of all nature.

This lack or loss of harmony with God's creation causes a further rift or separation in what was intended to be a common bond between God and every living organism He put on Earth. Rather like nature being the conduit channel of communication between the Creator and those He put on Earth to live, man's total mismanagement of the planet's vast resources leads us today into man made natural disasters. The on-going disregard for the planet which continues almost totally unchecked causes the gap between man and God to continue to widen. Man's claims to have the environment as his concern and its protection as his aim, are little more than protestations of minimal value or worth. While money, power and global control are at stake, only token gestures are being paid by those in control and the environmental groups who represent those most concerned lack the political power to actually influence the destruction of the rainforests or the melting of the icecaps.

The age of technology has also coarsened man into accepting the image rather than the reality. The great art forms have become corrupted and warped. The triumph of fantasy over fact and fiction over truth has led generations of young people into the realm of transformers and transponders rather than into the lives of great scientists, saints and scholars. "All you need is love" according to the song, and indeed the sentiment is correct, but it is the love of God and of one's neighbour which is required for it to make sense, a sense of love which in the developed world is by now almost well and truly lost. Nevertheless there is hope that in some of the poorer countries, in the underdeveloped regions of the world, all is not lost and hope still flourishes. At the synod on the family in Rome the German Archbishop,(Emeritus) of Rottenburg-Stuttgart, Walter Kasper, was put firmly in his place, having made a most disparaging remark regarding the quality of some of the Church thinking in Africa. Little do we know how reliant the developed world may become over the coming decades to the Church in Africa and even further afield. It is very possible that unknown to us at this moment in time the church itself maybe standing at a crucial crossroads in history and the future is poised to reach upward or spiral downward out of control.

Witnessing the ongoing assaults on the Catholic Church in the Middle East and further afield the lack of personal and private prayer by Catholics worldwide to help overcome such attacks must be evident as Christians everywhere are needed as never before to give witness to God's love for mankind. That God so loved the world that he sacrificed his only Son to save mankind is the great mystery the Gospel unravels and presents to us; yet in one of the very shortest periods in mankind's history the Greatest Story Ever Told, is being ignored, maligned and mocked by those it seeks to save. How this is the sad situation mankind finds himself in today is the mystery this book seeks to try and uncover and in some small way help solve.

The question man needs to address is, how having fulfilled his need for prayer and adoration of his various Gods for 4,000 years or so, in less than 100 years Man has now rendered his need for God almost obsolete? From being the central core part of every society the instinctive belief in a single omnipotent Deity is now relegated to little more than a minor psychological support system, in the lives of countless millions. To what extent this diminution in belief in the life of Jesus Christ, His Death and Resurrection, is a question that the Catholic Church must not simply address, but make every serious effort to illuminate and answer. The Church with millions upon millions claiming membership, yet fewer and fewer accepting its doctrines and its goals is no longer the Church that Christ founded; it is rather a synthetic copy church lost in its own confusion.

In today's world of noise, hassle, consternation and stress the reality of prayer is blocked from view, or virtually hidden from reality. Prayer is the loving conversation we express with our soul while it rests for a moment with God. In prayer we seek God's love, His grace and His mercy. Prayer is the feelgood-factor one experiences through one's soul as God breathes grace into us. This experience on a daily basis is what keeps one in communion with God, in the love of God:- "Prayer without ceasing," the constant awareness and inclusion of God into everything we do on an hourly basis.

Today the tremendous power of the sacraments is ignored and the response to them amongst many Catholics is that there is far too much ritual. That the opposite is the truth, and it is in the ritual that truth is unlocked, is seldom dwelt upon. Over the past 50 years a substantial amount of ritual was dispensed with, and it was this vacuum Pope Benedict XVI recognised during his Papacy and the urgent need to reinstate it. Whether his successor will reinforce the emeritus' Pope's efforts remains to be seen, but that it should be 'supported' is without doubt. In the Gospel and throughout the centuries the necessity of ritual was always quite evident for just as any jewel must be placed in a golden setting so also must truth be placed only in a worthy liturgy.

Spontaneous prayer and the speaking through tongues only attained popularity after the Second Vatican Council and once more, through the Catechism of the Catholic Church the need to understand the spiritual realities of prayer must be highlighted. The need to unite with the Communion of Saints, to gather together as a community to give God our love, must not continue to be so misinterpreted and misunderstood. These ongoing misconceptions, due to a deficit in religious knowledge, are the cause of so much adolescent and spiritual immaturity, that the need of a forceful prayer life for the individual and for so many living together as a community is not just a necessity; it is an essential.

Sadly it is not uncommon today to hear people complain that having prayed, they experienced nothing. Furthermore they did not receive what they had sought; Prayer at this level is almost fruitless and it is guaranteed to leave one cold and frustrated. These all too misguided encounters are put forward as some form of an indictment of their religion, of God, and indeed of everything and everyone connected with the Church. Such convoluted approaches to prayer are almost meaningless, as they represent little more than a series of demands made without any genuine expression of love or sincerity. Just as the supporters of both teams who battle for supremacy in the Super Bowl may pray ardently for victory, the obvious reality is that both teams cannot win."

When questioned by the apostles as to how they should pray, they were left in no doubt that "Thy will be done" is the prayer that Christ himself taught us all to say when he invited us to use the word "Father". The Lord's Prayer itself encapsulates the Love of God, Love of Neighbour and our salvation, and was given to us so that we all would have the courage and confidence to call God our own 'Father' asking Him to bring us home.

The Gospel never fails to bring the need for prayer and obedience to those who communicate with the Father into one's daily life on a constant basis. This is because there are those who have reached the stage of understanding what such clear obedience and prayer means. Christ for his part always instructed his Apostles to do likewise even when He was aware of how lacking or tired they may have been. In the Gospel Christ commands Simon,

> "Launch out into the deep and let down your nets for
> a draught, and Simon answering said to him: "Master,
> we have laboured all the night and have taken nothing,
> but at thy word I will let down the net." Luke 5: 1-11

Here one can actually feel and somehow experience the tiredness and frustration Simon felt, yet in obedience to Jesus the net is played out and, perhaps for such abject devotion he experienced the love of Jesus in the most practical, way. Whether he ever realized it as a massive sign of approval one can only guess but his reaction was totally encapsulated by St Luke as being 'wholly astonished!' at such a huge catch, 'the like of which none of them had ever seen fishing the Sea of Galilee.' Falling on his knees in front of Jesus, overcome by the magnitude of what had taken place, all he could do was to cry out in a loud voice:

"Depart from me Lord, for I am a sinful man." Luke 5;8

CHAPTER

7

Prayer is no different when recited by many people, as individuals or in a congregation. The same words are said, the same sounds are uttered, yet for each person the experience differs. It is only in the heart of man that the soul's passion stirs. The longing for a closer unity and deeper intimacy than the one already has with God intensifies.Like a fire the more it burns, the more fuel it needs and the heat grows the closer one moves towards the fire. It is this urge to grow within the love of prayer and, only after much painful self-awareness has been experienced, that the actual power of prayer begins to be realized. It is this depth of awareness that governs the prayers of saintly men and women, offered to God throughout the world that secures for mankind the protection and graces needed, to combat the fearful global power of Satan.

The enclosed orders, the hidden communities, the monastic settlements, the ordained and lay hermits living the rule, all combined, concentrate on such intense prayer, in order to protect mankind, and save sinners from being lost. As the world goes about its everyday business it is the power of prayer by such hidden people that brings relief to so many distraught and desolate souls.

Prayer can never be isolated. It is never alone, an empty cry waiting to be heard, but rather instead a coming together, a consummation, in which a togetherness is felt and experienced as God's love reacts to any prayer however small and insignificant or great and majestic.

Saint Mother Teresa spoke of the great pincer-claw pains of poverty and loneliness, yet it is in the spiritual realm we must realize the depth of her wisdom. What would it merit a man to gain the whole world, if he were to then lose his immortal soul? Likewise the loneliness of the soul divorced from God is a loneliness far greater than that of a physical loneliness so often forced on families by emigration, migration, sickness and other social and economic conditions. This great loneliness of the soul is the result of living in a continuous state of sin. A state in which no mercy, no spiritual light exists and only shadows lead one further and further into a life of total misery and despair.

The life of prayer combats that predicament and advances the presence of God in our lives, whilst the absence of prayer moves one further and further into the barren wilderness, where one is only left with self for company and the isolating waves of loneliness which eventually washes one up onto the deserted beach of spiritual oblivion. This terrifying conclusion is all too often heralded by one's own physical extinction through the horrible sinful act of suicide.

By inviting God's presence into our lives through prayer, one is automatically welcoming both His love and His mercy. Sadly few choose to exercise the power to formally invite God to join them in their daily lives. In this very troubled world it is easy to understand why; yet God in His infinite mercy always remains ready to take one's call. To exclude God from so much of our daily lives through indifference, if nothing else, is one's own free choice, and for many the need to commit to prayer in even a modest way is not seen as important. For so many, Catholicism is seen as little more than a package of Mass on Sunday, some small prayers, like grace before meals and perhaps at most Confession once or twice a year. Why this is the case is something that should be seriously questioned. What also must be debated and reconciled is why there is a need to make God central in our private prayer life, in our homes, and in our place of work.

Unless such open discussions take place and are positively reconciled, there will be no reason, to raise our game. Other faith paths make far greater demands on their congregations, and formal prayers and observances bond them much more solidly with their beliefs. The Islamic faith today spreading once more throughout the western world leaves its followers in no doubt as to its rules and obligations. One of the five Islamic 'Commandments' Muslims are expected to adhere to is their rule to pray five times a day, preferably within the mosque. How or why the followers of such a prophet submit willingly to such a regime while the majority of lay Catholics, chosen as sons and daughters of God, decline to commit themselves to any similar daily prayer obligation is a sad reflection. Everyday prayer bringing one into God's presence not only gives us the grace needed to maintain our sanctity but it also infuses us with the knowledge that we can easily develop a far greater friendship with God. As in any of our temporal relationships, our relationship with Christ is no different. Once it reaches a certain stage it is also two-sided, and just as one would touch base two or three times each day with a friend so also should one seek to speak with God.

In this way the urge to pray is manifested within one's spirit which then responds to the call by seeking some solitude in which to pray. How indeed can the relationship be otherwise, the more meaningful and loving, it becomes? For just as one is revealing oneself and one's plans to God, He too is revealing himself to us in return. This may seldom if ever take the form of a direct communication; nevertheless through prayer, the sacraments and living the love of Christ, one can be assured that He is continuously making His presence felt in whatever way He chooses. Christ Himself reassures and comforts us with the beautiful words,

"blessed are they that have not seen, and have believed."
St John 20: 19 – 31

Prayer which flows like a mighty river is almost incomprehensible to define, insofar as its depth and flow are impossible to gauge. Every day, worldwide, the cumulative number of Masses said, plus the offerings of prayer, combine to give glory to God, to seek forgiveness for Mankind's transgressions, and beseech Him to renew Man's faith, redeemed through the Passion, Death and Resurrection of Jesus Christ. It is the great omniscience of grace drawn down on Mankind by this daily offering of Masses which forestalls Satan. For whereas the goodness of prayer is total, the badness of sin from which Satan draws his power, is in itself deceptive and false, empowering in appearance, yet at the same time impotent in ability.

Reflecting on prayer, it is only by catching fleeting glimpses of its true beauty that one feels the need to pray. That is why the need to understand payer is almost too difficult to define. The desire for such knowledge to have everything explained in great detail, is beyond the reach of the most casual enquirer. Even with all the social media platforms available worldwide the vastness of limitless subjects defies comprehension. Truth, fiction, fabrication and lies compete for time and space. Unless a more indepth and thorough means is obtainable one is at the mercy of whatever here-say is being promoted.

Participation in a full and vigorous prayer life promotes another path, a different route. Although scorned by many as if to pray is somehow beneath one's intellectual prowess the need to pray for guidance can bring positive results. To ignore the practice is a most foolish and presumptive arrogance and only motivated by deep feelings of inferiority.

The providence of God must always be seen as that of enabling the faithful to understand that on the Day of Judgement the inconsistencies of this world in which it appears that the good suffers whilst the wicked prosper, will be evident and clear for all to see. The Gospel explains fully that it will only be after the harvest is saved, that the separation of the wheat from the chaff will take place and whereby one will be saved the other, standing beside him, will not.

St Augustine of Hippo, the great doctor of the Church, spent much of his life bringing the reality of this parable, one of his favourites, into his preaching and everyday focus. His writings underlie and underpin this and many other Gospel parables and passages. After Vatican II such teachings were sadly set aside, and the idea that all would be well and there would be room at the banquet was the new thinking that was widely promoted.

To a certain extent all sinners were thereby somehow encouraged in the belief that God's mercy prevailed above everything else and God's justice was almost decommissioned. Popular though this concept was and continues to be, it is without any foundation or doctrinal support and cannot be substituted in place of the original teaching on presumption. This being the truth the Church must again reiterate so that there is no room for any doubt or ambiguity in the mind of those who are undergoing their life's mission. Once this takes place the need to know will be replaced by one's need to believe. For faith, the Church has always taught must surpass reason and, until time ends, this must remain so.

Prayer then is always based on faith but centred on God, the faith to believe in God's love and the faith to have full confidence in His mercy. To pray is to seek the presence of God where one needs, seeks or wants Him most in order that His will is accomplished. Having taught us to pray Christ made it clear that as a community where we come together, He wll always be present.

In this age of self-assurance in which one is forever tempted to see oneself as superior to one's neighbours, the heart is often too hard to receive or give love. Very much like a team player who refuses to train with the less talented members, or the lead singer who prefers not to join the group in rehearsals, the need to pray, apart from times of private or particular solitude, should whenever possible be designated as "community". It really matters not if some people are wonderful on their own, unless they can come together as brothers and sisters in Christ, their love may easily be misdirected inwards towards self, rather than outward towards all those in need around them.

To pray then is to seek to raise the mind and heart to God, for only as one knows God can one only hope to share His will, it is in this way the saints find their own pathways to sainthood. Their prayers have brought them so close to God that He allows them a fraction of the intimacy they seek; that fraction is enough as it takes them within His will in somehow allowing them to witness somehow the mystery of His Life, Passion and Death on Earth.

In prayer we have been assured we are bringing down God's love, graces and mercy on all our brothers and sisters and it is this invitation to prayer we should consistently seek to receive and extend to others. To shower down prayers on our families, friends, communities, our dearly departed loved ones, these are the normal everyday groups for which we honestly seek God's graces, yet these are only the beginning of what our prayer catalogue should and could contain.

Those in need of prayer today are far too countless to list. One need only think of all those who are physically or mentally suffering, all who have become marginalized, those who are daily experiencing deteriorating ill health, prisoners, low paid labourers, conscripted soldiers and sailors, misfits, homosexuals, transsexuals and of course the millions living in poverty to name only some, who are just too worn out with the miseries of the world to have remained true to their faith. It is these souls who having become drained of all hope, confidence, and belief in the love and mercy of God who are so urgently in need of the prayers of those who remain steadfast. By such prayers, countless souls are still out there to be somehow touched by the finger of hope and the possibility of being rescued.

When thinking of prayer and calling on God's love to be present, where can one begin? Where indeed in today's world is God's grace and mercy not sorely needed? Geographically there appears to be no corner of the globe where some degree of serious social or economic problems do not exist. One is tempted to believe the forces under Satan's command are so strong that the trail of havoc they continue to spread across the world seems at times to be almost out of control. Yet we know this is not possible. Regardless of appearances or that somehow a period gap in time now exists that allows Satan an interim advantage, his ultimate defeat is inevitable.

One aspect remains however, and that is, whereas Satan cannot consolidate his forces, his powers of destruction are mammoth. His desire to destroy Mother Church, in whatever 'true form' she exists is the purpose of his existence. So total and complete is his hatred of God's creation that his on-going corruption of Mankind is his prime objective and the most sure route for him to attempt to succeed in his purpose.

As Man abdicates control of his free will to Satan, and chooses the earthly temporal pleasures which he believes the state of sin will provide him, God wills his priests and faithful followers to listen to his voice and hear his message. It is through the Gospel, through Mother Church and through those entrusted to spread the good news that the faithful are encouraged to set out and secure their salvation; a salvation of love, one which will include all those whose lives one touches whilst on Earth, influencing them also as much as possible to complete their mission. When one receives the invitation to take up one's cross and 'follow Him for:

"the harvest is plentiful whilst the labourers are few,"

the temptation is always there to ignore or set it aside for a more convenient time until one is "ready." This temptation is one must never succumb to. For God the time is always "now", the restrictions of previous or future weeks do not exist for Him and so our minds are distorted by such time frames. The Gospel makes clear the need is not only to heed the word of God but to live it, and live it to the full on a daily basis, not in the past and certainly not in the distant future, but forever in the present.

To seek faith, to desire belief, to nourish the growth of truth are all fundamental aspirations which are common to men of goodwill, save the very few whose life's journey from birth appears as if they were born into this world only to suffer. That some such persons exist seems totally inconceivable, yet God's plan is not revealed to man or, for him to question. One has no need to know the reason a paraplegic or a Downs Syndrome infant is born into one family rather than another. The purpose of such a life is as real as any other and perhaps even more essential and worthwhile than one can ever tell, yet its meaning will only be fully revealed on the Last Day and the reward so well earned by the handicapped person in this world may far exceed that of so very many normal people in the next. For the vast majority who have eyes to see, tongues to speak and ears to hear insofar as they choose to look, speak and listen, God's invitation to come closer to him is always there.

The deception of Satan is that there are those who will always appear to others as if they were pre-chosen and have the whole hologram of Christ given to them at birth. Yet this is nothing more than a further lie designed to defeat the weakest. Rather one should always pray that all who labour in the vineyards, regardless of when they arrive, they also will obtain their rightful place in the Kingdom of Heaven.

Why God permits the launch, arrival, birth, colour, health, destination, status and parenthood of each single individual who today achieves life on earth is due only to His providence and the parameters of man's free will. In the Gospel more than once it is stated that, "indeed to whom much has been given, much will be expected." This quotation stands over those who, through no fault of their own, are born into lives of abject misery, degradation, poverty and despair. In the Gospel the compassion of Christ for those in any form of cruel poverty is all encompassing and evident; by the same token His anger is powerful towards those with excess wealth, status, possessions and talents who fail to make proper use of them.

The premise therefore remains as to what must be expected of those who were born directly into our Mother Church and who immediately after birth were admitted into the mystical body of Christ. It is for all of these children to remain steadfast to their Baptism and royal priesthood, to share their spiritual wealth with those less fortunate fellow travellers.

In order to share the Gospel, one must first seek to secure the salvation of love, for until one has some degree of this security one has little to share with the few, let alone the many. One must strive to live it, to work it and to share it. One must desire to know, love and serve God through an intimate relationship with Christ for it is only through Him, with Him and in Him that one can reach the way, the truth and the life. To identify with Christ must mean that one not only acknowledges Him as their Lord but one accepts the totality of the relationship and the necessary conditions and demands the relationship makes. There is no way one can offer God one's love until one first appreciates to some degree the love which God holds for us all as His children, both individually and collectively.

As is so often stated, God has no favourites, He could not have, for His love for each of us is total. One's fear, that one may be receiving a degree of love inferior to the degree being offered another, especially a person one may totally dislike, is baseless and makes one's own feeble attempt to love so limited and restricted that it fails to fan the flame of intensity vital for the pure love of faith to flourish.

It is this harsh, demanding love then that so few ever achieve, but which every son and daughter is encouraged to seek and make central to their lives. This is one of the reasons for maintaining the rule of celibacy for priests and religious orders so that they are given every opportunity of achieving greater unity with Christ while they are still on earth. St Pope John Paul II for his pontificate chose the words "Totus Tuus" (Everything for You) to emphasize his devotion to God's Mother as his source of inspiration and protection in bringing her Son's name into the mind and hearts of man.

When St Augustine spoke of love in relation to keeping the Commandments, he stressed that love must come first, for without love there would be no reason for keeping them. This seeking is the urge to share love and serve love by bringing Christ into the lives and hearts of man, just as any son or daughter who represents their father would do so in the full confidence of representing him.

Saint Patrick, Patriarch of the Irish wrote,

'For it is the wise son that is the honour of his father'.

It is in this light as sons and daughters of God that one is invited, not just, to express one's own love of Christ but rather to express Christ's love for each one of us. How well then can one know, become intimate, and love Christ in a way that will withstand the tremendous onslaughts such devotion will attract? How will the temptations and doubts be overcome? Is it possible that one's motivation will become corrupt? Can pride ever be totally vanquished? To these and so many other questions the only consolation one has is that the greater one's knowledge and understanding of Christ is then the greater one's love and faith in Him is supported and assured. It is this assurance in which one's faith is firmly secured that can be described as the "Rock." Peter the first Pope chosen by Christ used the word "Rock" for strength, and made it clear:

"that the gates of hell shall not prevail against it," Matt.
16:18

and it is for us even as sinners to realise that as part of this rock, this Church, Satan can never destroy us as long as we remain loyal to our Father our salvation is secured.

The Gospel illustrates for us the Incarnation, Life, Death and Resurrection of Jesus Christ. For Catholics seeking to return to their Mother Church its long lost familiarity must be once more re-examined with serious adult awareness, appreciation and understanding.

The private interpretations which the past 20 or 30 years have gained much popularity are meaningless if they are not in accordance with precise Catholic theology and church doctrine. For some this is an easier exercise than for others, for just as some will gain great pleasure from a piece of music or a picture, the Gospel will likewise affect many differently. Effort and a genuine desire to learn, bounded by prayer, will bring the light of the gospel into the poorest person's heart, regardless of their mental prowess. The Gospel, however factually detailed it may be, was given to us in order that we should know and experience Christ on a one-on-one basis.

The Son of God was born into this World and committed to living his Life, Passion and Death in order that each one of us could be redeemed and given the place prepared for them in God's Kingdom should they wish to secure it. Christ preached that it is only through Him we can 'seek to find'. He has also told us the path He has left us to follow is not an easy one, nevertheless, He has told us that He will sustain us in all our efforts. With such encouragement then we need to read and study the scriptures, in order to seek and find some depth of understanding. We need to realize the Gospel truth and in accepting it, to become part of it.

The Gospel ordained by our Mother Church is primarily the authentic collection of the texts of the four Evangelists, Matthew, Mark, Luke and John, concerning the life and teachings of Jesus Christ. These accounts and others such as "The Acts of the Apostles" approved since the earliest times by the Church are believed to have been those directly inspired and influenced by the guidance of the Holy Spirit and written by those closest to Christ and who witnessed the events described. In addition to the four gospels, The Acts of the Apostles, the Epistles or Letters of other writers such as St Paul all contribute to the body of knowledge endorsed over many centuries by the Magisterium of the Church.

To any Catholic who has received a basic and fundamental religious education in junior or junior high, these levels of sacred scripture texts are easily recognisable albeit on a superficial level. This causal knowledge however without being grounded in any firm or appreciative bed of faith can hardly be expected to withstand the onslaught of materialism let alone the real temptations of Satan during one's life. However for a great many young Catholics today such is the case. Knowledge without meaning, meaning without understanding, understanding without love, all contribute to an overloading of such enormous proportions that one's spiritual sensibilities become almost obliterated. The core beliefs of Catholic doctrine on which one must draw regularly if one is to spiritually exist are no longer firmly anchored with the reverence and awe they should command but rather instead treated in an almost differential manner.

In the Creeds of our Mother Church, our doctrine, our belief, our faith is laid out formidably and forcibly for all to see. Elsewhere it is written, it is spoken, it is pronounced, it is recited. It is within each one of us however that it must be lived. For it is our faith, and only our faith which will lead us to know, love and serve God. The need to love God, and the need to understand how one is loved by God are the two greatest mysteries of life, for with them anything is possible and without them everything is almost impossible.

In the two most popular Creeds of Mother Church, the Nicene and Apostolic, the birth of our saviour Jesus Christ is close to the beginning. It confirms one's personal belief in church doctrine, it was that by the power of the Holy Spirit, the Incarnation of the Word took life through the Blessed Virgin Mary, and was made Man.

This is the greatest of all God's mysteries, for love was reborn, and mankind was about to be saved, through the Passion, Death and

Resurrection of Jesus. The enormity of the Incarnation and what it meant for mankind can never be totally comprehended, because it is a sacred mystery, one beyond belief. What one can only hope to achieve is a degree of realization that God was prepared to accept the living sacrifice of his only Son on behalf of Mankind in order to free Man from sin, and welcome him back into Paradise. The Paradise lost to Man by the sin of his first parents, Adam and Eve, divorcing humanity from God, being finally regained. This Original Sin however still had to be atoned for through the sacrifice of the Son of God. That God sent His only Son into the world as a man to pay this supreme price was, and still is, inconceivable and far beyond our ability to comprehend in its magnitude. Nevertheless our Creed is our belief, and however hard one chooses to struggle with one's faith, one is left in no doubt as the Gospel proclaims that,

"the Word was made Flesh and Dwelt amongst us."

In the liturgical calendar the Feast of the Annunciation falls on March 25th. This date has many meanings, one of the most beautiful being the appearance of a new star in the East on this date which inspired the Magi to commence their odyssey. Over the following nine months the star finally led them to a shepherd's cave in Bethlehem where at last they were allowed to behold and adore the Messiah, a newborn baby infant, the saviour of all Mankind.

It is central to the faith of all Catholics that the Archangel Gabriel was sent by God to Nazareth to assure the Blessed Virgin Mary not to be afraid, to tell her she had found grace with God and that she would conceive and bear a son, and He would be called Jesus. That Mary was comforted, and that her mind was put to rest, enabled her to agree fervently, declaring herself to be,

"the handmaid of the Lord let it be done unto me according to thy Word."

This is the very keystone of the New Testament because of it and on it, the entire truth of the Gospel rests. If the Annunciation and

Incarnation were not true then the entire Gospel would be untrue. To believe in Jesus it is necessary to believe in Mary His Mother. The choice of Mary to be the Mother of Jesus was made by God Himself and so one must ask if one is uncertain, what is there to doubt?

In perhaps the most simplistic way one should logically meditate on what if the Incarnation never happened, how then did the life of Christ ever even get reported? If the initial account of the Incarnation never took place then how did the actual Nativity happen? At what stage did the factual and real birth of Christ take place? It would be almost impossible to believe in the birth of Jesus without the shepherds, without the angels and without the star. To believe in the Incarnation then is a true act of faith, an act born out of desire, a desire to make a declaration of fidelity, to establish one's first real belief in faith.

To believe in the birth of Christ confirms our belief in God the Father, as now it is being made clear through the Word made flesh that all things come from the Father. In reading the gospel of St Luke one senses that the marvellous meeting between Elizabeth, the mother of John the Baptist and Mary must have been a most truly wonderful occasion. The older woman acknowledging in whose presence she stood, the younger woman the handmaid of the Lord, joyfully proclaiming her Song of Praise, the most beautiful Canticle of all Canticles.

The Annunciation and Incarnation therefore is where one must try and understand the true beauty of this wonderful mystery in which the unity of God is shared again with all humanity. Through the Immaculate Conception of Mary, Jesus, true God and true Man came into this world. For all who struggle with this doctrine, the secret of the Incarnation and its understanding always rests with Mary and her personal devotion to her Son. In the Gospel as Christ's life unfolds, His divinity and humanity are both constantly being revealed and restated in order that one can continuously wonder or meditate upon. Prior to His birth, the truth was retained by Mary His Mother; from the moment she accepted it, it became God's Will. It is so important that this doctrine, this original seed of faith, is truly loved, for it was the love of the handmaiden for her Creator which fostered the greatness of the mystery of the Incarnation and allowed it to take place. The secret and the need to begin our mission again then rests here with Mary Ever Virgin giving birth to the Saviour of Mankind, Faith Itself, the Word Incarnate made Flesh, to dwell amongst us. Her giving Life to Truth gives life to all truth. Her role as she herself has said throughout the last 2,000 years has been and is to bring us, her children, back to her Son. The Mother of Jesus, the Mother of Holy Hope can lead any wayward son or daughter back through her love to Her Son.

The ultimate prayer used by the beatified Servant of God, John Sullivan SJ, whilst giving retreats, was to beg forgiveness of God, and that even if one's own actions would not prove worthy, one's salvation would still be possible through the intercession of the Mother of God. Such faith as expressed in this way is what one should always seek to attain throughout one's mission, and Mary leaves no child of hers without a Mother's comfort.

St Louis de Montfort puts it so beautifully when he writes;

> "It is through the most Blessed Virgin Mary that Jesus Christ came into the world and it is also through her that He continues to reign in the world".

To see Jesus as the infant, the boy and the man it is difficult to focus on his ordinary basic humanity. It is also hard to appreciate his role as that of a loyal son, growing through his teenage years to manhood, yet there can be no doubt that his lifestyle of obedience, serving the temporal needs of Mary and Joseph, especially after Joseph's death, was central, ordered and an intrinsic part of his humanity. One interesting speculation being considered today by many biblical scholars is that during this period the enormous Roman fort of Sepphoris was being constructed by Herod Antipas, only four miles from Nazareth and historians wrote at the time it took 40 years to build. The demand for craftsmen must have been great and it is more than likely that Joseph the carpenter and his Son Jesus may have worked together on the colossal building site.

The fact that Jesus grew to become fully man in the adult sense of the word is not without significance. Furthermore His entrance into public life was in no way premature. The need was for his ministry first to be introduced by John the Baptist. The elderly parents of John the Baptist; Elizabeth and Zachary were themselves blessed by God's grace, and knew of the Divinity of Christ before all others except, of course, Joseph. Zachary had told his son he was to be the Precursor, and he was to proclaim the way of the Lord. John was only six months older than Jesus when he first appeared as a mature man on the banks of the Jordan preaching repentance, humility and goodness. Earlier prophets had for centuries preached the coming of a saviour, a Messiah, but it was to be John the Baptist who would directly introduce Jesus as such when he proclaimed:-

"Behold, the Lamb of God who takes away the sins of the World",

Once Jesus was baptized His mission for Man's redemption was ordained and His public life began. He took over from John the Baptist whose role was destined to diminish. From then on Jesus would baptise not only with water, but with the Holy Spirit. As the long-awaited Messiah promised by John the Baptist, He was the Good News, the Word made Flesh, born to save Mankind, yet throughout His ministry His message was one of repentance, salvation and the Kingdom of God. The mercy and love of God was what Jesus offered to all who listened to Him. Today is no different for those who are baptised, who seek to be baptised and indeed all who hunger for the word of God.

Baptism is the indelible seal on one's soul, and once it is bestowed the spiritual responsibility of making every effort to seek God becomes the great longing which can never be satisfied until one is finally welcomed on Re-entry into the Kingdom, as a "Child of the Living God".

From the beginning of His ministry Jesus spoke of the Kingdom of Heaven. As a journeyman preacher with His followers He moved throughout the lands of Judea and Galilee attracting both small or large crowds wherever he went. As soon as a sufficient number had gathered around He would bid them to sit, and begin to outline and explain the passage of scripture He wanted them to understand. On this occasion it was a sermon that would become known as the "Sermon on the Mount," As always the gathering was curious to hear what He had to say. He could see how weary and weak they were forced to live and work under Roman rule, and to offer them hope and consolation He explained to them the meaning of being "blessed."

He told them of God's great love for all men and rejoiced in those who were prepared to lead such lives under the most difficult and trying circumstances. Living under the strict Roman authoritarian code was not an easy regime for either the Jews or Arabs, who both suffered considerably from the might of invincible Rome. It was by remaining resolute Jesus comforted them with the following thoughts:-

THE BEATITUDES
(Mt 5; 3-12)

Blessed are the poor in spirit: for theirs is the Kingdom of Heaven.
Blessed are they that mourn: for they shall be comforted.
Blessed are the meek: for they shall inherit the Earth.
Blessed are they who do hunger and thirst after righteousness: for they shall be filled.
Blessed are the merciful: for they shall obtain mercy.
Blessed are the pure of heart: for they shall see God.
Blessed are the peacemakers: for they shall be called the children of God.
Blessed are they who are persecuted for righteousness sake: for theirs is the Kingdom of Heaven.
Blessed are they when persecuted in my name, for their reward will be great in Heaven.

To meditate on any one of these Beatitudes one should always pray for a deeper understanding and in what way it's meaning can be incorporated into one's own life. One strange observation was made by Leo Tolstoy who claimed that "We must take the Sermon on the Mount" to be as much a law as the theorem of Pythagoras". And so reading them, one is almost overcome by the number of questions which spring to mind:-

- Does poor in spirit mean humble, without vanity, without pretension?
- Are those who mourn blessed because they seek to help others, perhaps in Purgatory?
- Jesus praises the meek, not the weak, Does this mean, "be strong, but be gentle"?
- Likewise, those who stand up for the truth must they always be commended?
- Blessed are those who are always generous enough to forgive others!
- Those who bring reconciliation rather than strife should always be praised!!!

How much does one need to suffer for their faith as witnesses to Christ is there any limit to it?

How does one get sufficient courage to accept such sufferings when facing intimidation or ridicule for our faith?

- How can one be a true witnesses and not back down or worse still run away?

Seeking further insights never ceases to bring rewards and sometimes, as above via L Tolstoy, in the strangest of ways as through the power of the Holy Spirit, we are assured that one must 'seek if one truly wants to find.' Again and again The Gospel emphasizes that;

> 'to whom much has been given; much more will be given'
> 'to whom little has been given, even that shall be taken
> away from them'

In reading such accounts one is tempted to question the fairness of such a scenario yet it is obvious that the penitent who keeps looking and searching will gain help and reward while the person who never seeks will never find and in addition surrender up what they already have received.

Jesus used parables to teach his disciples in such a way that the lessons would be understandable and remain relevant to their lives. One example of the effectiveness of this method was not so much the actual parable of the Sower and the Seed in itself but rather the interpretation of its contents which Christ Himself went to great lengths to explain.

"Don't you understand this parable? How, then, will you ever understand any parable?

The sower sows God's message. Some people are like seeds that fall along the path; as soon as they hear the message Satan comes and takes it away. Other people are like the seeds that fall on rocky ground. As soon as they receive the message they receive it gladly. But it does not sink deep enough into them, and they don't last long. So when persecution or trouble comes because of the message they give up at once. Other people are like seeds sown among the thorn bushes. These are the ones who hear the message, but the worries about this life, the love of riches, and all other kinds of desires crowd in and choke the message, and they don't bear fruit But the other people are like the seeds sown in good soil. They hear the message accept it, and bear good fruit."

The apostles felt the need to question Jesus in more detail about the meaning of this parable as it was obvious that it contained a deeper message of some sort. After He explained it further He cautioned them that they would need to develop their faith further, if they were to understand it even more. It was for them an obligation and only after they made this greater commitment would they receive deeper knowledge. If they were not prepared to do this, what knowledge that had previously been given to them could well be lost.

Jesus made this point elsewhere, as in the account of the centurion with the sick servant who astonished Jesus by saying:

"Lord I am not worthy that Thou should enter under my roof, only say the word and my servant shall be healed."

Matthew 8:8

Jesus turned to the multitude declaring how great was this centurion's faith, and to emphasize the point, he tells them plainly that there will be those who will gain entry into the Kingdom of Heaven as strangers, whilst those already chosen as children of God will find they have been excluded. To listen to such a harsh message and not to hear its content is today's great threat to mankind and yet it is painfully clear throughout the Gospel that one's own Baptism in itself is not enough to guarantee one a place at the banquet. One's need to deepen one's understanding of one's faith is an obligation the same as the one facing the apostles 2000 years ago and that obligation is to deepen one's understanding of one's faith. This is the commitment one must be prepared to make.

Baptism as stated makes us all Children of God. It gives us the obligation to know, love and serve God and yet it is only a royal invitation which one must validate oneself if one is to respond positively. This is one's own personal right, one's own personal choice and if one chooses to forfeit it for whatever reason they will be excluded from the Kingdom of Heaven. Should we fail to listen, or try and understand then eventually one will cease to comprehend the Gospel itself, and the message of salvation, God's greatest gift achieved for us by Christ's sacrifice will be lost. No fate could ever be worse or more terrible to bear, yet today's church, its hierarchy and its clergy appear almost unwilling to discuss the Four Last Things in any detail.

Who, having heard the parable of the foolish maidens, failing to trim their candles can have had much sympathy for them as they ran out of oil and were subsequently locked out of the wedding? (Matt. 25: 1 - 13) Likewise in the parable of the master having given his servants their respective "talents" (Matt. 25: 14 - 30) fully expected them to be used and not buried in the ground. To have received the gift of faith through Baptism, the Gospel continuously stresses that one must not only allow the Word to grow, flourish and spread but rather roll up one's sleeves and make every effort to ensure it flourishes and bears fruit. The barren tree receives nothing. The great gift of salvation offered to each of us through the Sacrament of Baptism must be recognised for what it is: the ultimate glorious invitation for each one of us to accept. In today's world one hears so many times that God loves the sinner, but hates the sin. One also never ceases to hear of how great God's mercy is, and indeed it is for those who seek it. What is seldom heard however is that even though God loves us, it will be according to how we fulfil our missions that He will reward each of us.

In trying to live the Gospel as an everyday lifestyle choice, how does one make the parables relevant in today's society? Keeping in mind or in one's daily prayers the Beatitudes; one of the central themes constantly portrayed is the need for justice and forgiveness. "Insofar as you have done it to the least of mine, you have done it to me". This is an open opportunity or invitation each one of us receives on a daily basis; Take for example, The Rich Man and Lazarus (Lk. 16: 19 - 31), and The Good Samaritan (Lk. 10: 25 - 37) what more powerful parables or examples can one be faced with? An even more meaningful and significant parable in today's selfish world and particularly apt is that of the Unmerciful Servant (Matt. 18: 23 - 35) who not only took advantage of his Master's generosity, but in turn showed no mercy to the man who owed him money.

There are few torments in life comparable to that of remorse; regret allows some room for compassion, but remorse seldom does. For this reason, the opportunity to help, which one is always blessed to be given, if rejected or denied, is gone and usually gone forever. Later the realization of one's total selfishness, meanness or hardness of heart always returns to bring one face to face with the local Lazarus on the pavement that one passed by without so much as a second glance.

Again in choosing the Gospel as one's life-choice in our world of today, under the guidance of our Mother Church we witness the constant call for humanity to identify with Christianity. Its message for mankind is the same as it has always been; to realize that Christ died for each of us so that we may claim our rightful salvation. Mankind must wilfully accept the teachings of Christ, and listen to the word of God. The Church guided by the Holy Spirit forever strives to enlighten and guide all men of their Christian, social and moral obligations to themselves, their families and their communities.

In the global hierarchy of The World Bank, The International Monetary Fund, The UN, The European Central Bank, The Russian

Federation and the rising superpowers of India and China, domination and dependency are constant. These powerhouses of empire all compete to muscle in to take control and manipulate the less fortunate developing countries in every way possible.

Within such a material and secular world the role of the Roman Catholic Church is not simple. Seen not in its true role as the Mother to Mankind, but rather as an sinister force its presence is tolerated rather than welcomed. Sad as this maybe for the less fortunate inhabitants of so many countries, the Catholic Church sees the urgent need and necessity to speak the truth of Christ unequivocally as she has done over the past 2000 years. This is her obligation and her right, and from which She has no reason to stray.

Professing the one true faith, the Pope, the Holy Father is expected to take up the Cross of Christ, and enduring whatever suffering he is called upon to bear, it is his duty to continue to preach the message of God's love for Mankind expressed through the life, death and Resurrection of Jesus Christ.

Over a hundred years ago our Mother Church under the pontificate of Leo XIII published the very famous encyclical "Rerum Novarum". This set down the principles which guided the Church's teachings on social obligations as they needed to be applied, relevant to the Industrial Age, which was at the time ushering in the 20th century. Pope Pius XI 40 years later wrote his encyclical "Quadragesimo Anno" as an addendum to Rerum Novarum and to meet the new needs of the social classes which were by then becoming consumer-driven.

Seventy years after Rerum Novarum the well loved pontiff St John XXIII issued his encyclical "Mater et Magistra" to stress the need of not only a fair wage, but also the importance of the dignity and participation of the worker. He was also conscious that in addition to the needs of industrial workers those in the most deprived sectors such as agriculture should not be excluded or treated in an inferior way. Paul VI issued "Populorum Progressio" in 1967 which broadened the entire social and ethical fields into one of total global awareness. He in turn insisted that economic development should not be restricted and limited by economic growth.

People trying to escape from endemic disease, illiteracy, hunger and other forms of misery deserve the support of the richer nations if for no other reason than that of their most basic need for survival, justice and peace. Ninety years after Rerum Novarum first made its appearance, St John Paul II issued his social encyclical "Laborem Exercens" in which his Polish identity, affinity and determination were most evident by his call for human solidarity and work as key to all equitable economic life. In his writings St John Paul II often stressed the need for the dignity of man to always take priority over the demands of capital. As the most worldly aware of Popes in contemporary history, with his personal experience of work his role allowed him to also call for the Church to play a role in the spirituality of work. In 1987, he issued "Sollicitudo Rei Socialis" to mark the twentieth anniversary of "Populorum Progressio". Solidarity again was central to this encyclical which sought to push the boundaries further back than ever before.

Global demographic problems, debt crisis, economic resources and the help to poor nations were well within its gambit, and the sharing of resources between nations was again emphasized. In addition to the economic dimensions, the moral, cultural and social aspects were highlighted as being necessary to incorporate into the full and true order of society. The equality and solidarity of all peoples must, it stressed, be found in unity: the unity of equitable belief, the unity of equitable work; the unity of equitable living. For the 100th anniversary of Rerum Novarum in 1991, St Pope John Paul II decided to return to the social needs of society, and how best they could be attended to by Mother Church. In his "Centesimus Annus" he reappraised the original issues and dwelt on the failure of socialism in its many guises including that of Liberation Theology. A most paradoxically titled theology as never has any revolution, rebellion or Marxist uprising brought liberation in its wake.

The attempted use of an iconic Christ as some form of freedom fighter was seen as a blasphemous attempt to 'use' the Messiah. St John Paul repeated the Church's teachings on social doctrines and condemned the spread of materialism based on human exploitation and consumerism. In his rejection of totalitarianism and liberal capitalism he made quite clear that the responsibility of Mother Church was to teach the gospel: this was its primary function.

These seven Papal encyclicals covering Church teaching on its social responsibilities and obligations to meet the needs of Man over the past hundred years, can leave no intelligent person or serious seeker of truth in any doubt as to the tremendous concern the Catholic Church has, not just for her immediate children, but rather for the entire family of Man. Of the three encyclicals written by Benedict XVI, Spe Salvi, (21:10:2007) 'In Faith We Hope' the Pontiff outlines that the true destiny of man always lies in hope and it is in hope we seek salvation.

Today's Bishop of Rome, Pope Francis I began his Pontificate with his encyclical, Lumen Fidei (29:06:2013), The Light of Faith. The encyclical letter is primarily addressed by the Holy Father to the College of Cardinals and Bishops throughout the world and as such is a somewhat technical reading in a spiritual sense. It is hard to read and the labyrinth of views expressed are difficult to navigate. The views outlined are those of the Pope and the topics expressed are the topics he chooses to interpret as he sees them. Of course as with any powerful and thought provoking document it was written in a very high-church form and so not intended as an easy read for the layman.

His second encyclical, Laudato Si (24:05:2015), Praise Be To You, could not have been written in a more different or upbeat manner. It was written for all the faithful and therein lay the conundrum for such a modern written encyclical, On Care for our Common Home is a breakaway from all previous encyclicals. In the past it would have been addressed to the bishops of the Catholic Church for their personal edification and adherence as if being formally addressed by the Vicar of Christ addressing his Apostles. In so doing it would have demanded their attention and sought their support and the support of their relevant pastors and congregations. Today instead this document is written more like a Spiritual Secretary General addressing the United Nations. It is global and it is all encompassing but it is not in a classical sense a Catholic document. Its deliverance contains no radical type moment when Catholics in particular were singled out by their own Holy Father bringing them to task as to how they are responsible for the environmental world situation and how he now wishes and instructs them to deal with it.

Instead it seems more like an introduction to Environmental Catholicism for non Catholics or any non believers who maybe interested in what the Catholic Church leader has to say. It may well be that the Pope's method is the new way forward and now as a global figure he has the right to address everybody worldwide in this manner. However, for such a popular world figure it is quite possible the Holy Father sees the World as his 'church' and with co-operation of other world leaders in the global fields of the Environment, Evangelical and Ecumenical spheres his goal of unity. A world of church unity, or a world of united churches, yet at the same time as it would be a church without unification, it would cease to be Catholic.

Sadly whatever his own personal and private thoughts are he has a distinct and unique obligation to share them with his universal flock and not just with his parochial confreres. To teach, inform and guide his own hierarchy is however the true role and the first obligation of the supreme pontiff. It is for him to nourish, to tend and to call his bishops to order. They in their turn must likewise inform their front line priests as to how the Catholic Church sees any serious problem and how as a Church we must all deal with it. By such witnessing to Christ and His creation it is possible the Catholic Church will then be seen by today's' agnostics atheists and modern day pagans in a new light which will prompt them to ask,

> "How can we join with you and together be followers
> of your Christ"?

CHAPTER

8

It was only upon reaching the age of 30 that Jesus emerged from Nazareth as a journeyman preacher and prophet. His life from boyhood through to manhood moved slowly into the public domain. From the Gospel account of the Marriage Feast of Cana it appears at first He was somewhat reluctant to begin his public ministry. Only on the prompting of His Mother and after acquiescing to her wishes He performed His first miracle, demonstrating His power by changing the large stone vats filled with water, into vats filled with wine.

Being fully aware of what lay ahead of Him, His humanity instilled in Him a fear that could not be avoided. If anything, it greatly intensified His awareness of what suffering He would have to endure and how well His courage would be tested when the time came. He knew the necessity of the sacrifice He would have to bear. Being conscious of how His life would end would, from His first days as a preacher, never be too far away. He knew in order for mankind to be saved His sacrifice would have to be undertaken and born time and time again over all ages in great agony.

After the wedding celebrations at Cana with what must have been a heavy heart and a measure of sadness, he said goodbye to his parents and friends and headed south. Leaving Nazareth He headed for the Jordan valley where he knew His cousin John would be. Once he had arrived there He was at once baptised and His mission was publicly heralded by the Holy Spirit. Now, as if finally ratified, He at last was set to begin His ministry. To all who were prepared to listen his was a message of good news, simple enough for all to understand. It was one of hope, redemption, salvation and above all else, God's infinite mercy and love. It was through Him who had been sent by God as the Old Testament foretold that mankind would be saved.

Mighty as the mission was, and overwhelming as the good news it contained, Jesus took the simple role as that of a journeyman preacher and teacher to deliver it. To all who would stop to listen to what he had to say, he patiently outlined texts from the Old Testament explained their meanings to those who gathered around. After some time had passed He choose a small group of fishermen as his selected companions or followers to remain with Him as He travelled throughout Judea and Galilee spreading the good news of God's mercy and Man's salvation.

Reading the Gospel and the various texts giving detailed insights into the public ministry of Christ is the undertaking of a lifetime. After acquiring an intimate and detailed knowledge of it in one's own language the next step is to further explore the texts in the languages of the period, Greek, Coptic Syriac, Armenian. For the most intense scholar such research may take a lifetime, yet, for those who engage in such work, it is necessary and time well spent.

The interpretation of so many accounts, of so many descriptions, of so many opinions examined by the most knowledgeable and learned intellects of every century for the past 20 centuries, is an equation that is complex. Allowing for each 100 years to have had three, even four, generations of scholars dissecting every core belief makes it almost impossible to calculate how much time has been spent examining the life of Jesus Christ. All one can surmise is that the amount of time, effort and reflection which has gone into exploring every known fact and detail relating to the life and death of Christ over two millennia is without equal. That He existed and walked the face of the planet is indisputable, that he died is also indisputable; that he rose again from the dead in order to save every single man and woman is what the Catholic church has always taught, continues to teach, and will continue to teach until the end of time is perhaps disputable to those without faith, but not to Catholics who practice their religion in the service of God, helping others.

To the faithful everyday lay Catholic who in a general sense is far removed from the world of theology, his fundamental religious information is usually based on the quality of the teaching and reading he has undertaken over the years. This interest may or maynot be substantial but from the sermons one hears, the informal discussions one takes place in, the newspaper and media accounts one is exposed to will give any normal person a reservoir from which to draw their own conclusions.

When the life of Christ is under discussion or being examined in detail the chronological series of events which take place over the final few weeks normally referred to as the Passion are those eventful weeks in which Jesus is hailed as the Messiah, glorified riding into Jerusalem, betrayed by Judas, tried before Pontius Pilate and crucified at the insistence of the Jews. The preceding three year condensed time period highlighted in the Gospel allows every seeker of truth to acquire a sufficient knowledge to qualify them as a follower of Jesus Christ. The teachings of Christ are very simple in the sense that one is obliged to follow the Commandments, love God and one's neighbour as best one can and lead a good life. For those more intent on living a life in a full and complete imitation of Christ's, this way is all the more demanding in that one must radically change one's lifestyle, take up one's cross and follow Him. This is the path chosen by those who not on a casual basis but on a 24/7 time schedule, working on behalf of one's fellow man sometimes loving them sometimes not, but always in the name of Jesus Christ.

Christ said quite plainly many times that unless one is prepared publicly to acknowledge Him, He will not acknowledge them as they stand before the Father, awaiting their own judgement. This clear and unambiguous statement may appear rather harsh, yet one would do well to remember it as it is a failing all too easy to make. To try and fully understand some of the direct instructions in the Gospel it is necessary to realize that what is valid and understandable in our everyday life must also be even more so in our spiritual one. There can be very few people who have not experienced at one stage or another a sense of being ignored or overlooked by a friend who failed to wave, or offer to help when it was badly needed. Christ likewise therefore cautions us never to turn our backs on Him when he tells us:

"The fear of the Lord is the beginning of all knowledge,
but fools despise wisdom and instruction"

Proverbs, Ch. 1:7

Our premier responsibility therefore always remains the same, to know, love and serve God. Once this Commandment is lived as God intended it to be then one is in a positive position for every choice one is called upon to make.

The life of Christ, as described in the Gospel and the Acts of the Apostles contain most of the facts and events in Christ's life. During His short ministry as it became more widespread and gained many followers as news of his cures and miracles spread. This almost unknown preacher from Nazareth began to gain a formidable status as an exceptionally holy man and powerful preacher. As time went by and as they do more and more people heard Him preach. He was becoming well known not just in various parts of the countryside but also to the Jewish elders in Jerusalem where he would preach intermittently in the temple. In an age where word of mouth was the only common means of communication, over a period of time His reputation started to become serious as it spread further and further afield. As one Rabbi after another would attract listeners by the quality of his sermons so it was also with this Jesus from Nazareth. It was about midway through his ministry that Jesus began to talk in more serious detail of what was about to happen to the Son of God to His small group of disciples He had gathered about Him. By this time they had witnessed many healings and great events and were committed to Him their master to serve Him whatever way they could.

The more time passed the more they were prepared to hear, see and believe whatever He told them especially in relation to the future and any details He would reveal to them. Christ, knowing what was in store for them all, began to be more explicit and demanding in His teachings. He asked them to consider what it would profit a man to gain the whole world, and having done so, lose his own soul? He told them that to follow him they would have to lose their lives first in order to find them again. He stressed that they would have to serve rather than be served, and it was the lost, rather than those already in the fold, who would have to be saved. It was these and many other parables He preached to them, all the while explaining that the dark days of Jerusalem's shame lay ahead and His final days were beginning to draw closer and closer to hand.

It has always been obvious that without Christ's Resurrection there would be no Christianity, just as it is clear that without night there would be no day. The magnitude of this one central mystery of faith, the Resurrection, is the most enormous truth contained within Christianity and the very rock on which so many non-believers are doomed to perish. Without the gift of faith this truth is almost too hard to accept let alone comprehend. Nevertheless by prayer, effort and persevering some of God's greatest sceptics have made the journey, and having made it after battling with many demons along the way, have at last embraced the divinity of Christ and acknowledge Him as their Lord the one true Son of God.

Interestingly for many eminent biblical scholars lacking the true faith, the death and crucifixion of Jesus is fully acceptable as a landmark historical fact yet His actual Resurrection surpasses their reason and so the grace necessary to accept this mystery of faith is denied them. The paradoxical situation these scholars find themselves in is that even though they are somehow able to promote and refer to Christ as the holiest of all the prophets they cannot come to terms with His Resurrection as if it were too big for them to understand. This one indisputable fact believed by all faithful Catholics is the very greatest of truths. It is held onto even to death itself as the jewel of martyrdom.

To those who choose to disregard Christ as their Messiah the let-out is to base their unbelief or their lack of knowledge on some form of intellectual laziness or indifference. That this one historical person's life changed the Julian calendar from BC to AD proves that the life of Jesus of Nazareth was truly unique. For Catholics there is no ambiguity or debate: Church doctrine cannot be altered and all faithful Catholics are obliged without reservation to accept that Jesus Christ is the Son of God, who rose from the dead, and after a brief period of 40 days ascended into Heaven. This blind acceptance of dogma is a reality of Catholicism and must be seen as such. Faith is what one is given freely as a gift to accept, not to understand or question, just as one would not behave in receiving an expensive or priceless gift in real life.

Looking at the reality from another angle just as so few people understand the laws of quantum physics or chemistry one lives and profits from them. Likewise nuclear fusion, advanced engineering, scientific and mathematical formulae are all subjects way beyond most people's understanding, yet very few sceptics demand to see the proof of such knowledge.

To dwell on the Life of Christ in detail is not the purpose of this book, nevertheless it is all-important that one attempts to try and accompany Jesus briefly through the horrific events of Passion Week which He endured on behalf of each one of us. The Catholic faith teaches that Christ undertook these events not for us all en masse, or collectively as "mankind," but rather, instead, for each one of us individually. His sacrifice would have been undertaken if only one or two were to gain paradise by His sacrifice. As His life on Earth was coming to an end. He spent much time in preparing His disciples and His followers for the terrible culmination of events about to begin in order to bestow on them the knowledge they would need to bring to the followers of Jesus after His Resurrection and Ascension into Heaven.

As He spent the last weeks of His public ministry, journeying throughout Samaria, Galilee and Perea, He preached the need for the sanctity of marriage, he cured lepers, He told His disciples of the great need for humility and, when He arrived in Jericho, much to the annoyance of the Pharisees, He stayed, not with one of the elders, but with a tough common little man, a tax collector for the Romans, called Zacchaeus. In choosing such a despised host Jesus wanted to demonstrate to His followers that He could have just as easily stayed with any one of them. It was not the wealthy merchant or the landowner with the olive grove He chose but a hard working honest man like His own foster father Joseph, whose humility and devotion to his family were the hallmark of his strength and sainthood.

When He and his disciples left Jericho they travelled the 20 miles or so to Bethany which was no more than five miles from Jerusalem and less than an hour's walk away, the train of events leading up to the memorable week were beginning to unfold. Time was beginning to move at a faster pace and the Passover was about to be celebrated. After three years of hardship and preaching throughout the length and breadth of Judea, the incredible confrontation destined to save Mankind for eternity was about to begin.

The raising of Lazarus from the dead four or five weeks earlier was an incident of such magnitude that it refused to disappear or fade away. It may have been yet a further "cure" or "miracle" of Jesus of Nazareth, but it astounded all who had witnessed it and those who had heard of it. Extraordinary and amazing by any degree of human understanding it had left the people bewildered and the neighbours and friends-were still talking about it weeks later in whispered tones.

Jesus was now of course engulfed in notoriety, His fame, his radical proclamations, his seemingly on-going defiance of the elders of the Temple were turning Him into a legend, a major prophet, perhaps even the Messiah Himself, some of his constant followers murmured. To celebrate His raising of Lazarus from the dead, an anniversary meal of the blessed event was organized by a man called Simon. Mary, Martha and of course Lazarus himself along with the Disciples, were all present and at some stage in the evening in a display of adulation and thanks, Mary anointed the feet of Her Lord with a costly and delicate ointment. This seemingly expensive gesture greatly irritated Judas, the disciple in charge of the group's finances, His annoyance and frustration at what he saw as a waste of money began to take a firm hold of him, and Satan moved closer and deeper into his ear. From that exact moment as the temptation of Satan began to grow the tidal torments of Passion Week were set in motion and the terrible betrayal of Jesus moved slowly and surely into position. For Man to once more gain admittance into the Kingdom of Heaven the price was the crucifixion and death of Jesus, and it was this price God's only Son was now preparing Himself to fully accept and pay.

Nobody was quite sure on the Sunday before Passover what the coming week had in store, but everybody had heard that the famous Jesus of Nazareth was staying in Bethany and that He was due to arrive in the city, and maybe preach in the Temple. The air was charged with excitement, anticipation, apprehension, rumour and intrigue. The ordinary people felt the air charged with the unknown.

Rumours ran wild that the Pharisees had had enough of this upstart from Nazareth who kept treating them without the respect they believed they were due and demanded. The population of Jerusalem was overflowing for the annual festival and as always the Roman soldiers were tense and jittery and let it be known that no mercy would be shown to any person who stepped out of line or got in their way. It was always at this time of Passover that the murmurings of some form of 'rising' against Roman authority would take place, and so all leave was cancelled and the garrison was put on full alert. With so much tension in the air and with little or no idea of what to expect, Jesus and his disciples made their way slowly towards the city. As He rode on the back of a white foal from Bethany towards Jerusalem the Gospel describes how the people came out from the city waving palms to welcome Him and addressing Him as if he were already royalty, "Son of David" they chanted as if paying homage to a new ruler or a new king. The Gospel recounts that on seeing Jerusalem in the distance, Jesus wept, not on His own account or for what lay ahead, but because of the role the Jews themselves were about to choose. He entered the city amongst a tremendous fanfare with huge numbers of admirers and other travellers from various parts of Palestine. For the Passover, people came from lands far and near some from as far away as Greece. For a city normally numbering between 2,000 and 3,000 the population for Passover could grow to four or five times that size. Jesus, seeking solitude so hard to find at such a time spent most of the day in prayer, preparing Himself as best He humanly could for the terrible suffering He knew now lay directly ahead.

On Monday, accompanied by the Apostles he again entered the Holy City and having reached the Temple precincts found it inhabited by traders, stall holders and money changers dealing with the demands of the huge multitude still gathering for the Passover. There can be no doubt that Jesus and his Disciples could normally not have evicted such a collection of stall holders by their own physical force; but somehow like determined crowd control marshals they bore down on the traders and swept all before them clearing the precincts of the temple. The Chief Priests were furious with Jesus as he had yet again taken control of the chaotic situation and upstaged them completely. They knew there was nothing they could do as the crowd by this time was again entranced by this amazingly impressive yet gentle preacher. They were all too aware of His enthusiastic following, as the previous day's welcome had demonstrated, and so they left Him alone to spend the day in prayer and preaching.

Tuesday morning started differently however as by this time the Chief Priests were much more determined and organized than they had been during the previous days. Now they had formulated a strategy or plan by which they believed they could ensnare HIm. They waited until Jesus had commenced teaching, and then began to try and entrap Him. Jesus fully conscious of their efforts to put him down not only again turned the tables against them he began to preach some very powerful parables, by way of almost identifying the Jews in their complicity. The "Two Sons" (Matt. 21. 28-32) the "Wicked Husbandmen" (Luke 20. 9-18) and the "Wedding Feast" (Matt 22. 1-14). The Pharisees were in no doubt that these parables were addressed to them as the message of each made clear the need for them to obey God and not attempt to usurp His Kingdom. As if ignoring His teachings and the messages they contained, the Elders still pressed ahead, demanding to hear what He believed was the greatest commandment of the Old Law? Jesus told them that, above all else, to love God was forever the first and greatest commandment, and secondly to love one's neighbour. With both parables and His direct speaking they could make no further inroads or criticism, sufficient to indict Him. He therefore continued and elaborated to the congregation on the hypocrisy of the Scribes and Pharisees, predicting that the old order was about to crumble only to be replaced by a new order. Upon leaving the Temple, Jesus noticed the contribution of the two mites made by an elderly widow. He praised her genuine generosity as it was her "all" that she had given, and in that lay its greatness which He marvelled at. This was the last visit Jesus would make to the Temple. On the way back to Bethany He stopped at the Mount of Olives to pray, taking with him Peter, James and John.

Of the four evangelists, St Matthew's Gospel is perhaps the most explanatory as Matthew presents Jesus as the "teacher". In the first of the two following parables he describes the attitude of the two sons who, when having been asked by their father to go and work in the vineyards, reacted so differently. The first son out-rightly rejects his father's request and refuses to go. The second appears to have no problems acquiescing to his father's instruction and assured him that he would go right away. However, the former hotheaded son, having time to reflect on his father's request, realizes he was wrong and took himself off to carry out the work.

Meanwhile the second son who by now having met up with some of his friends is easily led astray, putting the work off for another day. Jesus teaches that the right way is when he who listens to the word makes the effort to understand it and carries it out. Whereas others hear the word but make little effort to listen and so do little about it. Those who go through the motions, saying fine things, are all too often those who do the least.

It is by actions and not words that men will be judged and the Pharisees who heard were aware he was identifying them as men of words only. In the second parable (St Matt., 22. 1-14) Matthew tells of Jesus talking in terms of a King who, while preparing a wedding feast for his son, discovers that the invited guests are too busy to attend and make their excuses to his servants. The king's anger is swift and ruthless and he quickly throws open his house and fills it with anybody and everybody who happens to be passing by.

The Pharisees again were forced to listen to Jesus clearly identifying them as the original invited guests who were too busy, indifferent or arrogant to attend whilst the humble and the poor, the followers surrounding Jesus, would instead be those that would be made welcome. Here was the formal direct notice that the Old Covenant was about to be replaced. The Pharisees shocked by this new awareness made them realize it would be the Gentiles and not the Jews who would now receive the New Covenant and become the new chosen people of God. To them this was unbelievably heretical and no matter how it had to be done or at what cost Jesus the Nazarene had to be stopped once and for all. Regardless of the means, or what it would take to make it happen, Jesus of Nazareth had to die.

On Wednesday just two days before Passover Jesus had gathered his disciples around him and told them quite plainly what was about to take place. This was not the first time he had informed them of what lay ahead; even now it remained a scenario too complicated for them to understand. As ordinary plain fishermen they just could not get their heads around what he was trying to tell them. He appeared in their eyes to be at the pinnacle of His power, popularity and influence. To them the last few days had proved conclusively that the common people loved Him. He had been hailed as Son of David, had been publicly addressed as King of the Jews and no greater honour or title could have been bestowed upon Him. The people were crying out for Him and wanting Him more and more as some type of leader or ruler. His Disciples felt that what he kept telling them was impossible to reconcile with what they were looking at and what they had witnessed. Over the previous three years they had continuously walked, weary and exhausted, along every dusty and dreary road in Judea, all the while the gatherings had grown larger and larger until it seemed to them that all Jesus had intended to achieve had been achieved.

How could he now be describing such a cruel backlash of faith, followed by the most barbaric death possible under Roman Law? All this was incomprehensible to them. The uncertainty of where Jesus was going and where he was taking them was still way beyond them but they did not care. As things seemed to them at that moment, Jesus could do no wrong; in fact it was possible he could do nearly anything he wanted to as the people were clearly and totally behind Him. The fact he was not seeking to establish a new Jewish kingdom, free from Rome, was however the cause of great bitterness which finally erupted from deep within Judas who at last was beginning to understand what was unfolding and taking place.

The support Judas had always given Jesus was always based on the assumption that Jesus would be the founder of a new kingdom, free from Roman domination. Now it was all beginning to make sense. As the future Jesus had spoken of was beginning to crystallize Judas realized he was now never going to further the ambitions he had personally desired for so long. For this reason Judas decided in pure spite and hatred to destroy Jesus. It was for this reason that he had not gone with them earlier that Wednesday into Jerusalem. On his own he had gone into the city very early with evil festering in his heart and revenge in his soul.

He had never loved Jesus: that was his treachery, his hypocrisy and his sin. He had only seen Him as a potential leader or figurehead who could be used by him and other Jews determined to overthrow the empire. When Jesus had spoken of a kingdom, the apostles were never sure what He meant and spoke of it amongst themselves. However Judas had always chosen to believe it would be an earthly power base, a kingdom on earth. This state which he imagined to be all powerful, prestigious and one in which he would be made a senator or similar which would provide him with all the trappings of wealth, power and privilege. Once he realized at the banquet in Bethany that Jesus was who He claimed to be, and that he never had any intention of leading a popular revolt or insurrection, he was livid. The truth of His Master's teachings bore down on him and as far as he was concerned all the meetings, gatherings and public rallies had been for nothing. The last three years had been a waste of time and he had nothing to show for it. He therefore set out for Jerusalem that Wednesday morning, consumed by a deep hatred. He knew where to find those only too ready to assist in destroying Jesus.

For the Elders and the Sanhedrin it was essential if they were to capture Jesus and stage a mock trial they would need do so in as isolated a spot as possible. Judas was more than able to convince them that he could identify Jesus as he knew when and where He would be. Being pleased to have such treacherous person prepared to act as their spy who would in turn oversee the capture, the Jews were happy to pay him 30 pieces of silver.

For Judas money itself was always the goal, his own personal weakness and the one which would now destroy him. Greed was always his motivational power and, as bursar for the group of disciples, he was constantly aware of the power and control the purse strings gave him and the deference money commanded from all with whom he had any dealings.

On Thursday morning Jesus sent Peter and John into the city to make arrangements for their Passover meal, which was to take place in the house of a friend. The meal was the solemn feast, the highlight of the Jewish calendar during which all the rituals and formalities would be fully observed. Who would sit where and with whom would be decided and not for the first time the disciples speculated as to who would have what role and status in the coming Kingdom. Even at this stage they were still unaware of their immediate world's impending collapse. Jesus took the opportunity to wash his disciples' feet and emphasized to them the need to see themselves as servants to others doing what He was doing, so that the love of God as shown by Jesus to them would likewise be shown to all men. Yet it was this central message of service to all men which still remained hidden and unrecognisable to them as they celebrated the solemn feast.

During the meal Jesus told the 12 that one of them would betray him, to which they all, including Judas, voiced cries of consternation and denial. Nevertheless Jesus was adamant and after He had initiated and distributed the first Eucharist Judas left. This was in no way seen as unusual as often one of the disciples would remove themselves to carry out some task or instruction they had received from Jesus. After leaving Judas then proceeded immediately to meet with the Sanhedrin and tell them of the group's plans for later that evening. Jesus meanwhile told the apostles that in due course He would send the Holy Spirit, the Paraclete to enlighten and commission them. He also spoke of his relationship with his Father and now of their forthcoming direct relationship with Him also. When the meal was finally over they left the house to return to Bethany.

On the way there they stopped at a junction of olive groves called Gethsemane at the base of the Mount of Olives. Taking Peter, James and John, Jesus went a half mile or so upwards to steady himself in prayer and meditation. The realization of what now lay ahead was beginning to take hold of Him and the grip of fear held Him so tight that the sweat on His face turned into beads of blood. It was well into the night after reconciling His will with that of the Fathers to 'take the chalice of salvation' and fulfil His mission. No sooner had He completed praying then Judas appeared with the Temple Guard followed by an unruly mob, to seize and capture Jesus of Nazareth.

As dawn was about to break He was brought in front of Annas who even though deposed was still recognized as the High Priest and the major figure of Jewish authority in Jerusalem. Having questioned him, Annas had him then sent before his son-in-law, Caiphas, the Roman figure of power. It had been Caiphas who had earlier said that it was better for Jesus to die rather than the whole Jewish nation should perish. His thinking being that were Jesus to be the figurehead of some insurrection against the Romans their response would have been swift and terrible. Having assembled the Sanhedrin that morning the trial was quickly called and brought to order. As it progressed the sham procedures started to become obvious and the proceedings exposed as little more than a farce.

Caiphas moved quickly to take control and sought to bring matters to a direct head. He commanded Jesus to say under oath, "I order thee by the living God" to say whether or not he was the Messiah, Jesus replied that He was the Messiah as,

"Son of the Living God."

Caiphas being the Rome-appointed High Priest declared this testimony to be blasphemous and so was able to approve the Sanhedrin's demand for the death sentence. Whilst all this was taking place inside the palace, Peter was outside in the courtyard cursing and vehemently denying again and again that he even knew Jesus. Until, in the distance, he heard a cock crow.

It was only then that the pain, shame and black agony of his infidelity struck him almost physically tearing his heart out from his chest.

Later that morning Jesus was brought in front of Pilate because, although the Sanhedrin had passed their death sentence on Him, they required the approval of the Roman Governor of Judea for its implementation. The Jews had the authority to condemn and stone a religious miscreant to death but in this instance they were seeking a Roman sanctioned crucifixion which would publicly mask their own fear and hatred of Jesus while affording them the refuge to hide behind the Roman verdict and the sentence they sought. The blood of Christ by this sentence would not be on their hands. Pilate, being a shrewd and experienced Governor, could see the dispute for what it was, little more than a sordid and bitter internal Jewish feud. He was well aware his office and authority were being compromised to meet their needs and the fact that Jesus was being used as a scapegoat did not sit easy with him. In fact his own wife told him of a dream she had had and warned him against being involved in "this Man's death". For these reasons he then tried to appease the situation by having Jesus savagely flogged and beaten. He also tried his utmost to have the authority for the execution issued by Herod Antipas, Governor of Galilee, who happened to be in Jerusalem over the festive period. When these ploys both failed Pilate, in full view of the crowd, publicly washed his hands, signifying he would not be the one responsible for the death of "this man".

In one last final attempt he proposed to the crowd that in accordance with the tradition of the festival he would release a convicted person under sentence of death. Promoting Jesus as the choice he was prepared to make, the crowd who had been encouraged and bribed by the Sanhedrin objected strongly to it and instead called for the release of a violent cruel killer devoid of any mercy named Bar Abbas. Pilate listened to the mob's scornful contempt "let His blood fall upon us and our children", realizing he was compromised acquiesced to their demands and released Bar Abbas while at the same time handing over Jesus to them for crucifixion.

Dressed in a robe with a crown of thorns beaten deep into his forehead, Jesus was shoved out onto the street in front of the house of

Caiphas. Numb with pain from the tremendous beaten and laden down with the heavy crossbeam on which some hours later He would hang, with staggering steps He began the way up the hill, through the maze of lane ways and alleys to the place of the skull called Golgotha. Along the way He stumbled and fell three times only to raise on each occasion while atoning for the sins of mankind.

In excruciating pain, severely cut and lacerated, He half-carried and half-dragged the crossbeam along the way. As time passed the sheer weight of the crossbeam which by now had worn down the flesh on his shoulder increased His agony a thousand times. The weight was almost crushing Him into the ground. With each step He stumbled forward while the intense pain in His chest added to the tremendous difficulty He had in breathing and step after step became harder and harder to make.

On the way His own Mother stepped out from the crowd. The physical pain He now had to bear was almost doubled by the agony He saw in her eyes as she tried to contain what she was feeling in her heart. She could do nothing to help Him and He could do nothing to help her, his own Mother. The soldiers kept shoving Him on and she could only try to bear her own sorrow that was also crushing her, as she watched His slow progress. Heavier than the very Cross, was the burden she bore for him in her Immaculate Heart, as the parade of merciless pain inched its way upward. The soldiers, hardened as much as they were, seeing that Jesus was in danger of collapsing again and, fearing he would lose consciousness or even die, forced a Cyrene by the name of Simon out from the bystanders in the crowd to help Him shoulder the heavy wooden crossbeam. Another woman, Veronica, seeing the appalling countenance of Jesus, sweating and straining with the effort to keep going, stepped forward and wiped away from His face the blood, sweat, spittle and tears which were blinding his vision as he gasped frantically for each single breath of life.

Between his second and third fall another group of women in the crowd, who were also overcome with pity for the now almost half-dead, half-broken Nazarean, stood out from the spectators weeping at his plight. Jesus consoled them by telling them not to cry for him, but rather for themselves and their children. Goaded, mocked and spat upon, by the same people who had five days earlier hailed him as Son of David, King of the Jews, who had laid palms before Him in his honour they now looked on at Him in pity as He at last reached Golgotha. There the Roman soldiers roughly prepared him for his crucifixion and death.

With little or no ceremony Jesus was stripped of his clothing that would later be gambled over by the toss a dice, stretched out on the cross in the Roman manner of crucifixion and held down whilst the heavy hammer delivered the terrible blows required to drove the nails through his hands and feet, the excruciating pain continued to grow. It is impossible to imagine the seething spasms that shook His body as the cross was hoisted into an upright position. For those who now came to bear witness, Jesus hung suspended on the cross for three long hours enduring the most brutal and horrendous death Roman law could inflict.

The Gospel details the duration of those final three hours as Jesus hung there one can almost feel a numbness at the cumulative savagery inflicted on this one single human being, Jesus the Messiah, Son of God, Saviour of the World.

Only three days earlier while in the Temple Jesus had preached the parable of the "Wicked Husbandmen" (Lk 20. 9-18). This parable tells of the owner of a vineyard who is seeking to have his tenants pay their rightful dues. As his previous emissaries had no success in collecting them and so in a final attempt he sent his son.

This parable clearly identified Jesus as the son of the owner and the Jewish elders as the tenants. The tenants being totally ruthless decide that if they murder the owner's son their debt to his Father would somehow or other be cancelled out or left in abeyance as being uncollectible. Then the estate would revert to their common ownership. Jesus told His listeners in a firm and very direct interpretation what message the parable contained and what the actual outcome would be. The anger and fury of the Father in avenging his son's death was swift and harsh and having put to death the treacherous tenants, new ones He could trust, were found to replace them. The elders who listened to Him, ashen faced, understood his words were addressed to them yet they followed the same exact course of action. In less than four days after Jesus had preached the parable it had been fully re-enacted and the Son of God was put to death.

Beginning about noon that Friday as Jesus was raised, nailed to the cross, a major and significant deterioration in the weather began to take place. A desolate darkness spread across the sky shadowing the entire land. The Gospel describes how nature itself reacted violently upon the death of Jesus as the earth trembled and rocks were split apart. According to the Gospel account, the roman centurion standing at the foot of the cross proclaimed as the heavens opened:

"Indeed this man was truly the Son of God" Matthew 27:54

CHAPTER

9

That Jesus rose from the dead is well documented in the Gospels, as is the culmination of His Passion which He undertook to redeem mankind. It is church doctrine and obligatory for every Catholic who wishes to remain faithful to the church. While Satan exists however, the element of doubt is always there. The ultimate test of one's faith nevertheless rests in one's belief in the Resurrection. Here is where one must eventually find oneself knocking on the door and waiting for it to open.

The Resurrection of Christ as Saviour of Mankind brings meaning to everything. Once one chooses to accept the Resurrection one is raised to a supernatural level and one's contributions can be incorporated into God's Kingdom. If one chooses to disbelieve, one continues living a shadowy earthly existence as one who is spiritually dead. Furthermore, once one declines to believe in the Resurrection, one also declines the invitation extended by God at Baptism, to participate in one's own resurrection and re-enter God's Kingdom. The great sadness of today's lost Catholics is their preferred belief in the "nothings", the "it doesn't matter", or "what difference does it make?" syndromes to those actively seeking the truth that awaits all those who persevere

The Gospel speaks at great length of Man's indifference, and the

Catechism of the Catholic Church, and UCAT introduced in recent years helps to lighten the heavy load of ignorance being sustained by so very many of today's young Catholics. The enormous and ever growing erroneous amount of inaccurate information that has been allowed to take hold of so many young catholics must be challenged and dispelled. Can any oversight, carelessness, or laxity by those responsible for teaching Catholic doctrine, do more harm than allowing the prevailing mood of such indifference to sweep through so many of our schools today? The sin of presumption is a serious sin against Hope. In pre-Vatican II Council days, there was little if any ambiguity as it was clearly defined as follows:

> "Presumption is the foolish expectation of salvation without making use of the means necessary to obtain it".

In the Catechism of the Catholic Church/Compendium this definition is now elaborated in two distinct parts: Firstly, man presumes without God's help, that he is entitled to enter the Kingdom. Secondly, Christ's Passion, Death and Resurrection assures him the eternal glory he fully expects. This salvation is thereby seen as guaranteed without any real effort on man's part to merit it. To talk to some of today's Catholics in such terms would provoke some criticism but that is exactly what is needed. The ambiguity that exists in this mammoth catechism is overloaded and almost optional. Unless a definition on the presentation of the truth is clearly stated, the triumph of Satan inches closer the whole time.

One hears today of young people asking to be heard, listened to, and taken seriously, and it makes one wonder just how lopsided society has become? There can be little doubt that the voices and opinions of the young should be heard, but surely the teachings and truths of eminent scholars, teachers and saints must also to be reinstated in seminaries, colleges and schools? The Church must present a case outlining the wisdom of the elderly, expressed and appreciated by Piers Paul Reid the historian who wrote,

"Jansenism was condemned by Pope Clement XI in the papal Bull Uigentus, 1713. Today it has no adherents perhaps because no one worries about the possibility of damnation. Salvation is a universal entitlement: we are now all the elect."

In doing one's utmost to re-establish a relationship with God through the Gospel, one must read and indeed re-read the words our Saviour spoke to those closest to Him, His closest friends. Two parables in particular convey a wonderful insight into the mind of Jesus the teacher; first is "The Sower" Mk 4 (1-20) and secondly "The Rich Man and Lazarus" Lk 16 (19-31). Here is "The Word," the teaching given, as are all parables, for those who are not only prepared to listen clearly but also to make every effort to try to understand.

In the parable of The Sower, one sees the Seed as The Word of God, flying through the air some of it falls on stony ground, some on ground devoid of any growth, some without any depth and some where bushes already cover the surface. The birds of the air come, the sun beats down harshly and, inevitably, much of the seed is lost without having taken root or produced a yield. The major reason the seed fails to germinate being of course the quality and condition of the soil onto which it falls.

Every individual has the responsibility for the care and maintenance of their own ground, their own soil. Farmers know that the land must be well prepared in advance before it can be sown. One's own spiritual preparation is very much the same. In order to listen to the word of God one must prepare, one must be genuine, and must be ready to accept and protect The Word; otherwise, Satan, will do all he can to destroy it; for even if it succeeds in taking root he will still do all that he can to ensure it does not survive.

The Seed needs rich fertile soil in which it will withstand all the ravages of the birds, the worms and the weather, so as to emerge confidently, seeking the sun for the completion of its growth. This parable like all others encourages one not just to hear The Word, but to heed it, and to keep it carefully in focus throughout one's life. Without any doubt the best fertilizer for one's soul is the Sacrament of Penance followed by the Eucharist which keeps one's soul in perfect condition for receiving, tending and growing The Word of God.

In the second parable of "The Rich Man and Lazarus" the lesson, like so many of the others is double edged. The first obligation is the need for the fortunate to take care of the less fortunate, the need to distribute a proportion of one's wealth to the poor. This act in itself should not be seen as an act of generosity but rather an act of necessity in which the benefit is to both parties, each gaining from the other. This distribution of resources is a constant call for one to see and identify where a practical need exists as the Lord said, "the poor shall always be with us". One need only pick up a daily newspaper to read about the needs of the poor, locally and globally. Whenever one turns on the TV one must witness the constant string of natural disasters across every continent and ocean. For those fortunate enough to have access to surplus cash it is clear their responsibility is to make a donation or sign a standing order. The second strand of the parable however does not relate to the temporal status the two men achieved while they were alive, rather it is the dialogue which is developed between Abraham and the Rich Man after his death.

The Rich Man finds himself in Hades, and Abraham shows him Lazarus resting happily by his side. The Rich Man implores Father Abraham for a single drop of water and when this is refused, he then begs him to send Lazarus to warn his brothers of the terrible place he now finds himself in. This request is also declined as Abraham points out that the brothers should listen to The Word as it is being preached to them on Earth. The Rich Man agrees, yet makes a final attempt to enlist Abraham's help by begging for a messenger to be sent to his brothers, since they will not listen to The Word Abraham claims there is no point in sending a envoy, if the brothers will not hear The Word as it is preached to them on earth why would any messenger from the dead convince them? This then is the lesson clear and unequivocal for everyone, to make every effort to hear. Without preparation to receive The Word, without listening to The Word, without praying to seek the graces to understand It, how can one hope to be rewarded with the vision,: the beatific vision to see Christ as the Messiah, The Son of God, and Saviour of Mankind?

When the Rich Man was on earth he neither cared nor shared his good fortune with Lazarus. He choose to ignore the Word of God. Today every person, Christian or non-Christian, is faced with choices and lifestyles which encourage them to accept or reject the Lazarus outside their own gate. Unless one is prepared to accept this responsibility, however difficult, it is presumptuous to expect to receive the grace to share in the vision of the risen Christ.

To return to the Gospel of Our Lord's Passion and Death; it is easy to see that justice was not well served. Much to the chagrin of the Sanhedrin, Pilate who had been uneasy and on edge throughout the entire episode, insisted on having the official proclamation "Jesus of Nazareth, King of the Jews" nailed to the top of the cross. It was to some extent his way of showing his contempt for the Jews in making them realise in his own way how he appreciated Jesus and His life so much more than he did the Jews with all their rituals, finery and hypocrisy.

By agreeing to allow Joseph of Arimathea take possession of the body, he further aggravated them as, it concerned them that the remains might possibly be stolen. Should this happen the Jews maintained, it would enable the followers of Jesus to claim, as Jesus Himself had predicted, that He would arise from the tomb.

Pilate acknowledging such a development would cause him more problems and ordered that the tomb, containing the body, be sealed and a Temple Guard mounted for three days to prevent any of Jesus's disciples interfering with the remains. The detail of soldiers given this duty, were left in no doubt, as to the severity of the punishment, they would face should they fail in this duty. They were therefore more than determined than ever to carry out Pilate's orders in guarding the tomb.

On Sunday morning the women who were the most faithful followers of Jesus, decided to go to the burial ground even though they were filled with deep apprehension. The events of the past week, and especially the last three days, had greatly traumatised them. Approaching the tomb they were confounded to find it empty, yet a stranger dressed in white stood alongside it, as if waiting for them to arrive. The Gospel recounts plainly the words he spoke:

> "He is not here, He is risen, as He said He would. Go quickly and tell His disciples."
>
> Luke 24:5

Now even more dumbfounded, than ever before, they hurried back to Jerusalem where the Disciples were staying to tell them what had happened. The Disciples on hearing the news, made great haste themselves to the tomb. On arriving there faced with an empty tomb as the women had said they were so stunned and frightened by this unbelievable turn of events that they were now even more unable to comprehend what had happening. It was quite beyond their understanding and they had no way to intellectually grasp it. The situation was so far beyond their understanding.

They gathered together in the room where they had celebrated Passover on the previous Thursday evening. They were now more terrified of the Jewish authorities than before, as they had no way of knowing what reaction the Sanhedrin might have, should they decide it was the Disciples who had broken open the tomb and taken the body:

Suddenly out of nowhere, He was there, in the room, right amongst them. They were petrified. Slowly and calmly He reassured them, He comforted them. He talked to them. After He had shown them His wounds and having spent some time explaining the need for all that had happened, He gave them the understanding to begin to realize what the previous three years had been all about. He told them He would send the Holy Spirit down upon them to assist and enlighten them so that they would fully understand everything and until that took place they were to remain as they were, quietly contained and withdrawn from the city.

Our need today is neither lesser or greater then the disciples and after Easter each year one should invite the Holy Spirit to give them some further enlightenment and encouragement in going out into the world to spread the Good News. There will be no day during one's mission when one would not benefit from such help or understanding; Our Lord's Resurrection is so overwhelming that one must struggle to absorb such knowledge as it is only through prayer that one is capable of containing a deeper and more intense meaning of Christ's passion, death and resurrection.

The Resurrection of Christ and belief in the Resurrection are two distinct issues. From a historical viewpoint it would only be the very few, the most naive and uneducated who would deny or debate the existence of Jesus Christ as a man. Far greater would be the number who would deny His Resurrection, and far greater still the number who would deny His claim to be The Son of God.

Following His Resurrection Christ remained on earth for about 40 days. During this period much still had to be reordered and reaffirmed. He appeared to the Disciples in small individual groups continuing to instruct them. They were now acutely aware of recent events, yet they were still having difficulty coming to terms with the enormity of it all. Nevertheless, the completion of their novitiate was upon them and they had to grow more in spiritual confidence and authority. They would need a final period of reflection before the Feast of Pentecost when the Holy Spirit would descend upon them.

The reconciliation of Peter, who had had no opportunity to make his peace with Jesus since denying him three times on the night of his arrest, also had to be achieved. It was after his triple declaration of love for Him that Christ ordained Peter in his role as the first Pope in its totality, and the arrival of the Holy Spirit was heralded. In this manner and order the church was formed.

Simon Peter chosen by Christ Himself was given the virtual, and symbolic, Keys, authority and powers as the first Pope. The disciples gathered around him were to serve as his bishops, subservient to him, not as equals but as auxiliaries. Today over 2000 years later it is Pope Francis I who holds the Keys as Vicar of Christ and today's bishops are obliged to remain as they should in the subservient and auxiliary role. Those cardinals or bishops today who dispute this secondary or servile position to the Chair of Peter are in serious error and should be seen as such. The arrival of the Holy Ghost filled each of the Disciples with grace and knowledge and infused in them the power to preach the good news with both great fervour and authority. Their commission, now, as confirmed Apostles, was to go forth and share the Good News with all people, whoever would listen to the message, truth and meaning of Jesus Christ.

The role of supreme Pontiff which over the past 2,000 years has been secured by both holy, and less than holy men has never been under the scrutiny it is under today. Reading any history of the Papacy the lives, trials and tribulations the popes suffered leaves one in little doubt why so few of them ever achieved sainthood. The world's press and media cover every aspect of the Papacy, and the turbulent times it is presently experiencing, throughout its many arms and global ministries, from financial, through curial, to regional zones and national conferences. The intense interest is not always positive, in some parts of the world it is looked on with a certain degree of suspicion while in other areas it is treated with open hostility. Regardless of its standing however, within all secular and other pluralist countries, the task in spreading the Gospel of Jesus Christ must remain its core mission and moves to downgrade it must be resisted in every way possible.

When Christ spoke to the Disciples in detail during His short post-resurrection period he shared with them further insights into how the power of the Holy Spirit would enter them and how it would fill them with confidence. He told them that it was for their sake He would soon leave them because, until He did, their individual roles would not commence. It was necessary for Him to return to the Father in order that their mission to preach could begin and the gospel would begin to spread through foreign lands, reaching the minds and hearts of many.

On the day of the Ascension He walked with them and His Blessed Mother for the last time to the Mount of Olives, only a mile or so outside the walls, a place of great peace where He had often gone to rest and pray. This particular hillside had been one of His favourite places when seeking solitude from the crowds at the end of an evening. This day as they ascended the several hundred feet a slight mist or fog surrounded them. Upon reaching the top He embraced every one of them in turn and gave them His final blessing. Very slowly He rose upwards into the mist, and was gone. It was all over in a few short moments an anticlimax, of enormous proportions that almost passed them by and yet they descended the hill, renewed, rejuvenated and in great spirits. He had left them and they were somehow free and surprisingly able to accept His departure with great joy and happiness. The final words he left with them, supported by the knowledge they had pondered over in spite of never fully understanding, now seemed more easy to comprehend. The traumatic passion and death that had totally numbed them at last made sense, as did the reality that from now on each had individual missions. They were finally aware they were to speak as His Apostles, bringing the good news to those whoever would listen, they would forgive sins in the name of the Father, and above all they would be 'Fishers of Men'.

Their role from that day forward would be to baptise all who would seek to follow Christ. They also realised they would have to travel afar to preach, to explain The Word made Flesh, and tell all who would listen that there was a God whose Son had died for them so that they could be saved. They would convert sinners, they would heal the sick, they would tend to the needy and somehow they also sensed they might one day be called to lay down their lives for Him whom they now loved and understood without measure. The years ahead would be hard and yet they welcomed the challenge. Patiently they awaited the Holy Spirit to descend upon them as promised by Christ a month earlier, knowing their lives would never be the same again. The descent of the Holy Spirit upon the apostles occurred just 50 days after the Resurrection. The Gospel gives an account of Peter's preaching being so inspired on that day that several thousand were converted in one afternoon. The Apostles spoke in languages of which they had no previous knowledge, and indeed the miracle of their preaching was all the greater in that those who heard them speak were themselves enabled by the power of the Holy Spirit to understand what was being preached to them and accept it as the living Word of God.

During the following weeks and months those who heard the Apostles preach knew what they were hearing was special, it was unique and it was God's own living word. The conversions, baptisms and acceptance of the faith that began to take place formed the nucleus of the earliest groups who would become known as Christians and who in turn would form the first formal groups and communities. They recognised they had been especially blessed to have received the gift of faith and it was this faith, alive and real that has continued in all its traditional glory which has been handed down to today's Christians from these first communities.

The Living Word is not only a phrase but a reality, a continuation of what the first Christians witnessed, listened to and believed. They had every practical reason during the first three centuries to reject Christianity due to the tremendous persecutions visited upon them but they remained steadfast. Finally, 300 years later after the epic Battle of the Milvian Bridge, Constantine claimed the emperor's throne. The following year, 313 AD, the Edict of Milan was proclaimed and the practice of Christianity, along with all other religions, was permitted. The cruel age of Christian martyrdom had come to an end.

Constantine saw the need to unite rather than divide and the edict allowed all citizens to worship freely and all property that had been seized by the state was restored. For the Christians who had endured relentless persecution since the time of Christ their joy was boundless, as now they were free to build places of worship and publicly preach the word of God. Circa 330 AD over the tomb of Peter rose the church which today one venerates as the great basilica of St Peter. Seeing these earliest Christian communities as our own spiritual ancestors should perhaps be a humbling experience. Just as the church rose from a period of persecution it is not inconceivable that the time may well be approaching when it will face a further persecution. Over the past 25 years the rise in Christian persecution has risen and 2015 was the third year in a row it continued to grow. Of the top ten countries where persecution is at its worst the majority of the population is Muslim. Rather than forever being seen as the migrants of violence and oppression as in Europe there is substantial evidence that it is the Muslims in many countries who are the perpetrators of it.

As has been more than proven in the past year or so the world's media gets to pick and choose exactly what to highlight and what not to highlight. In as many hues and colors, shades and shadows the media spin and control exactly what hits the global daily news services. What is considered palatable for the masses and what is not very much depends on who controls all the major global media networks.

The statistics for Christian martyrdom for the last three months of 2016 in Northern Nigeria were almost nowhere reported in the Western press but from reliable Catholic sources it was calculated that 53 villages containing over 1400 dwellings were destroyed. The number of people killed were over 800 and 16 churches were destroyed. These appalling statistics come from a country of 36 states of which 12 are governed by Sharia Law. It should be with little sense of incredulity that accounts of such modern torture and martyrdom are on the increase in many Muslim states. Some obviously are more militant than others but nevertheless until some reformation of Islam is undertaken by a national or international Caliphate, rogue armies such as Islamic State/ISIS, will press on with their 'unholy' Jihads. In more than half a dozen countries where Sharia law is enforced acts of gross brutality and barbarism can and will continue to take place as Christians are seen as infidels who are entitled to no mercy. They are easy prey for militant Muslims who see them as people who can be beaten, tortured and killed almost at will. That some first world countries are forever doing their utmost to avoid reporting such incidents let alone acknowledge such atrocities thereby guaranteeing their oil supplies is reprehensible.

In one's own Western secular society the presence of an anti-church, anti-Christian "sophisticated" opinion or mindset is never too far away and in the food hall, the workplace, the gym, the golf course it may suddenly surface. All the faults that can be laid against the Church are openly aired and the usual chestnuts as to why the Vatican does not sell all its treasures and give the money it receives to the poor. To counter this popular mindset it is of course necessary to point out that for one enormous gesture of financial magnanimity once completed it is done and gone for ever. Maybe the better way is to maintain what is in place so each and every year those parts of the world in great need and sections of society with little to hope for benefit in so many different ways. Few of those who complain the loudest are usually those who fail to recognize the fact that the Catholic Church is responsible for the running and maintenance of 140,000 schools,10,000 orphanages, 5,000 hospitals and over 16,000 health clinics globally. The overall aid package supplied by Catholic charities globally is estimated to be between $3,000,000,000 and $5,000,000,000 billion dollars annually and this figure does not include the further large sums gathered up at local parish level for their own pet projects around the world. For the Catholic Church with all its faults and negative press coverage it is perhaps the largest non governmental organization/donor in the world. By citing such facts and figures it is possible to ask even the most die hard critics of the Catholic Church to at least reconsider their secular animosity and hostile views

For the hurt or damaged individual who bears a loss hard to sustain, the degree of comfort one offers, must always be one of outreach. Whether the result of, a bad marriage, a tough confrontation with a unsympathetic teacher, a put-down from a vicious Catholic cleric these and many other reasons can always leave a whole group of individuals ready to pronounce on their experiences. It is more than possible they are fully entitled to hold the most negative anti Church opinions but that does not mean one should always remain cowed or too timid to launch a defence of one's faith when one is called upon to do so. Unless one is prepared to stand up and be counted, one's silence gives credence and authenticity to the attacker. As is too often the case, in such moments of embarrassment or angst, the need to pray for courage to remain steadfast, and vocal, if necessary is vital.

When the Angelus bell rings or when one passes a Catholic church the instinct to bless oneself should always be followed and fulfilled, that is what the meaning of 'follower' is. The temptation to deny Christ is there because Satan puts it there and each time one succumbs by not blessing oneself at home or in a restaurant then one is lacking in commitment to their faith. It is by showing courage and strength in one's faith that one may gain the respect in others, who in turn may follow the firm example.

Perhaps one of the great psychological differences between the early Christians and today's Christians is that the power of the Holy Spirit is not appreciated in any understandable sense. Our earliest ancestors, enthused by the Holy Spirit, made every effort to live the Gospel day by day, so why do today's Catholics fall so short? Among answers to this question may be the fact that our commitment is not as forceful as it should be because, rather than being a religion that offers great hope and joy, it appears to young adults to be one that is forever dull, bureaucratic and dogmatic.

The fact that the Bishop of Rome has singled out this fact and appears determined to do something about it leaves little doubt that it is a problem needing attention. Whether he will accept the guidance of the Holy Spirit, the advisers who participate in his inner circle or the vagaries of those whose words make too much sense to ignore, will help grow his papacy and set the tone for the future hurdles that lie ahead. This is frequently the case with popes who seek to establish their authority and primacy for all to see. On the other hand if the young Catholics of today do not witness the present Holy Father's efforts being genuine or his outreach positively touching their lives in any real and meaningful way than he will be in danger of losing another generation of young Catholics who are earnestly searching for the true meaning of their faith.

Over the past 50 years every individual pope has attempted to reform and revitalize the Church on the strength of the documents of Vatican II and yet it must be said the very opposite has proven to be the case! How two of the participants, Pope, St John XXIII, and Pope St John Paul II, both ardent supporters of reform were canonised and elevated to the sainthood in recent years, still requires a most detailed clarification and examination yet to be undertaken. That these two pontiff's (and Pope Paul VI) refused to divulge the Third Secret of Fatima as requested by Our Blessed Mother would appear to be an act of the greatest collective disobedience, and yet, their elevation was undertaken by the present Bishop of Rome. There can be no doubt that the canonization of these two popes will in the years ahead raise more than one or two interesting points. Regardless of how much pressure was exerted by the Polish hierarchy for the canonisation of Pope John Paul II the amalgamation of John XXIII only tends to cloud the issue further. It is ironic that both the greatest and not so great papacies are those only realised and recognised for what they were many years later. The last canonized Pope, Pope St Pius X was dead almost 50 years before his sainthood was formally declared.

It may well be the problems facing today's church are not that they are too progressive or radical but rather they are based on a flawed mindset which originated with the papacy of John XXIII and the liberal alterations that have been introduced since Vatican II. Regardless of how one considers today's situation, it cannot be balanced by applying the wrong solution to the right problem, anymore than applying the right solution to the wrong problem. As the Papacy and the Church per se struggle to identify and decide what exactly are the problems the church is facing, so each conference, each country and indeed every participant must try and become actively aware of their own shortcomings. If the Catholic Church can ever reach the process of renewing herself, than each person will have to undergo a similar task or program, spiritually rebuilding and renewing his or her own self. The most positive response given by an adventurous priest who, when facing up to this question, put it quite bluntly when he said:

"we had all better up our game."

This short but sweet remark, however flippant it may appear, perhaps does contain a nugget or gem of great wisdom, the more one reflects on it. The late saintly Cardinal George of Chicago, spelt out his view of the overall situation, a year or two before he died when he said,

> "We are at a turning point in the life of the church in this country. Liberal Catholicism is an exhausted project. Essentially, a critique, even a necessary critique at one point in our history, it is now parasitical on a substance that no longer exists. It has shown itself unable to pass on the faith in its integrity and its inadequate, therefore, fostering the joyful self surrender called for in Christian marriage, in consecrated life, in ordained priesthood. It no longer gives life. The answer however is not to be

found in a type of conservative Catholicism obsessed with particular practices and so sectarian in its outlook that it cannot serve as a sign of unity of all peoples in Christ. The answer is simple Catholicism, in all its fullness and depth, a faith able to distinguish itself from any culture and yet able to engage and conquer them all, a faith joyful in all the gifts Christ wants to give us and open to the whole world he died to save."

This perhaps is the statement which should be emblazoned on a plaque and hung in the entrance vestibule of every church throughout the land as the 'Mission Statement' of the Catholic Church for many years to come.

These words of Cardinal George emphasize very well with Spacespeak terms (used in this book) as they equate with what astronauts refer to as the 'Overview Effect'. If anything they would appear to encompass and endorse the solidarity of space terminology. The experience referred to in space jargon is the immensity of the cosmos when viewed and experienced from a spacecraft or space station in high orbit. It may well be the view is restricted to those astronauts fortunate enough to mentally relate to the phenomena from such a location, nevertheless, it is a reality that exists and once experienced remains. The definition of the term could be referred to as the 'them and us' syndrome in which the 'we-us' is always right, and 'the, they-them' are always wrong. In circling Earth every 90 minutes, the very notion of an us and them vanishes from the vocabulary and in its place the overview effect reduces the pluralist 'us'/'them' descriptions is automatically reduced to the singular term, OURS!

The simple cardinal's quotation does likewise, as it obliterates the divisions which are harming our Mother Church today and attempts to bring us all back into 'One';

> "'joyful in all the gifts Christ wants to give us and open
> to the whole world he died to save, Amen.'"

To revisit then the most central, fundamental essence of our being, the need to know why we exist, and for what purpose we are here must again be re-examined. Sadly, no matter how many times the answer is given, millions prefer or choose to ignore it. Every single individual infant is created by God and born, to know, love and serve Him on this Earth, and through the death and resurrection of His Son Jesus Christ our redemption was gained so, we may be re-united with Him forever in Heaven. This is the very alpha-point and the basis of faith from which each son and daughter of God's may draw considerable strength throughout their lives.

Jesus came to teach, he came to serve, he came to fulfil scripture, he came to free man from sin, in order that man could himself gain salvation through his love of Christ. In dying Christ gave Man a new covenant, a new beginning, a new awareness and a new knowledge of God's Kingdom. The Holy Spirit came to bring the love, the light and the life into the New Church, and the first Christians were baptised in order that they would be the living salt, the new witnesses to Christ, whose death had redeemed them, as it will all who believe in Him.

The Mystical Body of Christ, the Universal Holy Roman Catholic Church with Jesus Christ as its head, brings all of the baptised sons and daughters of God in unity with the Holy Spirit into the eternal realm. As a Church, this mystical formation exists in such a way that the happiness and joy of one benefits all in what can be called the 'common good,' and so the good of the Church. The Mystical Body has been evolving over the past 2000 years in times of both great spiritual health and poor spiritual health when it was under severe threat from attack and major heresies from both without and within. During these turbulent periods the Church was being sustained through the prayers, sacrifices and sufferings of its most faithful sons and daughters.

The church, as the Mystical Body of Christ, exists on three distinct and separate planes. First are those who have already been welcomed into the Kingdom of Heaven and who are known as The Church Triumphant, those who are already secure in God's paradise. The second level comprises those who are prayed for every Sunday at Mass, the 'Faithful Departed'. They are those experiencing the painful period of purification called Purgatory through which each person must pass having gone through the door of death. These souls are also referred to as 'The Church Suffering'. While experiencing Purgatory they are unable to help themselves yet nevertheless they can ceaselessly work to help those they have left behind on Earth. In addition they pray for the protection and safety of the Church itself.

Lastly there are the millions of Catholics currently living their everyday lives in whatever circumstances and conditions they find themselves. Some are attending to their faith and their Catholic responsibilities as best they can, while others are barely coping with their everyday lives. This enormous conglomerate of multi-persons from every crevice and corner of our planet is called 'The Church Militant'. It is this final 'People's Church' who today are tasked with the defence and protection of Christ's bride, the Catholic Church, against Satan and his legions who are dedicated to its total destruction and the destruction of mankind.

The Church, with Jesus Christ as its Head, was formed after His Death and Resurrection encompassing all who receive the Sacrament of Baptism. For Catholics who receive this gift of faith at birth is to be within and belong to our Mother Church. This singular honour bestows not only great privileges but in turn demands its own obligations and responsibilities. Those who are members of other faith communities and congregations who acknowledge Christ as their Saviour claim the right to be known as Christians but, by removing themselves from the sacraments and sanctifying grace, means they remain 'outside the walls' until they come to accept the full authority and doctrine of the Catholic Church.

The Communion of Saints includes the unique spiritual register of those sons and daughters who through their life's work in Christ have already risen to sainthood directly on death, foregoing any need for a period of purification in Purgatory. This doctrine of Mother Church is highlighted in the Creed as, 'One Holy Catholic and Apostolic Church, The Communion of Saints'. In trying to understand how precious is the spiritual life that one has been given at Baptism, it must not be seen as simply a life secure within the Church, but rather a life with a membership that must be constantly maintained and updated. It is this special individual mission guided by the Holy Spirit that each person is called upon to fulfil. This role chosen for each individual at birth is a single role which no other person ever born will be called upon to duplicate. It not only has a personal dimension and the goal of being invited into the Kingdom of Heaven but also a participating role in the overall collective, the Communion of Saints.

At baptism the invitation given is to become a saint; no one is excluded. It is the pinnacle that can be reached by anyone and everyone on earth, but achieved by only a minute few. As the whole process of canonisation is formulated and driven primarily by a hierarchical clerical system, there is always the possibility of a black swan being so elevated. In such cases the canonization may remain in situ on earth but obviously not in Heaven. Likewise there are also the many many saints who even forgo the public elevation in true humility, that will only be acknowledged on the Last Day. These are the saints who have passed through life with no interest in their own well being but rather have totally dedicated their lives to the service of others in every possible way.

Even if one does not achieve sainthood there is the great joyfulness experienced by the glory of one's own soul reuniting with its Creator, while also participating in the union of all the other souls who form part of the Church Triumphant. There can be no greater joy than the happiness of any son or daughter returning home knowing he or she has completed the mission they were given. They now know, regardless of all the misconnections, faults and failures they encountered on their mission, that they remained steadfast and true to the task they were given to accomplish. Though they may have stumbled and fallen behind on so many occasions, through the many graces of God and the help of Our Blessed Mother, they kept the faith.

The Church Triumphant adores God whilst at the same time interceding on behalf of the Church's Suffering and Militant. The Church Suffering lives through the temporal punishment earned and necessitated due to the numerous sins committed during one's life and the on-going cumulative effect. The petitions, novenas, and intercessions earnestly requested through the Saints, worthily accepted and offered up as a gift to God never go unnoticed, and indeed so it is with each son and daughter.

Even the most hard-hearted sinner, devoid of all sanctifying grace while still alive in the temporal world can and does benefit from the prayers of those who love him. What is not a presumption but rather certain is that God never refuses the prayer of one for another, no matter how far into the wilderness the recipient has stumbled. One need look no further than the life of St Augustine to understand the meaning and power of prayer. This incredible saint, who had lived a most sinful life, in later years acknowledged it was the powerful intercession of his mother's prayers that secured for him the Catholic faith that not only would he embrace but nourish so much that he would eventually become a Doctor of the Universal Church, Anyone today reading 'The City of God' cannot help but be deeply moved by the beauty and spiritual clarity of this saint's thoughts.

To those who insist that their life is a distinction they never desired let alone requested, their protestations may or may not be relevant, but they often make such assertions either in desperation or despair without ever attempting to reconcile or rediscover who they are or what they have been given. They decide instead to destroy the sealed envelope without first opening it and examining its contents. Their disregard or indifference for their mission, which they have foolishly chosen to ignore, may well be the cause of their problems. Instead of coming to terms with them they choose instead to follow a negative path repudiating what was bestowed upon them at the very moment of conception, through birth and the Sacrament of Baptism. On the other hand there are those who overcome whatever obstacles are placed in their way and make their mission one of purpose; it is their loyalty and devotion to Mother Church which guides them through the hardships and problems they must overcome along the way. These are the sons and daughters who have learned to accept the teaching and authority of the Church, and realise it is there to help them especially in their darkest moments. They may find it difficult, they may find it irksome, they may find it at times frustrating, yet they live out their faith with a mixture of confidence, humility and obedience.

Sadly it is those who appear unhappy, dissatisfied and disgruntled for a whole variety of reasons who actually fight any overtures made to them to even consider Christianity as a conduit of God's love. Their rejection through some form of disobedience or disagreement with the Church almost destroys their mission before it has begun. This latter mindset however remain members in name who always want it to adapt to their viewpoints, and their demands. It is as if they are the active agents of Satan and are only prepared to pledge their loyalty, provided it is their views and opinions which are given preference. While such matters remain unresolved sometimes over years, their contributions are negligible, but their negative influence becomes more extended and widened, all the while causing dissent and division. To consider this situation within the Church Militant one must try and understand what exactly is taking place.

The threat to our Mother Church at present has been clearly demonstrated and identified as coming primarily from within. The active dissidents who claim valid membership of Mother Church but, who actively campaign for her demise and destruction, are determined to inflict as much damage as they can, all the time claiming they are acting in her best interests. Such persons especially those in authority within the hierarchy must be challenged and rebuked. For those in teaching orders or even ordinary lay people in roles of responsibility or governance they should be asked to explain their viewpoints and/ or asked to account for their Catholic outlook. This call is not to be seen as some form of witch hunt but the days of scandalous statements and dubious doctrine must be brought to an end. Those entrusted with professorships in Catholic universities should be the epitome of what the church expects from its finest theologians. This does not mean that all the radical theologians and progressive elements are rogue academics or wrong in their views but it does hold that view that those who contradict, obfuscate and muddy the waters must be brought back into the fold or denied their license to lecture or teach. The church has always had such thinkers and always will, but not all thoughts are valid or are they in unison with the established doctrine of the church. These are teachings which simply cannot be incorporated as they are at variance with the Magisterium and so must be rejected out of hand.

A further area of basic dissatisfaction or dissent is that the laity appear to reserve the right to agree or disagree in whatever matters of faith, doctrine, discipline, dogma, authority and liturgy they choose to. Such is the belief in the degree of individual freedom now within the church that there are those who claim to be pro-choice and pro-contraception who genuinely believe they have a conscientious right to spread such views whilst at the same time access the Blessed Eucharist. The multitude of those who claim this right, regardless of what the church teaches, is quite staggering. Many of the problems besetting today's Church in the Western World are driven by these New Catholics, both lay and clerical who, although they appear to be loyal and attentive members of the Church, could not in any way be described as loyal to its faith, dogma or doctrine. These Catholics are usually found throughout the media world voicing opinions which appear to 'be on the other hand.' They like to appear helpful, and from time to time give lectures on such topics as "why Martin Luther should today be seen in a far more progressive light" indeed welcomed back into the church. Their faith has long since ceased to live in the sense of being alive and nourished by sanctifying grace.

These self-professed 'Catholics' are those for example who have decided to discontinue receiving the Sacrament of Penance on a regular basis, preferring to believe that their own personal contrition absolves them of sin. This ill-founded attitude is again the lie contained in the sin of presumption that sadly man's pagan pride readily glorifies. Once these attitudes prevail the sanctifying grace being received by the parish en masse wanes, and a deterioration in the overall spiritual health of the parish increases.

The Church up to very recently has always taught that those receiving the Eucharist in an unworthy state are compounding their disenfranchisement by this serious sin of sacrilege. For the new and neo liberal Catholics taking their lead from Rome these people prefer to believe the maxim that the Eucharist is 'a cure for the sick, rather than a nourishment for the faithful'. The fact that the Pope and some of his cardinals choose such different outlooks can only be seen as a satanic blow struck to undermine the unity of the Church. As mentioned in the Fatima and La Salette Marian apparitions the time would come when cardinals would disagree with cardinals and bishops with bishops and church unity would crumble. To think or to even imagine we have reached this period in time should surely be enough to bring all catholics to their knees and their senses but instead the opposite appears to be happening.

It must be a momentous moment in time when truth fails to prevail and the lie gains the upper tier of belief. Those who now cling to a vanquished truth are left in isolation whilst those who have secured the upper hand establish their 'new truth' as the new enlightenment.

Gaining the enlightenment however must come with a price and that price is the Grace of God. This is the most terrible price imaginable as now the supporters of the lie, who for so many reasons, believe they are supporting a new and more meaningful truth have lost their only hope of redemption, and their access to eternal life.

Now, by not being within the state of grace they have placed themselves automatically in the state of sin, divorced from the Sacraments, and moving further away the whole time from their sole purpose in life. This does not mean that these souls are actively engaged in the promotion of evil but rather they are now predisposed to tuning into one channel rather than another to receive their daily updates and bulletins providing puerile and erroneous doctrine.

It is this secular band of information which over time controls their opinions and subsequent actions. Because of this on-going sacrilege the doctrines and teachings of Mother Church are inaccessible to them and what knowledge they once may have possessed they are now in the process of losing. What they once knew and believed will become riddled with doubt and in the fullness of time become more difficult and incomprehensible to them. They are those that Jesus spoke of in the gospel as 'losing what little they had been given'. To them as unwitting disciples of Satan the urgent need he demands of them will take preference and without grace they must comply.

For Satan the exploitation of all the divisive issues from contraception and abortion through to the relaxation of guidelines governing the reception of the Eucharist and the tolerance of new relationships, whether they are of a same sex nature or not, are issues which he will seek to contaminate in every way possible. These are some of the causes the New Catholics freely chose to subscribe to.

The traditional teachings of the Church are now today being portrayed as being out of touch with modern times and the early interpretations of the Bible no longer meets the needs of today's Church. With such diverse opinions being openly aired in Rome, Satan and his followers are able to recruit very many adherents, the majority believing they are actually helping spread the good news or what is now perceived as the 'new' good news.

For an assault on the finer theological points of contention being discussed by those who will shape church thinking over the next 30 or 40 years, Satan needs only the finest of minds, those whose egos and neo liberalism views are very well masked behind what may well be an outstanding academic and scholarly track record. Such New Catholic members especially those in the hierarchy and lay theologians of repute are his perfect recruits. It never even occurs to such exalted Catholics that they are being recruited. Once this takes place they, of course are now operating from a very different base.

It is not too difficult to fathom why today there is such an advent of these New Catholics within the Church Militant. It is because they see themselves winning on all fronts. It is not uncommon to hear senior clerics claiming, that unless boundaries are extended, progress cannot be made. Should they fail to extend such overtures they claim the Church will lose so many of her children and revert to the days of sackcloth and ashes. They see no firm central authority or real opposition to their demands that cannot be overcome as already senior levels in the Church harbour a number of cardinals and bishops who are most sympathetic to their views.

The degree of confusion being caused by these fraction is easily quantifiable as senior clerics and theologians appear to contradict each other's viewpoint at almost every synod and conference. How the Holy Father will come to terms with this new guard will again be a plimsoll line that will very much define his Papacy. One constant factor however must always remain in place for him, and that is, to guide Peter's barque; and to protect our Mother Church, the church of eternal salvation. There is no doubt that the church is always under attack in one form or another and will always cause serious damage if never challenged is the belief that love will conquer truth. This is the one lie that must never be allowed to spread.

Pope St John Paul II made clear his priorities in his book, 'Crossing the Threshold of Hope' in which he stated that,

> "People of our time have become insensitive to the Last Things."

Regrettably he did not specify how 'insensitive' they had become or whether 'ignorant' would have been a more appropriate term, nevertheless, whether it was the hierarchy the laity or a combination of both, as whatever was the case and he stated that anything in this dynamic is now possible. Many of our cardinals, bishops, our pastors and our priests have become almost immune and even indifferent to the actual Catholic eschatology of death. In recent years the deceased cardinal of Milan, the famous Jesuit Cardinal Martini did leave a substantial memorandum behind, as if he were indeed trying to rule from beyond the grave. The Martini reflections into his own thoughts and agenda, outlined a new progressive church almost unrecognizable to today's one. Sadly it was not only Cardinal Martini who choose to see such a church in isolation his thinking was shared by some of his own confreres. It is a flaw in the human character that having chosen to follow Christ over time some powerful cardinals lowered their guard just enough to have allowed the attractiveness of secularism to take more and more control of their own spiritualism. Inevitably the quality of their own knowledge, the strength of their preaching, and the depth of their understanding becomes like a river, over many decades silted up making any navigation almost impossible. The very emptiness of the great cathedral of Cardinal Martini of Milan today gives overwhelming evidence as to the degree of negativity the sermons preached there over the last few decades, had on the Cardinal's own laity.

Is it any wonder therefore that Satan today now moves so easily within and throughout the institutionalised Church exuding such strength and power? He has every reason to do so confident in the knowledge that he controls many of the finest and most corrupt minds at every level of the church.

It is also quite amazing that the lack of clear and concise doctrine not only allows, but actually encourages, whole schools of dissident thought to grow and develop beyond any spiritual recognition they falsely try to claim and establish. The collegiality of the bishops in their own countries consistently enables them to push their own agenda regardless of how it conforms with universal church thinking.

There can be no great transfer of faith, no continuity of teaching, no living tradition, no true allegiance to any Pontiff unless the laity is clearly aware of what the Mystical Body of Christ is, what the The Communion of Saints means and likewise what the other sacred truths contain. The insensitivity, the de-spiritualisation and lack of coherent sacred doctrine being taught and made available today has allowed a discipleship of three or four generations of Catholics to emerge without any in depth spiritual maturity. So much so, they are today making demands, seeking changes and insisting that the most liberal interpretations of Vatican II Council Documents be made and implemented within all church structures and bodies.

The demand for gender free partnerships, same sex marriages and redefinitions of the word marriage and its meaning is enough to make any Christian, let alone Catholic, wonder where all of this is leading, or more so, where it will end? Movements supporting these and similar causes, demonstrate the degree of belligerence that has allowed hostile pressure groups to assert themselves openly within the church at every level over the past 30 years.

These demands for change may have spread under St John Paul II but it was Pope Benedict XVI who rightfully classified the homosesual act as sinful and was not prepared to dilute the classification in any way. He was also aware of how modern liturgy had damaged the church's presence and was adamant that classical liturgy was to be restored as much as possible, and returned to its rightful place. The support and approval of the present Pope to his predecessor's wishes was readily given and remains in place regardless of those who wish and will do all in their power to reduce its status if not completely change it.

While it must be clear that the teaching and thoughts of today's church rest with the clergy, the laity over the last few decades appear to have also moved back apace from the concept of authority and tradition. Now for many active and New Catholics they would prefer a church of joint partnership and participation, one that appeals to both clergy and laity alike. The church today is based on a hierarchical leadership, one of a Pontiff, apostles, and followers, (vis a vis, clergy and laity,) as was established by Christ, yet this structure of authority currently is being pulled apart as national conferences are determined to promote the national concept of collegiology and a right to an autonomy of self governance which may well progress until it becomes totally removed from the authority of the Pope. This innovation may actually appeal to today's Pope or a successor of his in the future but it is a deflection from the path instigated by Christ and contrary as such to the Law of God. To discern and redefine the doctrine and dogma of the Church cannot rest with any individual Pope regardless of how good he believes the changes he would like to make may help guide the church. Regardless of the influence any Pope may try to command by seeking more and more involvement in media power plays, social networking and internet exposure, the Oneness of the Catholic Faith' envisaged by Cardinal George, RIP, appears to be receding further and further as time goes on. Present modern fast-forward pace of World Youth Days and Masses, festivals and ecmenical prayer gatherings may produce popularity poll-topping figures but these are only achieved on a superficial level, and beneath all the banners and bunting, the core Catholic faith is becoming more and more undermined.

The questions facing today's Holy Father and his cardinals are many and varied, one of them being; will the Bride of Christ become an evangelical Church, in a protestant sense of the word a church where the new truths and new up-to-date tolerance will replace doctrine? If so then "love is all we need" will indeed make the sacraments, the Commandments and the clergy superfluous. What one must consider today is what the past 500/1,000 years has taught us or have we had the sense to see it. Why did so many persevere in the faith? Why did so many face martyrdom? Why did so many saints endure such suffering throughout their lives? Why did so many missionaries toil an entire lifetime? Why did the hardships and prayers of the countless hermits and monks commit so many to the love of great spirituality or did any of these lives have no truth or meaning?

In a world where the Ten Commandments of God can be set to one side, where man can rely solely on the laws of man, is it possible the world, as we know it, can continue to exist? Is the Earth we inhabit more likely to survive under man's care? Will future generations be sustained by the marvels of modern medicine, and live on in a more beautiful planet than their ancestors? These are some of the questions which need to be spiritually addressed, examined and answered.

It is easy to understand why today's Mardi Gras mentality is so popular and so user-friendly; yet it is nothing other than a beautiful face masking the reality of evil. A new world in which the strongest will assert their governance and one that is currently being designed to control millions of people.

Strange as this may seem, countless people today appear quite prepared to accept this scenario as long as they believe it will not impinge upon them and their individual lives. There are those who choose to believe that the world's population is too big, the resources of the planet are finite and that the sooner some overall system of global authority and order is established the better for all mankind.

With such an impetus, highly educated and intellectual people are busily promoting schemes of country-wide contraception programs, from regional sterilisation through to wholesale abortions all done in the name of progress. Much of this heinous work is carried out under the aegis of so many governmental and non governmental agencies including the United Nations and there are millions of Catholics who freely choose to support such policies. These again are the New Catholics who can see nothing wrong with encouraging their teenage daughters to use contraception and who can, when it suits them, justify euthanasia.

These are the ones who pride themselves on their far sightedness and who devote their time and energies in demanding whatever changes they 'think' necessary. Should one of these demands be for a New Church for a new century than this is the ultimate goal they are now seeking.

This new world religious organisation is where they are attempting to take the Bride of Christ. But will it be dedicated to serve God or Man? This church of New Man will claim to be in full communion and in an equal partnership with God. A modern vibrant world church, fully in compliance with United Nations approval and having as its founder, the Emeritus Jesuit Tubingen Professor, Karl Rahner SJ, already ratified and approved by the UN, to be its leader, its 1st Pope.

CHAPTER

10

The purpose of this book is not to prove the existence of God, nor is it to prove the Catholic Church is the one true Church. Rather, it is to offer help to those who having undertaken their mission, now find themselves trapped in some galactic cul de sac with no way out. It hopefully will act as a beacon for those who are in danger and who are seeking a safe route out of the impasse. That God exists, that Christ Jesus is His Son and the Gospels tell the truth as it is are all, given. That the Catholic church is the one true church founded by Our Lord Jesus Christ is one the reader will have to discover for him or herself.

The one who disagrees with this premiss or the one who rejects its present day teaching and who is fearful of the direction in which the church is heading, is perhaps the one for whom this book was best written. If for any reason it was written one can only say it was done so in order to encourage those who are seeking to keep on seeking and continue to do so until they find the truth.

This purpose then being established it must be clear to even the most diffident sceptic, that God is a single entity and unless he controls all authority his existence makes no sense. Those who seek some form of power sharing collection of deities combining together to make a single God are misguided. Just as those who equate mercy with justice, and salvation without redemption could not be further from the truth. That man appears able to feel confident or arrogant enough to no longer see, or indeed see himself as a lesser being created by God, is incredible. Yet again if one were to equate it, it is no more incredible than the sin of pride encouraging and tempting man to always see himself as more important, more capable and more powerful than he ever can be.

To try and demonstrate just how out of condition one may find oneself in spirituality, maybe even secularity is not too difficult. If anything it is somewhat shameful and embarrassing to realise how shallow or false one may actually be. In fact to see oneself as others' see us was one of the famous wishes of the Scottish poet Robbie Burns who used to lament,

> "I wish we had the gift to see us, to see ourselves as others see us"

In order to achieve this self evaluation the assistance of another man of letters is necessary, the author of IF every boy's hero, Rudyard Kipling (1865–1936). From such a 'Rudyard-Kipling IF type questionnaire, one is left in little doubt as to one's own spiritual standing:

- IF one is not in the daily habit of praying or fasting to some extent …
- IF one is not contributing to the welfare of some people or a cause in need …
- IF one is out of touch with the Sacraments especially that of Penance …
- IF one is really only concerned with having a good time and material possessions …
- IF one has not been home recently or has failed to take care of one's parents or relatives …
- IF one can never see oneself in any way inferior or subordinate … to any other …
- If one cannot give oneself to one's spouse or one's children as one should ….

- IF one participates in any words or actions leading to a sense of shame …
- If one is more inclined to the tearing down, rather than the building up …
- If one seeks to escape into the life of unreality rather than reality …

These and countless similar questions, very simple to formulate, can leave one with very few places to hide as to the strength and commitment one has to one's faith. It is so easy to read between the lines and see just how Christ-less one's life can become with the passing of time. Edmund Burke (1729–1797) the noted philosopher said

> "the only thing necessary for the triumph of evil is for good men to do nothing."

In our lives it can equally be said that for us to disregard and lose our faith, all one need do is accept the modern present day comforts and conditions that seduce us in so many ways, moving us further and further away from the Gospel and drawing us closer and closer into the world of Man.

It is also simple to construct other obvious questions that enables us to realize how user-friendly a particular type of lifestyle can be and how hard it is to alter our own individual participation. Many forms of modern day media and entertainment leads one straight into a whole lifestyle of pleasure and recreation, at the expense of any degree of spiritual exercise or awareness. With this in mind then how does one begin to take firm personal control of one's life, one's faith, one's behaviour? Nowhere does one need to make any room for one's dreams, one's fantasies, one's thrills or one's disasters. Except on the most rare occasions when one chooses to idle some time away, life is always for the living, and dreams are always for the dreamers.

People today like to talk in terms of their 'bucket-list,' an imaginary to-do list of pleasurable things to accomplish before they die. If only it were so, life in the fourth quarter would be that much more enjoyable, but sadly it seldom is. The advanced years - even with all the aches and pains - do bring a certain degree of satisfaction and even in restricted lifestyles it is possible to contribute to a cause, to write a serious letter to a newspaper, or help somebody else in need of encouragement, or just in some way to make a difference. It always seems preferable to right other people's wrongs, fight other people's wars, advise on other people's problems, than address one's own.

In our own Mother Church such is far too often the case. The clergy do not fully comprehend the laity, the laity certainly to not understand the clergy, the hierarchy are always somewhere else. The women's' movements are seen to be militant, there are no impressive laymen's movements and what societies there are, are seen as either sinister or misogynistic. The young struggle to attain real identity, the old struggle to retain their gained status, both age-groups never appear destined to be in unison with one another. The rich struggle to remain on top, the poor struggle to become rich, and so it goes on and on. Where does it lead, where is the Gospel within all this chaos and confusion?

It is hard to see Jesus if one does not look, it is hard to listen to Jesus if one does not try to hear, it is hard to meet Jesus if one never goes near his house. It may well be that God will hear us if we all shout loud enough, but we need to know exactly how we must shout. Jesus knows our needs and our weaknesses, just as He knew how badly He was going to suffer on the cross, yet He never ceased to tell His followers how they could be with Him forever in God's kingdom.

Unless a person, a man or a woman, understands their role in life they cannot function. They can perform, they can hold down a job, they can get married and have children, they can participate, yet they cannot truly function as they were created to function.

A person may find they are working as an accountant yet internally they believe they should have been a musician or a doctor. This lack of a feeling of fulfilment is one that only grows as time passes, when it must then either blossom or wither. The sadness is that many will never reach even the middle ground as they lose interest in trying to be what they should, and instead remain what they have come to be. For those who fall between the two stools the pain is even greater. This is why the homeless and the jobless are so vulnerable, their role, their value, their worth is not just diminished, it is both disregarded and destroyed.

Our spiritual life is no different. Once one's role is gone, there is really nothing left; one is indeed spiritually homeless and truly lost. It seems so easy to grasp the concept, yet why if it is so easy does one not fulfill it?

The parable of the prodigal son gives a glimmer of what is happening insofar as he left home, he had a wild time, he went on a major spree, he spent all his money, and he fell on hard times. At this stage it must be reasonable to assume that there were many days of deep regret and many sleepless nights of anguish before he finally thought seriously of going home. Even so, between the time of first thinking of home, and actually contemplating a return, a lot of time passed before he actually turned to go home. What is clear at this stage however is what he was determined to say to his father when he got there....

> "I am sorry, please forgive me....
> I am not worthy to be called your son....
> I will be content to take any job.......
> Just to be back where I belong......"

One of the many facets of this most moving of parables is the fact that the prodigal son finally had come to terms with what he was, what he had become, what he had originally been given, and most of all where he actually belonged.

He had to face up to what he had demanded, what he had squandered and what hurt he had inflicted on others. Most importantly he had to accept the fact that he had grievously sinned. Having set it all firmly in place in his mind, he now had to do what was necessary; he knew he had to return home. He had to apologise and express genuine sorrow for what he had done, ask forgiveness from his father and accept a lesser role on his father's estate. It was this decision, this new determination which gave him the courage to begin his long journey home.

Our supreme ability should always be to see ourselves primarily as God's Children. No other role, no other title, no other function, only as children. Our duty is to fulfil as perfectly as possible our responsibilities and obligations according to our role as God's Children in this life. What priest, man, woman, son or daughter will walk through 'the door of death,' look Jesus in the face and tell Him how unfair, how uncaring, how unfriendly his Bride on earth was to them? Surely instead as a child would it not be better just to ask Jesus for forgiveness? Jesus told his listeners that unless they were as children they would not enter the Kingdom of God. It is central, it is crucial and it is so real that one cannot for a moment cease thinking 'Father/Abba'.

In one's ordinary daily life as a parent, one first holds one's baby son or daughter as infant, then as an a small child. The holding pattern may become less and less over the years, but the relationship never ceases. To know God as Father is to love God as Father, and 'only' as a child should one try to develop one's relationship with Him. Whether one seeks to be as a young prodigal son or daughter or instead perhaps as a more mature adult who has grievously pained a natural parent, the lifelong intimacy is there. It is unbreakable, unless the son or daughter is determined to break it.

To hold this image of God as Father will make one's journey so much easier and so much simpler to live with. To try and understand that there is always an outreach waiting to embrace one is the beauty of God's forgiveness. It is a forgiveness without any limitations that dispels all shadows all doubts and all shame.

Heading back from the fishing grounds after a long day's fishing looking forward to a clean dry bed gives one a great feeling. Even if the catch still has to be off-loaded and the boat washed down, the feeling remains. Cardinal Newman's prayer captures this feeling so very gently:

> Lord may you support us all this day long, till the
> Shades lengthen and the evening comes, the busy world
> Is hushed, the fever of life is over, and our
> Work is done: then in your mercy may
> You give us a safe lodging, a holy rest
> And peace at last.
> Amen.

In his best-selling book, Crossing the Threshold of Hope, St Pope John Paul II spoke of

> 'People of our time have become insensitive to the Last Things.'

His insights into Man's awareness of death, judgement, heaven and hell were somewhat more than benevolent. They could almost have been described as lenient or sympathetic, as this whole area of theology had of course been re-formulated very much more in line with the thinking of Vatican II. This 'thinking' initiated and extended further along a more modernistic and ecumenical outlook and was an eschatology far removed from what had always been considered classical Catholic doctrine. The new thinking highlighted by the Council, was that God, 'The Father Almighty' of the Old Testament, vengeful, stern and prepared to permit His only Son to be crucified on behalf of Man, had to be de-masculated and re-defined and shown in a more acceptable light. It was thought of as being too difficult for the laity to understand how God, as Father, could be prepared to sacrifice his son. A more benign and desirable deity it was felt had to be introduced and thought of as more merciful.

The fact that previous generations had been able to identify and live their lives with God as Trinity and Old Testament prophets, such as Abraham and Isaiah as acceptable figures did not appear to register with the avant garde council fathers. After their new formula thinking was introduced the stress on the New Covenant was evident, and emphasized that as a God of Mercy there was absolutely nothing outside His forgiveness. The love of heaven was to be portrayed rather than the fear of hell, and any mention of judgement with eternal consequences were moved to one side and seldom mentioned. To a vague extent the obligation to apologise or to seek forgiveness as a prerequisite to receive God's loving mercy, was also downplayed.

For those firmly committed to the new formulae of Vatican II, the basic clarity of truth expressed in the Gospel was a problem which still had to be circumvented. The condemnation by Jesus of those who by the multitude of their sins merit Hell did not resonate well with the new thinking that was being put into place and has since been very well established. In his book Pope St John Paul II pondered on the very awareness of present day eschatological preaching, when he mused on the following reflection:

> "Whether or not Man has chosen to stop, or just stopped, being afraid of hell!"

Having raised the point he failed to pursue it further, yet identified the need for a more thorough in-depth study of the laity's indifference. The fact that the fear of hell had been removed was not acknowledged yet the problem remained, how could the Church promote and teach the Last Things. Without such a study or clearer awareness of what these things actually mean in today's world, Man's faith must remain deeply lacking.

This call for clarification of such truths endorsed throughout this book, can only help draw aside the heavy drapes of modernity, which for the past five decades appear to have hidden rather than revealed the true light of God's love and mercy from reaching the hearts of men. Arrogance, pride, lack of obedience and indifference, are some reasons why so very many preachers today fail to portray clearly the existence of Hell as the ultimate and real destination facing so many souls within their congregation. The people must be made aware that they need to amend their ways and decide to submit their obedience to the teachings of their Church. Why Pope St John Paul II failed to address this question in the depth it deserved to be addressed is unknown. What is known is that as his health deteriorated he had no choice but was forced to move slowly onward leaving many problems that troubled him unresolved.

This stumbling block in relation to the Last Things remains like an equation waiting in the wings, to be resolved. Until this happens without any closure, the cult of the individual which has impacted upon the church over recent decades, with catastrophic results, will continue to grow.

The immediate successor to Pope St John Paul II, Benedict XVI 2005–2013, had a difficult and somewhat paradoxical Papacy. His legacy after a reign of eight short years remains to be evaluated and with the passage of time no doubt it will be well and truly judged. The very fact that he was the first Pope in 600 years to resign assures him his place in history. Few would say he did little, but what he did was excellent. Many would say he was too intellectual and too committed to the structure of the office. Perhaps the overall majority would claim that he failed to introduce enough reform into the Church and no doubt there is also a minority who would have preferred had he moved in a far more traditional direction.

What will never be forgotten was how badly he was served by those close around him and even more so by the group of cardinals who were already planning for the next Papacy over which they believed they would be able to exercise their collective influence. That such a dissident group were able to form such a clique while Benedict XVI was actually occupying the Seat of Peter is more than indication of the depths of deviousness some of the highest ranking cardinals in the church were prepared to go to further their own selfish aims and ambitions. The sychophant English Cardinal Cormac Murphy O'Connor, RIP(1932-2017) even though not eligible to vote due to his age acted as a ringleader of the group in lobbying for and on behalf of the then almost unknown Argentinian Jesuit, Cardinal Jorge Bergoglio.

The present Bishop of Rome, Pope Francis I, as he prefers to be identified, is seen by many as a man in a hurry and one who likes to get things done. Whether they are secular or spiritual he appears to be a man of action and one whose words can easily be turned into deeds. Whether this is so, remains to be seen. How he will deal with the many obstacles and problems he faces, both internally and externally, will become evident as will be the authority he exercises. The fact is that he is but another link in a very long chain of Popes and both his coming and going will be remembered one hopes with joy and reverence. If not then he will join another list of popes, those who failed both their master and their sheep What does remain constant to this most exclusive confraternity is the continuity of popes that have ruled the Church since it was founded by Our Lord Jesus Christ. That the church will remain as the Bride of Christ until He returns to claim her is doctrine and must be believed. Until that time regardless of whoever sits in the Chair of Peter whether he does so as an idealist a radical or an opportunist he does so with absolute authority. Should one pope or another choose to exercise their time in office effectively or ineffectively it will be evident to God whether theirs was a noble or ignoble tenure. In studying the lives of the popes over the centuries it is clear to see why so few ever actually achieved sainthood. What is even more erroneous is how some of them were ever even elected to the Chair of Peter!

The Magisterium, or teaching authority of the Church, is there to protect the sacred truths, and it holds this tremendous responsibility regardless of who holds the Keys of the Fisherman. The Magisterium cannot allow church doctrine or dogma to be added to or subtracted from the body of divine truth, and yet it is the interpretation of such truths that so many senior clerical scholars today are constantly challenging. Whether the question is the status of those in second relationships and their entitlement to worthily receive the Eucharist or how those in same sex partnerships must be treated are two of the many battle fronts being drawn up between various groupings within the church at the moment.

Representatives from both these lobby groups are seeking the support of the Pope for their cause and it must be for the Pope and the Magisterium of the Church to provide the interpretation of the truth in accordance with the Gospel.

In dealing with so many concerns both global and national the church has the responsibility and the right to address and challenge the local government departments, bodies and organisations which impact negatively on the affairs of the Church, its members, and the laity in general. The Pope if invited to address the United Nations, a joint meeting of both houses of the administration or as in Europe the European Council of Ministers, obliged to outline the official views of the Catholic Church. How well he performs addressing such assemblies is the challenge he must be prepared to accept and how well he presents the truth as defended by the church is the yardstick by which he will be judged.

Whether such secular bodies would ever alter their stance to accommodate the Holy Father's views is hard to know. What is clear is that when the Church does take an opposing view to an administration's program, such as the Obama-Care, plan in relation to contraception services, then the government will tend to do all in its power to coerce the church to alter theirs. The interpretation of truth, doctrine and dogma therefore lies at the very heart of today's Church. Whether it is looked at from a classical, progressive, modern or radical viewpoint, most basic and fundamental issues pertaining to Catholic faith should never be in any doubt. Truth is never debatable and always unchangeable.

Since Vatican II the Magisterium and other formal doctrinal bodies appear to have been overly tolerant of such modern theologians and philosophers as Rahner, Schillebeecks, von Balthauser, de Chardin and a host of other prominent names. It appears in hindsight as if the church only wished to engage with them in some half-hearted rearguard action or way.

The relationship between Pope Benedict XVI and Hans Kung involved two exceptionally gifted theologians, who established themselves more and more, to the forefront of modern thought, gaining all the while more credibility and prestige in the various colleges and universities where theology and truth are considered to be synonymous. Indeed why would they not seek to push and expand all levels and boundaries of truth in as many directions as possible? Such concepts as that of 'anonymous Christianity' and others, whilst forever attempting to add further meaning to the sum total of knowledge, instead allowed for, and were made acceptable to whole schools of 'speculative theology'. These schools of thought then introduced into many seminaries and universities such gray concepts and thereby encouraged students and scholars in turn to consider all sorts of pluralist theology, far outside the traditionally endorsed teachings of the Church.

The tragedy of such uncontrolled individual theological independence expressed on so many campuses was that of the 'uniformity of thought' based on Aquinas and others was moved quietly to one side, and instead replaced with a new spectrum of theologies all vying competitively for pre-eminence. In the field of eschatological theology it is now quite evident that today's thinking falls far short of what is acutely needed spiritually or inspirationally by modern man. This in no way suggests that a new theology based once more on fear should be reintroduced but rather one of understanding and trust in God's love, mercy and judgement. As things stand currently the derision of the Four Last Things likens today's 'self-practising' Catholics to one:

"From him all wisdom has already fled."

In one's awareness of Christ as Head of the Mystical Body, containing the entirety of all the faithful, both living and dead, the role of Christ must be re-instated. It is the Church of today as 'Body' which many disillusioned Catholics are finding so difficult to identify with and participate within. Nevertheless, as body, as nations, as communities, as parishes, as persons, as sons, as daughters it is clear that what is harmful to any member of a family is harmful to all its constituent parts. Should the Church therefore have a dissatisfied member or a conglomerate of members within, whether it be it that of a celibate clergy seeking the right to marry, or a group of women advocating the approval of contraceptives or even those in second or third relationships wishing to receive the Eucharist. There can be no doubt that the ramifications of these demands, if fostered, must by their nature create dissent and division for all concerned.

The Church as the mystical body of Christ on Earth, with the Holy Father as its Head needs to re-define its authority, its superiority to teach, its mission to spread the gospel and its role in the redemption and salvation of Mankind. This role is guided by divine inspiration yet its implementation must rest on human dedication. It must remain that Church can unequivocally state it is in the Magisterium or those acting with its authority who can and do rely on the guidance of the Holy Spirit.

The present situation of so many interpretations being available for every present development within the Church at each level, all carrying various degrees of support from numerous national bishops conferences, is a danger laden method of disbursing Catholic Truths, which needs to be re-examined and re-visited. In the world of today where the very meaning of the word 'marriage' can be re-defined, all multi-cultural interpretations of meanings gives testimony to this course of action.

In no period of a society such as ours have the rights and roles of men and women become so convoluted. To say that they have become confused and mutually incompatible is putting it mildly. The Kennedy Camelot era which promised much, yet delivered little, tended to establish new freedoms, new rights and new families which in themselves never actually existed, let alone developed. The traditional role of father, the traditional role of mother, the roles of son and daughter all morphed into somewhat counter roles, which resulted in harsh, competitive and unisex modes of behaviour from which no one section had much possibility of actually benefiting. The advent of the Rock n Roll era, the drug culture, the West Coast lifestyle, Vietnam, all overwhelmed within one or two generations, the mindset and value system established in the previous century.

The allure of easy money, easy power, easy sex and easy freedom so eagerly advanced an easy rider attitude which combined to create a glut of unhappiness, a dehumanization of family values and an acceptance of individual rights advanced by the Ayn Rand school of progressive writers promoting a 'self' centre of existence. Thirty years earlier such writings would have been totally at variance with the establishment and maybe challenged, but the upheaval of society that had taken place and 'rights' gained with serious obligations attached- was no longer the case. The opposite was to become the new order and rights, without responsibilities, were seen as easily attainable and by far the more prefered lifestyle.

The goal for the few that can only be achieved at the expense of the many has become an economic fact of life, never fully rationalised in the public domain. In the new order of the swinging sixties and post-Christian world of multiple relationships, double and triple marriages, favoured birth control, abortion readily available, drug abuse, social pornography, alternative lifestyles and money as the yardstick by which everything can be judged, has left little hope of a spiritual renewal. In a society where the role of man is seen as being the father, the provider, the authority and the strength, and the role of woman is seen as that of wife, mother, comforter and teacher of the meanings and realities of life are today looked at as more stone age than space age.

Nevertheless until these two vital roles are once more fully defined then the whole concept of a Christian family is under threat. The present interest in the family expressed by the Holy Father and his synods will only make sense if the basic building blocks of the family are understood and the foundations are well secured.

The opposite however appears to be the case as it seems the peripheral issues are the ones today to be most likely addressed. The more contentious these are the more they distract from where the real problems lie and that is redefining the role of men and women and enhancing the Sacrament of Marriage leading to the true roles of father and mother. How this can be outlined and enshrined in some form of Papal social doctrine is what is first and foremost needed and it is then for the bishops, pastors and religious to present fully support and present it:

> "The father the head, as the source of authority and the
> mother the heart, the source of love."

Even though the realities of such defined roles may be somewhat economically difficult to put in place, it is in the conceptual sense of what they contain that should be understandable and acceptable. The nuclear route where the traditional roles are disregarded means many children cannot grasp the distinctions between father and mother, they get caught in a social dysfunctional and fragmented world where clearly defined parental ground rarely exists and when it does it only offers the secular route which inevitably leads to more confusion.

The demands of two jobs or careers considering time and space make family life more and more difficult to progress on a daily basis as the demands of children increase with age. The children, or single child, as is becoming more often the case, but also tends to demand his or her space and attention and both being at a minimum, becomes harder to procure in pressure- driven living.

Under constant stress and demanding work schedules the most appealing and feminist side of the woman is greatly curtailed. Likewise the man who finds his work or job too demanding can become more moody and irritable and these out of character traits make living together as a family more and more difficult. More than ever before the role of the father, the mother, the son or the daughter, all need to be restored to their rightful place and seen and acknowledged as such for the family to be seen once more as the bedrock of society.

In the western world referring to the 'Man' as being the 'Head of the Family' often causes offence and the word, Man, is identified as derogatory being both misogynistic and authoritarian. Indeed it may well annoy or infuriate a certain feminine instinct who would immediately declare such terms to be both sexist and gender driven, and to a certain extent that may indeed be the case, but it is incorrect when used in the Catholic sense. The father as head of the family is the person who is expected to support and defend each member of the family from as many difficulties and dangers as possible, while at the same time providing the means necessary to look after their needs and welfare.

There can be very few women who would not concur with this description and in so doing have no problem with the title of 'Head'. Whether such terms thrown about today carry derogatory or gender driven intentions depends very much on how they are presented and who wants to interpret them. The Gospel has more than one reference to the roles of husbands and wives in marriage and states:

> "Wives, be subject to your husbands"
> and "Husbands love your wives"
> > Colossians 3, 18 & 19

In addition to this well quoted passage from Colossians the additional text is rarely included which is a great pity due to its relevance in today's families,

> "Children, obey your parents in all things:
> for this is well pleasing to the Lord"

Another text which is also perhaps to seldom preached is,

> "Bear ye one another's burdens"
> > Galatians 6, 2

this lovingly crafted text also has a further poignant ending which is, "and so you shall fulfill the Law of Christ". If the Christian family is to be renewed let it be renewed along these lines first so that the everyday family and community would gladly accept the responsibilities and burdens that are individually and collectively thrust upon them. These are the burdens, not of one's own brothers and sisters, but rather the strangers that may have never even heard of Christ. The husband and wife roles therefore should never be seen as, more or less, strong or weak, equal or unequal but rather bio-complimentary, each one making the other 'whole'.

There is no role reversal in the Gospel which states the woman is instructed to love her husband and the man is subjected to his wife. Society today has become so confused in a unisex or metro man sense, that it is almost engineering a situation where the established form of sacramental marriage will be replaced by a gender-neutral partnership of two people of the same or different sexes.

Remarkable as it may seem, what was once considered irresponsible or unacceptable behaviour is now to be considered as valid and acceptable and as normal as that of a traditional marriage between a man and a woman who are expected to bring children into the world and become the parents of the next generation. As society is moving forward into such a new world, where the meaning of words and the definitions of doctrines can be re-mastered, the value and continuity of truth will continue to be weakened.

In this period of careful deconstruction of the family which now surrounds Christian society the onslaught continues. Ireland, for so long seen as a Catholic bastion, not only accepted same sex marriage but actually embraced it, thanks to a secular and degenerate government who sought to curry favour with their European counterparts and so attract substantial amounts of foreign investment into the country. The saddest part of the whole equation was that the Catholic Church hierarchy, to their shame, stood timidly to one side wringing their hands pretending to combat the evil that was being enshrined.

A further chilling example is that of infant adoptions in the United Kingdom. The Catholic adoption agencies there worked tirelessly to provide a valid and powerful alternative to women who for many reasons were facing abortion. The agencies also gave hope and joy to childless Catholic couples seeking to adopt a baby. These agencies provided counselling, support and peace of mind to those forced to part with their babies who at such a misery-filled time in their lives needed all the support they could get.

Sadly these agencies are now having to close their doors as they are facing legislation which is totally contrary to their fundamental mission of placing Catholic babies with Catholic families. Under the new draconian law on adoption any couple of the same sex, transsexual couples and bisexual couples with quasi-marriage certificates, are now entitled to apply for any baby from any agency. This new law therefore may place the baby in the hands of any different or same sex partnership deemed fit by the secular adoption agency as to their suitability, regardless of the birth mother's wishes and who up now could insist on a Catholic couple rearing her child. The Catholic agencies denied their sole reason for remaining in business were forced out of this charitable and genuine meaningful work. Of course where evil is never confronted it will succeed.

In Paris when 11 staff of the lecherous satirical magazine Charlie Hebdo were brutally killed because of a freedom of speech issue, widespread support and condemnation of the killings came from almost every political and many clerical groups. The magazine chose to exercise its freedom to print by greatly insulting the prophet Mohammad thereby giving total and gross offence to members of the Islamic faith.

A case could be made that some words, deeds and indeed actions which were judged as vile and blasphemous a hundred years or so ago are today no longer classified as such, yet it is clear that to very many what was venomous and vitriolic a hundred years ago remains so still today and failure to realize and acknowledge this fact cost these journalists their lives. The same magazine has many times in recent years portrayed the Holy Father and the Catholic Church in equally appalling and revolting ways and yet the Church continuously turns the other cheek. Nevertheless, in season and out of season, the Gospel clearly states the truth that:

It is only the good fruit trees that produce good fruit!
Matthew 3:10

If one accepts such is the case then a satirical, cynical or seditious society is hardly capable of producing good citizens, let alone a good society. It is obvious that it is the family which is vitally important. To make it so: marriage must be the predominant and all-encompassing factor, in order that the children will grow; develop and live in the love of God. This is the foremost reason why one must always protect and defend the sanctity of marriage and promote the true Catholic family as the best possible hope for the future of society.

Today the Catholic Church finds itself compromised on many fronts and reduced in stature by the evil scandals and abuses of many rank and file clergy and more painful still, by some of her more senior sons who have remained well hidden for many years. These clergy, who for one reason or another denied their faith, gave great scandal and caused unknown misery, putting their own Mother Church to shame. So much has been said and written in relation to how such evil actions could have festered for so long that again, one need only keep reminding oneself of Edmund Burke's words:

"For evil to succeed all that is needed is for good men
to do nothing"

How more succinct must words be, or how flawed must we be, to keep forgetting them? Through fear, favour or complicity to have allowed so much damage to be done, these facilitators will have to pay a terrible price for their unfaithfulness, while those who remained steadfast will once more have to take up the collective cross and rebuild the structures called parish, church and home. The more today's Catholic Church is restricted, curtailed and ecumenised, the easier it gets for those determined to take advantage of it to succeed.

In the secular world Satan's plan of gaining control, causing unknown levels of death, destruction and misery, is all the while gaining momentum and control. His agents move silently throughout the world as they recruit the more powerful and influential individuals, who in turn are empowering those beneath them in taking over their communities and all the while taking more control of society.

The concept of a never-ending, on-going combat between good and evil is a spiritual reality which far surpasses any video game or application. Yet the church very rarely speaks in terms of how real this spiritual warfare is. Why it does not do so, as the evil it causes affects so many in their everyday lives, is a tremendous oversight and one which also must be put to rights. How one must be prepared to engage and defeat Satan, if called upon to do so, is what the Church must try to highlight and equip one fully for the call to prayer, fasting and the need to perform good works are all so much easier to understand once the need for their contribution is accepted and taken on board.

In order to do this another central core teaching of the Church must also be made crystal clear and that is the depth of the Love of God. This love which is limitless and freely given by God is entrusted to His Church, a love that must be freely and generously distributed to all who seek and request it. Those who have no knowledge of Christ must be given every opportunity to hear what the Gospel has to offer. To the followers of other faiths, hostile or otherwise the invitation must always also be made and always remain open.

It may be that there are those who prefer to choose a religion based on wealth and social status. It may be that some people will choose to follow a prophet or series of prophets rather than a Messiah, but it will always remain the mission of the Catholic Church to preach the Gospel. In passing down God's love for man it is through the Sacrament of Holy Orders a bishop empowers the priest to make known God's love for a person. No penitent having received the Sacrament of Penance fails to experience this touch of God's love. These priests chosen, not by man but by God, accept the religious vocation offered to them to help Him directly as modern-day disciples. In such men chosen as priests the love of God is set to shine and whatever sacrifices they make on their own behalf, or on behalf of their flock, they make with the will of God.

The terrible sex abuse violations of rogue priests on young boys over recent years can never be forgotten but it is for the faithful to rebuild a better Church for a better congregation who will never again remain silent when confronted by such evil. This is today's invitation to today's lay-Catholics and one that all are asked to participate in being active followers of Christ.

In terms of spiritual warfare the march of materialism, entertainment and technology presses down ruthlessly, making Christ's invitation hard to receive and harder still to follow as it requires constant spiritual work yet it is an obligation the laity must be proud to follow. Should one decide to withdraw one's support for their Church the Face of Evil is so friendly and alluring that it is within such a Mardi Gras atmosphere that the young people decide wilfully or not to follow Satan. The ease in which the deception of evil triumphs over the candour of good, is both swift and seamless, as it is adopted by those who are unconscious of the choice they are making.

The Church so often appearing to compromise its openness to facilitate those in need of education, in human sexuality, in contraception, in re-marriage, divorce, in numerous small and conciliatory ways today now finds itself making room, excuses and allowances for whole sections of society, organizations, groups, congregations and various altruistic bodies who promote their own causes, citing the Catholic church as some sort of sponsor. It is an enormous task to undertake, to preach in classical and traditional terms, a redefining of God's law in terms of the basic set of rules and yet it is a task that many claim is necessary and must be undertaken.

The description of 'enormous' however is just that, a single word, because no matter how large the meaning of this term is, it does not mean impossible. The role of the preacher is to win the hearts and minds of his congregation, not to impose on his flock a draconian code or set of rituals through obedience and ignorance. Laws which become laws due to some government objective, or held in place with a serious level of fines, cease to be laws of acceptance, and instead are laws of compliance. It is only the laws the public acknowledge are in place for their own good and are accepted as ordered disciplines that become valid and the way a true disciple of Christ will freely choose to live.

Our Mother Church has a unique Trinity which will exist until the end of time. It possesses the full truth of Jesus Christ in its entirety. Secondly it has, and will continue to have, the divine guidance of the Holy Spirit. Lastly it has the 'keys' to God's Kingdom, given to Peter by Christ and handed down to each successive Pontiff. This triad of Faith (That we may believe, Mightily), (That we may hope, Joyfully) and (That we may love, Divinely) however difficult or 'enormous' to understand must be represented by our Mother Church so as to make modern Man not only understand these spiritual truths within Mother Church but will also desire to grow them with a firm passion. In addition, the follower of Christ will seek constantly the forgiveness and the love of God which he then in turn can share with his family, neighbours and friends.

In everything that man says, thinks and does, his views, opinions and judgements are governed by his beliefs. It may be for a politician, an actor or a farmer that their beliefs will differ so much they will be unlikely to act, say or do anything with any uniformity. It is only when great emotions are in place such as a tragic death or natural disaster occurs that some degree of predictability is possible. Without a cohesion of community beliefs or emotions, man would only be able to act on the strength of his intelligence.

To challenge man by asking him to confront death intellectually with only vague beliefs seldom forces him to realistically struggle with the challenge of Faith and the invitation to seek perfection. In the opening chapters of this book, the metaphor introduced was that each person born into this world is comparable to an astronaut launched into space to perform a number of tasks before returning to Earth, having successfully completed his or her mission.

This analogy has its merits as there is little doubt, regardless of how good or bad one's mission goes, the safe re-entry and return to Earth eventually becomes the all- important, vital part of the mission. To the astronaut facing Re-Entry this completion of his mission requires his total attention to every detail because for him the actual moment of truth has arrived and the final and last challenge must be met and conquered.

In seeking to achieve this goal many procedures are necessary. The three most crucial stages are the overall de-orbit, the atmospheric re- entry and the actual landing. From an orbital height of about 200 miles and a speed of 17,300 mph the spacecraft has to find, locate and touch down on a precise runway at an exact Air Force Base on the distant planet far below him. This feat over the years has become so mundane that now it hardly merits mention on the main evening news; but to consider it from the viewpoint of the mission commander looking at the blue orb high above him suspended in space the view from the cockpit almost defies belief.

The most nerve-wracking period during the entire procedure is the 4/12 minute communications blackout period generated by the atmospheric re-entry envelops the craft in a sheath of ionized white heat so intense as to make any radio contact with ground control impossible. After this excruciating period when the spacecraft bursts through this barrier and successfully re-establishes communications, the moment of touch-down is usually only 12 minutes away and with all hands on deck, as it were, the touchdown takes place and Deo gratias' are murmured.

Using this space mission analogy however, it does becomes clear that there are some inadequacies which must be considered using this terminology. First the most outstanding and obvious point of reference is that, for the entire mission from beginning to end, the communications are only down, or non-operative, for the crucial 4-12 minute period; at all other times full communications are in place, whether in use or not. Secondly, all orders come from ground control and must be adhered to. Thirdly, there is usually a full and advanced detailed knowledge of when the mission is going to be terminated, and if it is to be shortened or lengthened it is discussed and agreed with the pilot and mutually agreed upon. It is only then, with full confidence when all systems are pronounced 'Go,' that RE-ENTRY is initiated with total confidence in its execution and success.

One's life on the other hand lacks such tremendous awareness, self-confidence and ability. If death is to be one's own personal RE-ENTRY, then one's eschatology and one's understanding of the Four Last Things, need to be re-appraised. Facing RE-ENTRY, what condition must one be in? If on leaving the launch pad and achieving primary orbit one then decides to sever all communications and proceed independently of ground control, it is hard to imagine how the mission could be undertaken and how eventually it could be terminated. No mission however well constructed is totally self-sustaining. Supplies of finite resources, or lack of them, almost automatically signals the end of the mission is approaching and alarm bells begin to ring. This being inevitable, a conclusion, either scheduled or unscheduled, will therefore have to take place, whatever the subsequent outcome.

Without communications: the vital information banks and detailed on-going streams of information; cannot be fed into the systems. Whatever alterations are needed, as they always are, must be made yet now cannot be discussed and decided upon. The detailed orders from ground control are also in jeopardy due to the lack of communications and without them the gravest dangers lie ahead. Finally, whereas an advanced date of RE-ENTRY is planned and mutually counted down, this out of touch craft without relevant information has no concept or idea of the countdown and so no state of readiness exists. With such a terrifying unknown situation developing, only the worst re-entry scenario is inevitable and must be considered a real possibility.

One further major factor in the analogy is that while the properly manned space vehicle has an entire pro-active support system, the life mission, the spiritual mission, that every baptised Christian undertakes has an enemy of major and terrifying abilities. One that from the moment of lift off at birth, is determined to capture, enslave and destroy them.

All this space jargon is of course only jargon, it means nothing and can easily be dismissed off-hand as sheer conjecture, but what cannot be dismissed or avoided is the stark brutal reality that every one of us must face their own individual death and what that will mean. This is the ultimate and universal bond which both unites and separates all men. This:

"Door of Death" Mt: 7, 13-14

is the gateway through which each and every one must pass.

Our Mother Church contains the entire truth, the guidance of the Holy Spirit, the Gospel, the tradition, the Magisterium, the successor of Peter, the Communion of Saints and all the sacred truths. The wonderful and beautiful Creeds all begin, 'I believe...' and finish in the same idiom, 'Amen'. To seek then the knowledge of the 'Last Things' one must first turn to the Gospel and seek the good news.

St. Paul's Letter to the Corinthians contains the beautiful line,

"O Death where is thy sting, O Hades where is thy victory?"

1 Corinthians, 15:55

This beginning signifies so much hope and trust in the Resurrection, as if Death itself is somehow to be held in contempt. This theme was common in the early Christian Church as the awareness of death before one could live in Christ was both understood and desired. To rise in physical form was a further threshold of belief sustained by the apostles and the early martyrs through their faith which so recently had been tested to its extreme limits in the catacombs and the Colosseum.

Death indeed has no sting, other than that of sin, for the Gospel reveals the Resurrection of Jesus was His total victory over death, and His gift of eternal salvation to all Mankind. By dying and rising from the dead Jesus freed all men from death spiritually and gave each one the gift of eternal salvation. The price of man's redemption was the shedding of Christ's blood.

The meaning of the Resurrection is our faith, it is our belief. Had Christ not risen there would be no Christianity, there would be no joy, and there would be no happiness. The promise of the Resurrection was that in dying we are born to live again, to live for eternity. Once Christ rose triumphant on Easter Sunday morning, the prophecies of the Old Testament were fulfilled and the sacred truths in the New Testament confirmed. The Paschal mystery of the Resurrection redeemed mankind from sin, and justified him once more to participate in God's Kingdom.

St Patrick, Patriarch of Ireland, was confident enough to write of Man's' death in the fifth century:

> "For on that day we will undoubtedly rise in
> the brightness of the sun that is in the glory
> of Jesus Christ our Redeemer, as children
> of the Living God."
>
> Conf. 59

So from this man, the greatest of saints we have this wonderful assurance that our redemption will be as 'children' of the 'Living God', what more could one possibly hope for?

It is only the sin of despair that promotes the fear of death and the more one subscribes to this temptation the more fearful one becomes, until the fear of death is translated into the fear of God. This cannot be, of course, as it was God who sent His only begotten Son to sacrifice His life on each and every person ever born, and this act in itself was the supreme act of love. What Father would show such love for his children, as Jesus, Himself emphasised when he explained to the gathering:

"Would any of you who are fathers give your son a stone
when he asks for bread, or a snake when he asks for a fish
How much more then, will your Father in Heaven give good
things to those who ask him?"

(Lk 11, 9 - 13)

Man's fear of Death must be recognised and accepted for what it
is, a fear of the unknown, a fear of dark places. The power of Satan is
masked by one of either two emotions, fear or greed, and Man fears
what he does not know or understand. Over 500 years ago in "The
Imitation of Christ", Thomas a Kempis wrote:

"If thou be not ready today to face death,
how shalt thou be ready tomorrow?"

This is the question which Death finally forces one to confront,
to consider and cope with as one seeks the truth. As Man has no need
to fear Death, why then does he tremble at its name? Throughout the
Gospel to the final week of Jesus's life, the entire message He presented
was one of repentance, mercy and salvation. Jesus constantly preached
that he had come to save, not to condemn.

The events of Passion Week, His Crucifixion and His Death all
add to rather than subtract from what went before. The Resurrection
of Jesus from the dead raises Man from eternal death, and breathes life
everlasting into him. Why then this dreaded apprehension and fear of
what should be greeted openly and accepted as a new beginning rather
than a dreadful end?

In the eschatological order of events, after Death comes Judgement.
It is this truth, perhaps this reality, rather than Death itself which forces
one to fear. In the Gospel it states:

"That evening they heard the Lord God walking in the
garden, and they hid from him among the trees."

Book of Genesis, 3:8

This was the first indication or mention of Mankind sensing fear. It was not however a fear of death they experienced but rather a fear or sense of shame. Both the man and the woman, having eaten the fruit, were fully aware that they had done wrong, through their disobedience sin was established, and even though they did not understand the magnitude of their actions they were ashamed. Whatever pain they had caused God, they sensed immediately they were solely responsible for and so they hid.

Man had perfection in Paradise, his soul was pure. The sin of pride promoted the sin of disobedience and so contaminated his pure soul with this stain of original sin. From that moment the knowledge and awareness of sin was always to be accompanied by a sense of shame. It is Man's ability to mask this realization or sense of sin today that is responsible for the hardness that is evident in people's' hearts. The purer the heart the greater the suffering sin brings it. This is what Christ died for, to save each person the terrible pain of sin and their personal suffering through life followed on by their suffering after their RE-ENTRY.

Once one chooses to reject Christ the choice, in effect, is to make worthless His sacrifice on Calvary and render his offer of salvation obsolete. Today in the most advanced technological civilization that has ever existed, Man's soul still registers sin, yet because of the World's indifference, sin now in its most appalling forms is rapidly failing to actually register greatly in people's hearts. It is the price of man's pride and stupidity that his awareness of sin today is so muted that God's invitation to enter His Kingdom is no longer seen as what each Christian should spend his or her life fervently seeking to embrace.

Each individual on his or her pilgrim path or mission will have many constant dark companions in competition with their own guardian angel which seldom, if ever, rests. Even in the most unlikely or unsuspecting moment they can present temptations hard to resist, and it is only prayer and the strength of prayer that continuously rescues one from falling yet again.

As one moves onward, one's sense of sin becomes ever clearer, more focused, depending always on the state of grace, which one surrounds oneself with. The sin of Adam and Eve as creatures of perfection was at once so recognizable to them in its fullness, that they had to hide in shame covering their nakedness, of which they were now conscious for the first time. For modern man living a corrupt life in a corrupt world, it is now easier than ever to sin and sin with impunity and brag to his companions the strength of his triumphs.

The gift of life and Baptism given to one also comes with the responsibility for every person to search for God.

> "and demands every effort of intellect, a sound intellect,
> a sound will, 'an upright heart', as well as the witness of
> others who teach him to seek God"
>   Catechism of the Catholic Church Par, 30

For Catholics who have been baptised as God's children and who choose not to follow this instruction but rather indulge themselves in a life of casual selfishness, the State of Sin is practically an automatic progression of existence as every day they are committing their souls to the possibility of eternal damnation. For those born without being baptised into the one true faith, the natural law of fundamentally knowing the difference between right and wrong is their only guide, their conscience, the voice of their soul. Regardless whatever situation one finds oneself this existence however pleasant it may be, unless it is moving towards God and not away from Him contradicts God's Law. The awareness of conscience, the realization that one is harming one's soul every so often reappears like the sun momentarily from behind a cloud, only to disappear once again.

This uneasy awareness somehow reminds one that they are actually in urgent need as they are spiritually starving. It is always so easy and preferable to compare oneself to some other misfortunate who is in such bad shape that the comparison almost forces one to look good. Yet, if one were to compare oneself to a saint, then it would certainly show one in a much truer light, and the image in the mirror would again make one recoil. These jolts to how adrift one has become flash like a subliminal message across one's mind, bypassing the very need of sight. No one is so blind as the one who has the most sin on his soul.

As the Sacrament of Penance frees one from one's sins, the lack of urgency that is taken avail of this Sacrament is quite incredible. Who, if totally blind would wait a month or two or even three, to avail of an immediate cure that would allow them to see again?

Judgement then must be recognised as clearly as Christ wants us to recognise it. His declarations of God's love and mercy are more than an assurance to give one the confidence to realise that God's desire is for every child to return to Him. It is His desire that no one shall be left behind. To those who refuse His love and mercy and whose lives are lived as a refusal will find they are not admitted, and the door will remain closed. The Catechism teaches that on death there is an immediate and 'particular' judgement, and on the Last Day there will be a 'general' judgement. How then do these judgements differ?

The 'particular' judgement will confront the individual, who having been born into the world with nothing, will similarly depart from the world with nothing. What good he has done and what sins he has committed will be weighed, and what awaits him will be at once decided. It will be final.

All souls will be judged: those who need to make amends, will face the temporal fires and pain of Purgatory. This purification will cleanse their souls prior to their eternal reward and entry into Heaven. Those who have strayed too far and rejected every offer of mercy to make a reconciliation will however face the fires of Hell. On the Last Day the appearance before God will be public, and on that occasion, every tear that ever was will be wiped away, and all will be made clear.

The providence of God which at times appeared to allow the good to suffer and the wicked prosper will be clear for all to see and understand and nothing will remain unresolved. How both judgements will be fully reconciled with one another is not for one's knowledge in this world. It is clear that Eternal Glory will be man's just reward, and Eternal Damnation will be man's just punishment.

It must therefore be believed that as God willed his only Son to die on behalf of mankind, God will indeed reward the good and punish the wicked. There would be no order or semblance of sense to creation should it be different. Christ's life is all meaning, then, now, and for all eternity. He invites every person He alone created to follow him. Insofar as one listens to Him and takes up one's cross, one is in union with God.

Whoever refuses, for whatever reason, it will be by their personal choice as God forces no one to serve Him. This is the ultimate responsibility, the price of freewill which man possesses. Those who deny Jesus in this world have been told by His bride, our Mother Church, that it will be the very same sinners who will choose to deny Him again on death and in doing so freely choose the path of the unrepentant.

The modern day overall or universal approach to eschatology within the Church 'collectively' has become in some commentators' opinion almost schizophrenic. The most progressive modern school of thought favours a heaven which is attainable by all bar a tiny handful. Many religions and religious groups as communities have become persistent in recent years in trying to promote the overall view that all of mankind, regardless of beliefs or indeed any belief, will reach God's Kingdom. If this should be the case then why, one must wonder, was Christ born at all? His life, death and resurrection becomes almost devalued, or to some extent some extent totally meaningless. The deaths of countless martyrs also cease to have real value and Christ's message to 'take up one's cross and follow him' is nothing more than a lie'

The classical school of catholic theology disregarded and demeaned by those who restructured Vatican II have always rejected such thoughts and proposals, and remains committed to the Gospel accounts and the warnings of the church fathers and doctors. If one were to actually compare the writings of such dissident theologians such as Hans Kung and Richard McBrien and try to relate them to those of John Chrysostom and Robert Bellarmine, not to mention countless saints, then one would have to be more than a little naïve to choose the cosmic road of modern thought.

The eschatology of the private individual trying to secure a deep relationship with God has somehow been put to one side, and what was once the sacred teaching, learned and accepted by so many, has today been turned into a such a swamp of confusion that few feel committed to follow it. Today to once again try hard to foster this need for a closer ever growing awareness of God, this desire for truth must become a living 'want,' a need for every person who sees their personal judgement as a graduation of honour rather than a minimal pass mark.

This re-awakening or re-defined central belief in one's faith is an absolute 'must' for the Church to acknowledge and teach again to all Christians seeking the truth, that there is only one truth and that is to restore all things in Christ as King, as only when this happens will perfection be once more achieved.

How the soul should then present itself to God is the most integral part of man's journey. The Church cannot continue to fail in this primary teaching responsibility. In today's muddy waters the need for preachers of outstanding virtue and ability has never been greater. Eternal life may become what one chooses it to be here on earth, and it is a choice which must be made in faith so that it grows and attracts those who come into contact with it. To live the Gospel life is to reject falling in love with self, but rather on falling in love with God, in each and every way that is open to it.

To appreciate Judgement before our Death, it is necessary to look clearly at the Last Things which await each person according to their gifts, hardships and talents. Of the three judgements, two are eternal, Heaven and Hell. Whilst Purgatory, as taught by our Mother Church, however painful, according to one's life and behaviour, is temporal in both elemental time and space. For the whole of humanity the existence of God, the love of Christ and the power of the Holy Spirit, are terms and truths which the providence of God alone will make clear on the Day of Judgement.

Catholics are baptised into the one true faith which the Creed emphasises in detail in its prayer. These rules, or the events referred to, are defined as dogmas and not debatable. Each Catholic is obliged to believe these truths and, should they choose to consciously disregard or reject them they then cease to be followers of Christ. Many of today's clergy go through their entire ministry preaching the truths the Creed contains yet, failing somehow, to give their words the interpretation to make them real to those who listen. It is for this reason the laity often appear to be so nonchalant. If one were to hear for the first time a religion that encapsulates:

> The Second Coming of Christ
> To judge the living and the dead
> The Resurrection of the dead
> The Life of the World to come.

Of course they would be interested, how could they not be? Sadly for so many Catholics today these phrases have been allowed to become so obsolete and well worn they no longer have the resilience needed to rivet one's attention. Yet again and again they are presented through the Gospel as the inspired Word of God. Is it possible that such words of wisdom can continue to be so lightly brushed aside in today's world?

What modern day help can the Catholic Church provide if what she teaches is completely confused, if what she preaches is somewhat distorted, and if what she offers is somewhat ignored? Without greater knowledge and deeper understanding of the true faith, the mission one is undertaking is precarious, dangerous and fraught with multiple obstacles. Nevertheless one is assured by Christ that one only need ask in order to receive all the love, help and support one needs on this hazardous life mission.

CHAPTER

11

With the realisation that before reaching God's kingdom one must first pass through the doorway of death, what else can one do but cry out for mercy. There is no escape route, there is no other way. Whatever time is left must be used to try and make amends for the foolish and sinful actions one has committed in one's life. If one fully understood and appreciated the Sacrament of Extreme Unction, this anxiety would be somewhat lessened

This 'end of life' Sacrament containing the most endearing and loving of all the graces is sorely needed by each individual, as they face death. It is the Sacrament that gives the greatest comfort to those whose lives have been riddled with both shame and misery and yet, as their mission draws to a close it somehow relieves those most in need of spiritual assurance. The fascination with death itself is something that gnaws in everyone's head momentarily going through life. Certainly the great English playwright and poet James Shirley (1596 -1666) left no one in any doubt in his poem,

'Death The Leveller'
concludes with the most wonderful lines:-

"Only the actions of the just
Smell sweet and blossom in their dust."

To those whose missions are nearing completion not all will avail of
this Sacrament. Some will be offered it as they lie in their hospital bed,
others may not. A sudden heart attack or violent stroke with no priest
at hand, may deny them this grace. How or why this is the case must
remain in the realm of God's providence, and all one can do is trust in
God's mercy. In whatever situation one finds oneself, the need to achieve
a successful Re-entry and make a secure landing is, the all-consuming
priority. Every pilot getting closer to their final 24-hour count-down
cycle, must be in the best shape mentally to both control and land his
spacecraft successfully.

As death is a new dimension and a destination that one has heard
of many times during one's life, the various accounts differ from one
extreme to another. Even Christ's own disciples hotly disputed their
future roles and status in the new Kingdom. We are no different. If
anything we are more concerned with rewards and titles than we are
likely to deserve, yet, for the very few who are the genuine saints of
today and who have diligently carried their crosses throughout their
lives, it is they who will experience the unknown treasures.

It is the fearful, those realising how close they are to Re-Entry and
knowing that they still need to be rescued even in their dying hour,
who can still be aided. For some the dreadful fascination of Hell is still
trapped in their minds. They may have heard a brutal sermon long ago
while attending a spiritual retreat or ceremony. Never was the topic of
eternity, especially the eternity of the damned, allowed to gather any
dust before retreats were finally brought to their end. Its inclusion as
the finale or last drum roll may indeed have served a purpose as does
the final nail in any coffin. The priest or preacher like a high roll
gambler may have staked his reputation in the belief that if he was
going to leave only one message with his congregation it had better be
a memorable one.

In fact, for many orders, particularly the Redemptorists, the final
address of their fire-storm retreats always focused on the Apocalypse

in one form or another. Today such is not the case. The writings of St John Chrysostom, St Alphonsus de Liguori and St Robert Bellarmine have had most of their most profound teachings on Hell rolled up carefully in tubes and consigned to the highest and most unreachable shelves, of the most inaccessible libraries in which they once took pride of place. The vast bulk of the damned genre has been set aside to gather cobwebs. These writings today are seldom consulted or even considered suitable for some research scholars to study. The love and mercy of God is now the most given route, detailed by the Church, for all who fully expect to enjoy an eternity in a most wonderful paradise. Pope Francis in presenting 2016 as a Jubilee Year of Mercy, underwritten by the love of God, made it almost appear that the very need for man to apologise for his sins was optional. Nevertheless in ignoring such saints and the writings of, St Leonard of Port Maurice and/or St Teresa of Avila, the knowledge one should seek regarding the final judgment leaves this life very inadequately prepared.

The advanced world of today with major concerns of huge proportions, finds itself enmeshed in so many complex and contentious issues that the political leaders are struggling to maintain a degree of global harmony and equilibrium. Rich versus poor, advantaged versus disadvantaged, natural resource provider versus natural resource developer, are all interests vying with each other to maintain their positions. The natural resources of the planet are, as never before, being decimated by the demands of the super nations, regardless of the harm they may be causing the planet itself.

The encyclical Laudato Sii written by Pope Francis outlined many of his views on the climate change scenario, and man's' treatment of the environment, was a most unique document. How original and how meaningful were the views expressed, remain to be seen. Some commentators felt they were well drafted and of major significance whilst the more cynical insisted that the overall context was little more than a reiteration of many similar views already well expressed with some new bells and whistles incorporated.

For the more diligent Vatican observers it was the perceived desire of the pope himself who felt the need to even write an encyclical on this particular secular subject, which they thought should at best have been left to the scientific community. As with many such Papal encyclicals and letters originating from the Vatican, it was clear that unless it was promoted by the bishops and their priests worldwide it would have little if any real effect and that indeed proved again to be the case. The subsequent Paris conference on the global environmental appraisal itself paid little if any particular attention to the fact that the pope had taken such an active interest in such a secular topic.

The vast majority of countries today are no longer run as sovereign states. Many instead opt for alliances or trade blocs in the belief that where there is unity, there is strength. Of course in certain political circles this may be true, but in the case of global resources e.g. food, energy, logistics, health care, control is being manipulated and dominated by the banks, multi media empires, transnational corporations, and ultra powerful clubs which have in the past and will in the future continue to package everything, every asset and every commodity, so why not 'eternity.'

The same metals, crops and financial properties are being bought and sold, 5, 10 and maybe twenty times on the various exchanges around the world. For brokers and traders who play these 24-hour global markets, like the spin of a roulette wheel, never stopping. Gains and losses are made up on existing and nonexisting options. Meanwhile as traders make and break markets over crops yet to be sown, groups of sub Saharan tribesmen will fight and kill over what scant remains of the same crops, once they have been harvested.

Within such a confused world, the next generation of mankind is being groomed as carefully as a paedophile grooms an innocent child. Children now receive their initial concepts of a Jurassic time and period through the eyes of movie directors, not just in California but in India, Europe Asia and elsewhere.

Wherever such futuristic films, videos and games are manufactured today is of little consequence. It is their design, application and capabilities which are being distributed on every continent that provides internet bandwidths, of the 4th and even 5th generations that enable today's children to engage in virtual warfare of the most harmful and dangerous kind. For parents, teachers and adults seldom if ever have reason to investigate such domains the actual difference between virtual reality and real reality is rapidly being rendered obsolete. These games such as the advanced military scenarios are now hosting the closest technological cousins to the pilotless drones that overshadow countries such as Pakistan, Afghanistan, Libya, Syria, Lebanon and Iraq each day looking for suspected terrorists. Todays 'game-players' whether they are the children of America, Russia, China or India will be the soldiers and technocrats of tomorrow. They are already being trained in all forms of virtual weapons and warfare and transferring their skills from where they sit now to some command post of tomorrow will mean little to them other than a new console or joystick.

These then are today's' children, teenagers and young people being moulded to be in charge of the world of tomorrow. All that will be of any value then may be gauged in personal status, affluence, lifestyle and possessions and regardless of whether it will be empires, countries, populations or individual persons all will find themselves being evaluated, judged and stress tested at interim periods as they go through a more cruel, demanding and Godless life.

While the secular, economic and political power blocks all struggle to maintain their status quo, belief in the Gospel, belief in Jesus Christ and belief in the Catholic Church has seldom been under such a global onslaught. In the last century the most vile and cruel dictators such as Stalin, Hitler, Mao, and Pol Pot, all promised the destruction of the Catholic Church whereas today the external threat comes from the fractured diverse countries, where hard core fundamental Islamic Sharia law prevails.

In these and other Muslim countries in which rights without responsibilities, justice without mercy, and servitude without citizenship are the order of the day such harshness and brutality are both understandable and expected due to their culture and lack of love in any humanitarian or global sense. The analytical and prolific skills of Hilaire Bellloc as a writer 'par excellence' were second to none and his appreciation of what Muslims choose to believe to be their rightful place in God's creation helps greatly to make those who seek to understand their mentality, possible.

What is not understandable is the hostility the Church attracts from within. This arises from the whole new mindset which likes to believe that mercy outweighs truth, conscience is always right, and love conquers all. Holders of such views are the tolerant and liberal people who claim there is nothing wrong in the idealistic behaviour of anybody, providing they are not interfering or harming anybody else.

This message or universal proclamation, which appears, over the last fifty years or so, to have grown at an exponential rate is of course unsustainable and yet like a pandemic it continues to spread like a virus throughout whole swathes of society. The haste and rapid advance of this avant garde mode of thinking is helping to fuel the move from the family-based unit of society to the maverick one. A century ago, words and terms like agnosticism and paganism applied to people one would seldom if ever meet, let alone talk to. Today such people proliferate as it is now easier than ever before to state one's preference in disbelief and paganism rather than a committed and structured life. The move away from the conventionally married committed family unit to a joint individual bank account relationship with optional children has begun and, it is now well underway.

In times past, the words 'consumerism' and 'materialism' seldom would apply to one's own life and technical definitions such as 'world wide web' and 'social networking' had yet to be introduced. Today with 24/7 satellite news and media coverage worldwide, the 'fast forward' tempo-world allows little, if any, time for those who are not prepared or able to keep up with the herd. The amazing National Geographic documentaries showing the weakest animal being left behind or the oldest member of a collective herd being set aside to fend for itself demonstrates how cruel the law of the jungle can be.

Catholicism however, is the exact opposite. It leaves no one behind. The sick, the poor, the disadvantaged, the weak, the destitute, the prisoners, even the perverted. The Gospel ensures that no one, too little, too young, too uneducated, too old, too ugly, too mean will be thrown to one side, to God each and every life is of value and must be treasured.

When the Catholic Church finds itself ostracised in any country it is usually because some disadvantaged section of society is benefiting directly from its help. By providing help to the aged, care to the sick, housing, education or some other medical treatment the Catholic Church reminds the authorities of its obligations to its citizens. These technocratic countries have little or no time for the Catholic Church or its teachings. The exodus of Catholics and Christians from so many Arab countries in recent years is a regular item on international news channels. The reasons and stories however are seldom detailed. In the host countries meantime children are forced to work long hours in factories, women are sold into servitude and prostitution, families are being broken up and evil continues to triumph.

To see the results of Satan's work globally it is easy to appreciate how well he directs his strengths and forces in carrying out his work. As with any fortress under attack, the Catholic Church is only as secure as its defences. To view any assault as it is being executed is a challenge to those entrusted with its care, but as history has proven time after time it is the enemy within that causes the greatest damage. This immediate threat today is of even more considerable concern as it is the force or strength of the New Catholics who seek to contaminate the message of Christ's eternal plan for the happiness and salvation of all Mankind.

The knowledge of eternity and the sacred truths which the Church holds perhaps can no longer be presented as they were in the past by the Doctors of the Church, yet as Pope St John Paul II said many times, these mysteries must be shared, examined and discussed amongst the faithful. To try and somehow implement this high definition Papal statement today appears to be an aspiration that is not even open for discussion The mental onslaught of special effect games, the ceaseless epic movies of aliens, galactic empires and planetary battles are turning the very vestiges of spirituality in young people into nothing more than a colossal fabrication of foolishness with no depth or meaning.

As proclaimed guardians of the truth the sooner the Church speaks out forcefully regarding the Four Last Things in terms that are understandable and believable in the minds of today's young Catholics, the sooner the call to holiness can be answered. For mankind's salvation and the good of the Church, it is essential that the faithful can once more give real Catholic witness to the gift that has been redeemed for us through the Passion, Death and Resurrection of Our Saviour Lord Jesus Christ.

In the RE-ENTRY analogy the loss of a space-vehicle can be understood, whereas the loss of a soul for so many reasons, cannot. On this point the clear knowledge of the Church's teachings must be reiterated in the greatest detail so that they can be if not fully understood, at least appreciated. The message is clear, the historical life of Christ is clear, the truths contained in the Gospel are clear and the details of Christ's death and Resurrection are clear. If any of these statements are false then there is no need to consider an eternity which will be determined by a judgement that must be faced upon one's death. On the other hand believing them to be true means there is a tremendous and urgent need for the Church to again preach in the most meaningful terms the reality of:

'What would it merit a man to gain the whole world,
and lose his soul?'

Mattthew 16:26

This permanent loss of any soul, its exclusion from God's Kingdom is contrary to God's plan. Hell was created for Satan and his angels; it was never intended to accommodate Man. Only after the fall of Adam and Eve when Man through pride choose to exercise his own individual 'free will' was Hell opened to him. The choice has remained 'in place' for each person since that day and will remain so until the Final Judgement when it will cease forever.

For those who freely decide to promote and serve Evil and in doing so to further the cause of Satan throughout the world, only one destination awaits them, Hell. The descriptions by the saints and mystics who have been given such visions are both horrific and frightening. Terrible though they may be, setting them to one side is perhaps even more appalling because these descriptions are being sidelined by the very people responsible for sharing them. By doing so one is forced to accept the fact that the clergy who deny these truths, somehow knowingly or unknowingly, are assisting Satan in destroying as great a number of souls as possible.

The faithful having been denied this knowledge need to equip themselves against these dangers that are now exposed. As time passes more and more of the classical teachings and knowledge are being pushed further and further into the background and more of tomorrow's children are being sold into a false world, a world of unreality. This future can be misrepresented in advance only to be exposed when it is too late.

Today some of the church's most prominent clergy prefer to promote Hell as little more than a glorified superstition or a source of modern embarrassment and confusion, which is both contrary to church teaching and gross falsification. Who in their right mind would gamble their soul on such a glossed-over interpretation? Sadly the answer to this obvious question must be those who have already been led astray.

Throughout the Catholic World the need to quantify eternity, to re-define eternal judgement as meaning exactly what it is, should be an ongoing theological challenge for some of the Church's most progressive thinkers. To say the opposite is the case, or that they are in a form of gross denial is perhaps an exaggeration. Nevertheless to adulterate what is core to the Catholic faith is more than a grievous sin against what Our Lord Himself made clear in the most unequivocal terms on more than one occasion. The fact that He did so while on Earth was to ensure there would be no room for doubt as to what 'unfaithful' Man could expect on death. The very words we use on a daily basis for those we love dearly "the faithful" are indeed the same for those who have gone before us when we pray for the souls of "the faithful departed."

Hell then, 'is' or 'is-not'. Who has gone there and who will go there will only be known on the Last Day. All faithful Catholics must believe that Hell exists and profess that belief each time they recite the Creed. However one can choose if one wishes to believe that even though Hell may exist, no person has ever been, or ever will be evil enough to merit the punishment of eternal damnation.

Should one choose to believe that then, one must wonder why our Blessed Mother allowed the children at Fatima the vivid and lucid visions of so many souls in such terrible torment. Sister Lucia, the last remaining child of Fatima described Hell in order that people would receive a genuine image of the appalling suffering, the real fire and the intense agony of the damned, so that those who listened to her, would determine not to risk their eternity by committing grievous sin.

Authentic visions and views of Hell which today are so rarely preached or lectured on are missing in a great many people's lives. It is debatable, if on hearing them how many would actually turn their lives around and change their sinful ways. For numerous 21st century psychological reasons it is, as stated, considered inappropriate and unacceptable to portray Hell especially to young people in such harsh detail as a place of only intense physical pain. Hell today if referred to at all, must instead be seen as a 'place of loss' where the damned must accept the lack of God's love as some 'terrible punishment'. It is this non painful interpretation that Satan and his agents promote incessantly in order to deceive mankind.

This visualisation places one in the position of being excluded from a royal banquet or being denied forever the beatific vision of God. These denials or exclusions may inflict severe suffering, according to some progressive theologians, who claim that Hell should be seen in this particular way. However, in comparison to what classical Catholic teaching has professed since its foundation, today's progressive 'lack of' actual descriptions seem incredibly inadequate and almost meaningless to today's sophisticated Catholics in any real deterrent sense.

To lose access to a real life of Eternal Happiness or be denied the beatic vision, albeit the divine Face of God that one will now never see, are punishments which some Catholics believe can be treated as being of little or no great consequence, is widespread. The fact is that this 'total lack of privileges loss' type Heaven means so little to many of today's new Catholics, is the reality that those in authority must somehow acknowledge. It is for the Bishops and priests of each parish to present the Gospel in its true entirety to their own flock and their own congregation. The more the preacher strays from the original text or decides to experiment and present it in so many different ways, the more the faithful continue to lose interest and walk away.

In this brave New Order where so much is promised and so very little is delivered, the church the most progressive new Catholics want is the Church of Tolerance which appears poised to take over from The Church of All Times.

Perhaps it could also be said that this Church of Tolerance will encapsulate this whole theme of uniformity which is so prevalent today and appears determined to offer open access to all other religions. One need not go very far down this road to see the senselessness in such a venture. From the beginning, the first moment, temptation triumphed over obedience, the battle lines were established, and there they will remain until the Second Coming of Christ. For each person tasked with completing their mission, their own log book, their calendar of events showing all their highs and lows will be plain for all to see.

The Church of All Times which identifies the Church that Jesus Christ founded and has remained in existence until today as the one Holy Roman Catholic Church should easily be identified as the Universal Church of Continuity and Truth. In its most authentic form it should be a church of obedience in which one gladly chooses to comply joining their will with God's thereby becoming an active part in the Mystical Body of Christ.

This desire of unification to be part of the whole is in itself a reward. However God wants to give one even more and that is the reward of salvation and complete union with Him. If the Church mutates to become the Church of the all Tolerant than it will be a church in which everybody pleases themselves, there will be no real need to accept a figurehead or authority, as committees and consensus will try to ensure harmony. Families will be self-structured, and an environment of non-judgemental rules and regulations such as keeping holy the Lord's Day will be optimal but it will be only for the best social reasons.

This new Church of false love, promoting many distorted and modern Gospel views is the great new deception of Satan. It is the wonderful fantasy of so many varying Christian cults including some New Catholics who are seeking to establish a format which will revolve around a whole new social order in an ecological, and Mother-Earth type world. Promoting equality in all things, championing justice and peace with common human rights and encouraging all to talk in terms of global good will produce a society that can be governed with ease. It will persuade and encourage people into believing that Heaven is for all and Hell, as long suspected, is just a silly myth. This design-packaged new religion, by its presentation, will hold the greatest appeal to the greatest number of people. Who would not prefer to embrace such a comfortable religion rather than live the Gospel of Jesus Christ which brings every one home according to their own individual merit rewarding the good, while punishing those who caused nothing but misery, pain and suffering to others while they were on Earth?

This life, this precious mission entrusted to each person at birth, is a gift not to be taken lightly, and all the efforts made by parents, grandparents, families and friends are to be seen and understood as to being part of that gift.

For a new order, a new religion, a new same-sex family unit of society to be chosen flippantly by an organized, free-willing luciferian order of Man is total anathema. The sad conclusion being that such a "new-age" religion has to be a savage lie, leading people further away from God and a total further deception through the seductive appeal of Satan. Without the true faith to stop him, Satan will continue to inflict misery and havoc throughout the world. Only if we pray, if we practise our faith, if we help others, will we be able to protect ourselves, our families and be ready for whatever lies ahead. To be recharged again with true faith that we are willing and eager to share, must be a central part of one's mission in spreading true devotion to God.

A shuttle pilot is more than fully aware of what lies ahead. He knows that he has to break through an atmospheric barrier which could almost incinerate his spaceship before he finally passes through it and gets ready for his actual landing. For all the mission was, might have been, or actually did accomplish, are now completed events that are far behind him. Of course they all have been itemised, logged-in and recorded in some data bank or elsewhere in some ground controller's workstation. To all the 'What might have beens' or 'what could have beens,' the pilot knows he will have to give an account of, on his return, but for now the only thing that matters is his descent and his safe landing. He may not be able to physically see where he is heading or where the actual landing will be, due to the weather conditions or nightfall but he does know for certain that the landing strip or runway is there, it exists, and it is being prepared to receive him.

His anticipation in meeting his family is intense, as is his arriving back from space, all of which makes his imminent return even more incredible and exciting. His problem now is not his destination nor whether he can see it, his problem is that, unless he can touch down in one piece, whatever he did or didn't do, will be immaterial for him as life may suddenly cease. For him the focus on landing is all that matters. Fortunately he has trained for this day, he has prepared for every possible scenario of what could happen and he knows that if he reacts accordingly he will maintain control of his craft and achieve a perfect landing. He has the support of his commander, his ground crew and everything that is in place to make the final phase of his mission the total success it was always intended to be.

For one's own RE-ENTRY however the situation may not be quite as clear or as confident, as one may not have any visual awareness of our destination. We know we have a family or a group of friends who will be awaiting us, we could call our pastor or our curate or whoever we trusted but how well trained and prepared we are now is what actually matters. Certainly we are aware that a de-briefing will take place on our return and a judgement call awaits us on arrival. With all the data boxes fully loaded and available, all our calls logged in and monitored, there is absolutely no chance of any event, item or occurrence being overlooked or mislaid. The possibility for such omissions just does not exist. If we were to look around for our own Re-entry manual with all the answers, would there still be time to study it and master what we now urgently need to know?

One thing is certain, we desperately do not want to fail on this final task. We want to get back safely into the arms of those we love and those who love us. We must focus and remember all the while that God's love and forgiveness is already ours, and all one must do is to formally seek it, but seek it we must. There cannot be forgiveness where there is no repentance. Heaven awaits and we are bound to find ourselves embraced by the Lord of Love once we pledge ourselves to Him.

How then can anyone turn their back on God and risk forever the awfulness of Hell? If such a place exists, how real is it? How bad can it actually be? How can such an enormity be so hidden from one's view? The great saints and doctors of the Church did not renege from the task of telling the faithful how awful Hell actually is. They saw it and described it as best they could, for them it was an obligation not to be avoided instead it was there to be shared if they were still to fulfil their own mission. If one does not know then it is their own intellect that must drive them to seek the truth what knowledge is there to share. However once one is in possession of such knowledge than the responsibility to pass it on is unavoidable. Today with much knowledge being distorted and the responsibility of passing it on being avoided, a true picture or attempt to create some accurate description is not easy.

Today's church has chosen to exercise the softest portrayal of Hell which almost obliterates its meaning as if lost in translation. Since the fall of Lucifer (aka Satan) and his cohort of angles Hell has always been, is, and will continue to be constant. It cannot be altered to suit the demands of some modern cosmic day theologians. It does however need to be once more reintroduced and reinstated as the ultimate place of suffering. The suffering of Hell has always been pain and the alternative 'withdrawal of privileges' introduced in recent years is little more than a modern myth lacking all credibility. Hell as it has always been described, we must believe still, delivers serious pain, excruciating in all its levels, on a constant and never ending fashion. The forcefulness of this one truth and the spreading of such knowledge must be brought back once more into focus as a central plank in church teaching.

For today's technologically gifted generations who can easily understand a giga-bite, quantum physics, quarks, soft maths etc. the comprehension and integration of digitized graphics can perhaps be both used and accepted as part of an everyday life, yet the concept of an eternity of pain in multiple forms and levels somehow does not appear understandable or acceptable. It is as if it were a locked room in a strange house very few choose to visit. This seemingly no go area is blocked off or out of bounds to one's intelligence. So much so it now appears that Hell is a place that nobody not only wants to acknowledge it has become a place of non existence. This maybe is Satan's greatest deception of all, he has managed to erect a mental barrier to obfuscate Man's awareness of the reality of Hell that is 99% effective

The soul, like an exploding star splitting in agony into a multi-million number of smaller celestial particles each fragmented state forever shedding more and more shards in ever greater pain and suffering, can in no way come close to what awaits the doomed individual. A soul forever sinking into black agony, into an endless infinity of pain, all the while aware that it is a pain that will never cease. Such descriptions paint only the faintest shadow of what the lost soul may expect to experience for all eternity.

In 2nd century Rome the scholar Hegesippus gave a vivid and factual eye-witness account of his Roman Hell:

> "Seeing some eighty prisoners being crucified at one time.
> While suspended on their crosses, the wives and children
> of each prisoner were brought in front of them to the foot
> of each cross and before the eyes of each crucified prisoner,
> their wives and children were gutted and butchered".

Hell not only has the dimension of tormenting the individual, but also the power to inflict accumulated pain due to the ripple effect it causes on all who were contaminated by the thoughts, words and deeds of the sinner. The banker who spread untold misery over his lifetime devoted to usury, the drug dealer peddling untold horror and death amongst so many youngsters, the porn star who posed for the centrefold in some pornographic magazine unleashing a tidal wave of lust and masterbation, causing a vast tsunami of sin.

Hell in terms of sheer loneliness, without companionship other than that which is harmful, painful or fearful, will be a terrifying part of the sinner's existence forever at breaking point. The Black Hole in deepest space, always falling, always alone, always in terror and always conscious of the tremendous loss of what was offered and what was so foolishly rejected will be the greatest pain of all, and one which will never lessen in its agony, not even for one single second.

Insofar as Hell can be given reality, and in so far as its existence can be established, our Mother Church is honour bound to disburse this doctrine to her children. The knowledge must be shared as a defensive guard for one's journey that gives the recipient every reason and resolve, to be forever wary and vigilant. Unless one is duly armed one's mission becomes all the more likely to be attacked, overcome and destroyed.

The realisation of Hell is in its presence. No person should lose sight of it or fail to dread it as a potential reality, it must never be disregarded. Just as St Augustine claimed that a fear of God was the beginning of all wisdom, it is this healthy fear that brings such realization. This wisdom bestows an awareness of God's great love for mankind, His great mercy and His great justice. It is an appreciation that he sent his only Son to suffer and die on behalf of Mankind, in order that each child of God can return to Him. The beauty of God lies in his forgiveness and in His mercy. His truth rests in His justice. According to the Gospel:

> "If your brother offends against you, seventy times seven
> in one day, and asks forgiveness, you are to forgive him."
> Matthew 18:22

This is what we are asked to attempt, to forgive our fellow travellers who may offend or hurt us constantly as we move through life. It also provides us with an insight into God's mercy, for if He wants us to behave in such a manner, His mercy for us must surely be beyond comprehension.

This is His continuous gift which is there to be availed of freely and with great joy, for there is no sin which is beyond the reach of absolution. To repent and say, "Forgive me Father" and truly mean it, is one's final obligation and the simplest prayer to secure forever the Kingdom of Heaven. To claim salvation, however, our prayer of repentance must be genuine; we must also forgive if we wish to be saved. The words mean nothing unless they come from the heart. Truth exists in God's justice.

It is through such a faith and belief that we can take our rightful place at the table prepared for all of us. Without that faith leading to one's salvation one's only alternate route is a refusal to accept God's mercy. Making such a choice by exercising one's own individual free will, one remains outside and so forfeits any claim to salvation. It is the most cumulative sin of pride, this blasphemy and what must become a total hatred of one's fellow men that will condemn the sinner to remain forever in everlasting misery and suffering.

Having passed through the Door of Death and standing before the Throne of Justice the exquisite feeling of joy and of relief will be boundless. It will be evident that however lacking one may have been on one's mission, or how far beneath one's promise one actually performed, one can now stand down because now one is finally home. The awareness of how one's mission went will also be clear, and the good that one achieved, will far surpass whatever wrongs one committed. With such an awareness, however, will come the realisation of all that one failed to do.

It will be clear that with all the talents one was given most were either lost or gambled away and very few were put to the full use for which they were intended. To seek desperately and make amends for one's shortcomings and offer some form of reparation for one's transgressions during one's mission a place of healing and purification is reserved for them in Purgatory.

Just as clean rooms have to be sterilized and iron has to be forged through liquid fire so also will it be necessary for souls destined to enter God's eternal presence to be purified. Being re-born to the level of full perfection, will enable us to attend the banquet in complete perfection as was the original intention of God's joy in creation.

Purgatory as outlined in today's Catechism of the Catholic Church, Pars 1030 – 1032, is treated with almost a degree of solemnity. It is central to the the Last Things and must be accepted as the means or manner by which imperfection can once more be made perfect through the process of this cleansing purification. It is not only of crucial importance to the Church Militant but also to the Church Suffering, whom one refers to on a daily basis as the 'faithful departed', that the doctrine of Purgatory is preached fully once more with far greater zeal, love and understanding. On the 'Last Day' Purgatory as a place, will cease to exist, but until that happens it permits the faithful departed to receive the purification needed before they enter Heaven.

This is both logically and spiritually justifiable. From what we know of our earliest ancestors it is now almost universally accepted that both primitive and non-primitive societies believed that death, burial and farewell were events of major significance and that some form of afterlife awaited the departed. Regardless of how the funeral rites were conducted or celebrated, the onward journey of the person was seen as another step forward.

Goods, food, precious jewels, pets, even favourite slaves were all possessions included in the ritual so as to make the journey in the underworld as comfortable as possible. Right down to the days of the Roman catacombs the care for those who died was seen as a most integral and formal part of one's faith's foundation. Over subsequent centuries with the accumulation of more knowledge, acquired through Christian revelation and teaching, the reality of Purgatory became more clearly defined and preached as it added to the enlightenment of the Four Last Things: Death, Judgement, Heaven and Hell.

For the saint, who in his lifetime on Earth, achieves total harmony with God, the Church teaches that on death the soul goes immediately to Heaven, to stand in the presence of Almighty God. For the sinner who shows no repentance, and who is adamant in his refusal to seek God's forgiveness at the moment of death his destination is Hell. These extreme cases however, fail to address the question of the penitent who, having died in the State of grace must now make amends and for the venial sins they committed. These imperfections are the stains of sin which must be removed before the soul can enjoy the love of God which awaits them. The purification process of Purgatory awaits them.

Of the many apparitions made by Our Blessed Mother over the last 200 years or so the theme common to each of them is a call for Mankind to once more seek Her Son through holiness. Our Blessed Mother beseeches mankind to repent, to turn back from the sinful path on which he is travelling and seek forgiveness. Her constant pleas are for devotion to the Eucharist and the love of Jesus. In relation to the 'faithful departed,' Our Blessed Mother stresses the need for prayer for those in Purgatory, all the while helping them to climb from the bottom of the ladder leading them on and upward to Heaven.

The accounts of Purgatory which have been given to some visionaries leave one in no doubt that the period of purification is one in which a definite degree of suffering is not just obligatory but indeed necessary in order to undo the harm, damage and distress one has left behind on Earth. This purification process through fire however painful will be born joyfully by the penitent who having become aware of the hurt caused by their sins will willfully and gladly accept their punishments, knowing as they do, they are somehow lessening their offences.

The question of time or period one will spend in Purgatory depends very much on what sins must be atoned for, and the amount of prayers offered for the person in Purgatory. The duration one remains in Purgatory can only be imagined in finite terms, for many the period maybe experienced in 'days' while for others, the time of suffering and pain may last many thousands of years. On the Last Day all souls will be reunited in their true physical form and will rise again, before God, to receive their eternal reward. It will be with this all-encompassing peace of mind that they will sustain themselves in Purgatory. On the Day of General Judgement, Purgatory will cease to exist, as on that day all redeemed and resurrected souls will be reunited and welcomed into Heaven, to attain the joy of eternal salvation, while those who mocked Christ and chose to follow Satan will return for ever into the fires of Hell

CHAPTER

12

"The Resurrection of the Dead, and Life Everlasting, Amen" so ends the Catholic Creed, as does our life, not in death but in Resurrection, the promise fulfilled. The promise being that for those who have spent their lives seeking God, they're seeking is at last over; for those who have knocked on the door, it is now opened wide; for those who have cared and shared with others less fortunate than they, unlimited treasures now await them in Life Everlasting. As the Gospel so triumphantly proclaims,

> "Eye has not seen, nor ear heard, nor have entered into the heart of man, the things which God has prepared for those who love him."
>
> Corintians 2:9

What greater promise could exist that does not ignite the heart with a sensation of excitement and, having attempted to describe Hell, how best can one now conclude in an attempt to describe Heaven?

No matter how hard one tries to imagine Heaven somehow or other it escapes one's vision. The terribleness of Hell with fire and brimstone appear easier for some reason to grasp than ecstatic happiness. What the reality of Heaven is defies our wildest dreams. A tiny pebble at the base of the Rocky Mountains or a child's bucket of water on a beach beside the Pacific Ocean, fails totally in feeble comparison to describe the joy that awaits the soul on its arrival home. One may just as well be looking upward at some dense overhead rain clouds under a steely gray ceiling while trying to imagine a clear blue sky with blazing sunshine, than to attempt to try and think of the beauty of Heaven while on Earth, the comparison is not possible to make. If there is a clue to the enormity of Heaven it must be contained in the Passion of Our Lord's death, who not only lived and died for everyone but truly suffered an intense amount of physical pain for each individual person, so that they could all individually achieve redemption and gain access to a life of eternal happiness. Understanding the mystery of Our Lord's Passion, His Death and Resurrection is the quest every person is on.

This mystery must make us aware that Heaven is almost outside any conceivable concept of human understanding. One must believe however that not only will one be ecstatically happy in glorifying God- but one will also be in complete harmony with everyone else enjoying the beatific vision. This vision between the soul and its Creator will not only be twofold but in addition will be cumulative, everyone simultaneously enjoying every other soul's individual joy. Rather like a stream flowing into a river or a star being part of a galaxy of billions of other stars, our sensation of pleasure will be raised to incredible heights individually joining with each other's level of ecstasy, incalculable.

So also as galaxies keep expanding, heaven and our individual vision of God will keep forever growing brighter and brighter and our integration contracting closer and closer, more intimately sensuous, an intimacy in which each and every being will participate fully in a copulation of supreme love totally perfect in God's divine omniscience. A Heaven of kaleidoscopic permutations and combinations forever expanding and contracting simultaneously, in a celestial ballet of unbelievable beauty.

In this world of the physical, the onward march of time takes its toll on the individual, on the family, on the community, indeed, on everybody and everything. One progresses through childhood and the endless days of Summer which appeared to last forever, while the whole mystery of what lies ahead unfolds one frame at a time, until the acquisition of a wife or husband and children appear as if from nowhere and the whole establishment of 'family' begins to blossom.

Seen from afar, or as one dwells in the final quarter of one's life while at Mass on Sunday, the existence of such young families makes one acutely aware that this metamorphism of individual first and sequentially family life completes its physical circuit and one must be acutely aware that the world one must pass through and the mission undertaken are the prerequisites that must be completed, prior to the eventual one being death or Re-entry.

Before Heaven can be reached however, one's mission must be finalised on completion and all tasks accomplished. The need to pray daily, to recite the Rosary, to constantly be aware of God's presence, are all the spiritual components to be used. The sacraments that have sustained one through one's life will more than sustain one through death

Also what must never be disregarded is the fact that we are God's chosen children. The Resurrection of Jesus, obtained for us through His Life, Passion and Death that was ordained by the Father and blessed by the Holy Spirit, The Lord the Giver of Life, The Bride of Christ being the Universal Catholic Church which Christ founded on Earth before his Ascension into Heaven represents the Holy Spirit, and will remain so until the end of the World. Regardless of the power of Satan in the world today it is temporal. The Church will prevail and Satan will be conquered. What more assurance do we need than that which is declared by Christ in the Gospel when He said;

> "Thou art Peter, and upon this rock I will build My
> Church and the gates of Hell will not prevail against it."
> Matthew 16:18

The Gospel being the inspired word of God remains constant; the message is truth and the truth cannot change or be changed.

"Take up your cross and follow me."

Matthew 16:24

This is the instruction all baptised Catholics receive and the church teaches, because Jesus is the Way, the Truth and the Life. The way to the Father is through Him and only through Him only. He told mankind to love one another and to keep His Commandments. He even made it more simple and more concise: Love God first, and then love your neighbour, doing both these things and doing them well is all that one is asked to do. Today is it possible to witness such love, to see a genuine love of God and a love for one's neighbour.

In war torn Syria recently a Jesuit priest appeared on TV feeding his own flock and his Muslim neighbours, demonstrated such love in the horrific circumstances of today's civil war, as he does not differentiate between sides, religious groups or political parties. He is simply meeting a need, feeding God's children. God's love provides such simple impressive examples as this priest, for the world to witness God's love in action. Loving one's neighbour collectively or individually is always a challenge and must be constantly taken up, otherwise one wavers and the moment is lost.

For countless people, living in the vast mega urban sprawls of the great cities, they no longer have any desire or need to know who their neighbour is. Countless flat or apartment dwellers could not even care less. In the world we have created, man has forged ahead bereft of faith without hope and indifferent to charity. Is it any wonder then that it is only a matter of time before vast numbers of unrelated people, preoccupied only with themselves and almost devoid of love, watch 'real human beings starve to death right in front of their eyes'.

The work of the Catholic Church is to preach the love and mercy of God and to seek and restore Man's obedience and love of God, regardless of how much hostility she attracts. This is Her mission and she must remain steadfast to it.

Love must be restored and the role of each practising Catholic is to begin within one's own self. This is where one must start, but starting is not an end rather a beginning, for if it remains within and goes nowhere, it dies. Love only comes to fruition when it is sharing and to be a follower of Christ, one must share one's love of God. The more one gives the more love one has to give. The great secret of love is that in its giving it grows and the more it grows the more one has to give.

The Church our Mother, was founded by Christ to teach, protect, guide and comfort all God's children. As head of the Church and her Bridegroom, Christ never left his Bride but rather through His Church He has remained to perpetuate in it His living sacrifice. Christ left a group of disciples whom he commissioned to spread his message and who in turn would authorise others to do the same.

Christ therefore, at the Last Supper/Passover inaugurated the Eucharist in advance of His Death, demonstrating to the apostles that this was what He wanted them to do as soon as they received the imprimatur from the Holy Spirit. Once this power was bestowed on them, they then had the right to consecrate the bread and wine into His Blood and His Body and to represent the sacrifice of Jesus in the Eucharist. This power of consecration given today to all priests at their ordination through the sacrament of Holy Orders is the re-enactment of the Last Supper ordained by Christ Himself.

This miracle of consecration is the miracle the congregation participate in daily at all Masses offered throughout the World. To follow Christ, through the priest at Mass whenever possible, one should always start by uniting oneself with the priest in order to participate fully with the sacrifice the priest is making to God, The Father Almighty. The Mass is the citadel for the entire human race, and it is offered on behalf of mankind from every corner of the world. The Mass being Calvary again, is the same offering being made but without the physical presence of Christ being nailed to the cross and His sacred blood being shed. This is the only difference.

To attend Mass is to be there, to unite oneself with Jesus in the glory of his sacrifice, for the salvation of Mankind. This act of divine adoration renews the offering made by Christ on Calvary. In the Mass, one's total gratitude is offered to God for the gift of eternal salvation. This gratitude can be offered on behalf of all Mankind, it can be offered on behalf of one's immediate community, it can be offered in particular for a family member or a friend. It can include our dearest faithful departed, those suffering in purgatory, those suffering from ill health and those close to death. One's power to help others, to share God's love is never greater than when one assists the priest in offering the sacrifice of the Mass.

Not only does the Mass allow one to pay homage, but it also presents a perfect opportunity to apologise and declare one's contrite sorrow for one's sins and the sins of others for which one is maybe in some way partially responsible. It further entitles one to petition God from the foot of the cross seeking his help. While we on Earth apply ourselves to our daily lives, the Mass gives us the opportunity to unite with Christ almost as if we were in Heaven, as the Mass is in essence, already part of the Eternal Kingdom.

By attending at Mass, with the priest called by God to serve others, one becomes part of the Mystical Body, part of the community where two or three are gathered. It is the community, representing all mankind, on which the Holy Spirit descends, and it is why the priest intones the following aspirations,

> "Let us pray / We offer / and Pray Brethren / that my sacrifice and yours" / "together, giving," / "all honour, and glory" / "now and forever."

Such all-inclusive terms spoken by the priest in the plural are not just on his own behalf but also on behalf of the congregation gathered around him at each and every Mass.

The presence of Christ in the Eucharist, in Masses throughout the world, makes God available to all Catholics. No other Christian religion has the Eucharist as the most holy Sacrament which pours down sanctifying grace, empowering the faithful to spread the living Word throughout the World. This crucial need of today must surely help Catholics realize the mission they have been given, which was never as important in the history of mankind as it is now. In a world created by God where Catholics number less than one in seven and only perhaps one-third of whom are practising their faith, the Church more than ever before, needs her missing children to return and be reunited with her.

Before many can do this they may need to investigate who, or what or how their loss of faith took place. For some it may have been a lie, a corruption, a cruel parent a wayward adult who stole from them the graces they received at Baptism and Confirmation, or they may be confronted with the fact it was their own free will that made them choose to turn their back on Christ. Why they chose to follow a forbidden path that denies them access to God's love, or just adapt other people's foolish ideas without first questioning their validity, is of little interest. For whatever reason they chose it encouraged them to stupidly set aside the gift of faith that had been given to them. If the world, in which they now find themselves, is a place in which their total satisfaction is through the abuse of money, power or prestige, now is the right time to look again at their discarded faith and consider coming home.

Once one realizes the depth of enmity in today's World of global proportions and disproportions, of economic bullying and dominant trading blocks, in which the individual barely matters if at all, the world ceases to be a very hospitable place. The alternative world of the Catholic Church, in which Christ is acknowledged as King and Ruler, offers each person a total life, a life shaped in the image of Jesus Christ, a life of love and hope.

This life is there to be chosen for what it is, Christian, spiritual, meaningful, and holding the key to eternal salvation. Why do so many fail to choose it? Is it because it is not offered freely enough? Are the terms and conditions too harsh? Can it be because it is incorrectly perceived? The true beauty of a Catholic life is not that it is not a self centered one, but rather a means to an existence in which one is a conduit for God's love to be offered to whoever one meets in one's life. It is in such stewardship and compliance with God's law that guarantees the son or daughter their eternal salvation. Here then is where one enters the Kingdom of God and forever after experiences eternity as a total and absolute full realisation of God's love.

All men and women of good-will who follow Christ, can and will become children of God within the Mystical Body of Christ while on Earth. It is as true followers of Christ they are promised that such is the eternity that awaits them. How can such an incredible promise fail to be taken up and grasped tightly in both hands?

For all travellers struggling to fulfil their missions and for whom this book was written, the primary reason was to once more reintroduce the true reason of life, and to invite those furthest from God to accept this outreach and turn their faces towards home, to where they belong, and begin their journey back. In doing so as a born-again Catholic, one must first repudiate and refute the arguments which are widespread in today's world towards the Catholic Church. For many reasons, the Catholic Church is presented by hostile governments, Satanic forces, media syndicates and nominal religions, in the most disparaging of ways.

Prompted by the temporal power of Satan and the on going stream of falsehoods his earthly empire produces, there are many "loyal" Catholics who buy into these deceptions and in so doing become Catholics in name only and are then destined to do all they can to harm the Church before they wither on the vine. How they come to accept, adopt, add and relate to such falsehoods of their own faith and Mother Church rather than to defend the reality of her truth and beauty, is due to the tremendous power of Satan.

The presence of some corrupted and most senior clerics in national hierarchies who have brought tremendous shame on the church and its affairs over the past half century, is without doubt and their ongoing influence, through their teachings and writings, must be identified and removed. Rather than react to such disgraceful and appalling lifestyles, as was done silently in the past, the Church needs to rejuvenate and reassert herself and lead solely from the Chair of Peter.

Whatever false doctrines and interpretations exist in schools and colleges today, they must be weeded out and placed at the door of the miscreant individuals responsible for passing on such adulterated faith. A new order of discipline based on the truth of faith must be restored. The faithful owe their Church the fullest degree of loyalty and fidelity which they should willingly demonstrate by their full participation in

Mass and the Sacraments. As members of the Mystical Body, all are fully expected to actively proclaim the good news and share the joy of being followers of Christ.

To hear the Church continuously being described as too tyrannical, too authoritarian, too cruel to women, too rich, too unkind to homosexuals, too patriarchal and so on, should make all adult Catholics seek to examine seriously the facts, before accepting or acquiescing to such accusations and fictitious generalizations. The qualities of obedience, of loyalty, of steadfastness, do not enslave any Catholic in some form of brainwashed subservience as is often claimed by those who seek to harm the Church. Rather it is for the well read and educated Catholics to be able to refute and disburse such mindless arguements foolish people with no great degree of knowledge or awareness of faith like to hurl.

The Church is the premier dispenser of truth and knowledge over the past 2,000 years, and it can never be compared with modern day 'churches' who operate in the realm of new age cults, or dubious figureheads. The history of the Catholic Church over 2,000 years, which fostered the birth of European civilization and culture, needs only to give testimony of its care for mankind, throughout so many centuries of world history, that its proven concern for the wellbeing of man is without equal.

Shameful episodes that occurred throughout the centuries should never be forgotten and today's transgressions and abuses must also be acknowledged. That all future events, assemblies and actions will, from now on, meet with full transparency is today's goal. Regardless of whatever happens and even though unintended incidents may occur they must never again be downplayed or diminished. The Church claims it is committed to ensuring that in the future only 'best-practice' guidelines are established and enforced.

In a similar mode the Church should never have the need to suppress or deny any genuine theological proposal put forward by any person, within or without, the Church. This belief in the freedom of speech endorses the right of any Catholic to express his or her opinion on matters that pertain to the good of the Church and to make that opinion known to the other Christian faithful, (Code of Canon Law 212, Lumen Gentium, par. 37). This right encourages all Catholics to freely express themselves. For those who have made their case and find the reaction and answer not to be to their liking, the need to seek further clarification can be sought.

If at a certain stage however, one is still dissatisfied, a withdrawal, resignation or acquiescence to the greater intellect is called for, because the question and its contentious nature will have either been resolved or rejected. This applies to the demand still being pursued for the ordination of women and the faithful are obliged, in fidelity, to accept the teaching on ordination as being the irrevocable and true teaching of the Church. As Pope St John Paul II himself reiterated, the power to ordain women is beyond the power given to him and so also must be the case with his successors.

For many Catholics and indeed others also, Pope Francis I is seen as an individual with an outgoing personality and charismatic spontaneity, which gives him his 'charm'. His unique way of doing things is seen as non-judgemental, heart warming and so appealing that his famous "Who am I to judge" remark must remain outside the bounds of any clarification. As a hands-on activist, he appears to be more concerned with the needs of the poor and disadvantaged than with the theological and doctrinal matters of the day which he leaves to his closest confidants and theologians to consider and advise him on. While this is perhaps the case, there is little doubt that his interests in modern financial and corporate planning are evident in the high profile stable of advisers with whom he has surrounded himself.

Among his closest advisors now established are McKinsey & Co, Promontory Financial Group, Ernst & Young and KPMG. These four giant global consultancy and accountancy firms are amongst the most prestigious in the world, their competency is perhaps beyond reproach; nevertheless, they are there to exert whatever influence it allows them to exercise and who is to say that a conflict of interests in the future may never arise?

The reliance of this Pope on this camarilla of experts is a move of such total originality that one can only hope and pray that the day of 'two masters' is not already being brought into play. The significance of the papacy and its relationship with any commercial world bodies, governments or banks as co-respondents to church affairs can only, at best, be regarded with extreme caution. What must always take preference for the Church, is not its financial or administrative well-being but rather its own well being as the Mystical Body of Christ and the salvation of mankind. The Pope as the vicar of Christ and the universal shepherd must, through his bishops and priests seek first the return of the lost sheep to the flock, and those in greatest danger of damnation.

Insofar as he keeps these and similar goals in front of him, he can do little wrong. Should however he become distracted or led away from this path to pursue other causes which may greatly concern him, his authority must waver and the structure of the Church begins to suffer. There is little doubt the weight of papal responsibility resting on one man's shoulders is tremendous and by appointing a circle of cardinals to help him, the Holy Father may well formulate plans to help guide the Church forward but any sought-after conciliatory innovation in the decision-making process of the Papacy in itself cannot be entertained for obvious reasons.

As time goes by the retention of the above mentioned firms may or may not be maintained by the next Pontiff but whatever is decided the needs of the Church can be best served only by those who love Her most. Today's Church in the care of the Bishop of Rome will only prosper in so far as he allows himself to be guided by the Holy Spirit and those whose advice he values having entrusted them with various responsibilities. In addition the Holy Father he is also supported and sustained by the prayers of all the religious and the faithful, who are obliged to pray for him at all Masses said throughout the world. Without such a formula it matters little whoever inhabits the Chair of Peter.

To consider momentarily that the role of Christ's Vicar on Earth has passed through the hands of 264 holders, with all their human frailties and foibles, it is easy to understand how so few of them achieved sainthood. The office has been held by saintly men and charlatans but it is the Church itself, the Bride of Christ, which will remain in place in one form or another until the end of time. This is the most significant point which has been guaranteed by Christ Himself in the Gospel. Were this not so the Church would have been destroyed many times over the centuries.

For non-committed and lapsed Catholics the challenge is to set aside the things of youth and accept the responsibilities of Catholic adulthood, of being true followers of Christ. Is there any greater challenge which can be offered which will make more sense of this present world? If one instead thinks of future generations of children destined to grow up in a more material, a more commercial, a meaner, harder, more difficult world, then all one needs to do is to remain committed to today's society of hostility, aggression and domination. We must accept the inequalities, poverty and manipulation of vast sections of humanity, while at the same time trying to improve their conditions. Nevertheless and regardless of such discrepancies in the structure of many societies harmful though they may be to the Christian way of life, we must with confidence believe in Our God reigns and it will be His, and His only Will, that shall be done.

This is the critical point of one's Christian existence: to live in accordance with God's Commandments or to live according to some Satanic form of Wall Street madness with its traders and jobbers screaming orders for others to fulfil. It must be obvious to even the most non-committed person that to try and promote a better, safer and more meaningful global community than the one in which we exists today is the challenge any right-minded person should be fully prepared to participate in. In the final analysis, one is faced with the choice of trying to make the world a better place with or without God's help. Without such help provided by His bride the Catholic Church the challenge is all the greater and almost impossible to achieve. The Church into which one was originally born is there to welcome back the absent son or daughter, who wishes once more to be involved. To those who return to 'help bear one another's burdens', the load maybe tough but the going is good and the rewards are ten-fold.

In seeking to return to one's lost faith, how must one plan for such a journey? For some there is a simple route, for others a more difficult way and for yet another group perhaps even a more hazardous one still. Nevertheless the Gospel gives everyone an assurance as it clearly states:

"Ask and it shall be given to you, seek and you will find'.
Matthew 7:7

The message could not be more direct or under written. For any mountaineer, explorer or traveller planning a hard trip, the first step is usually to secure the services of a competent guide. It would be to one's great advantage to follow the same procedure and take a little time to study. At the Battle of Pamplona, in 1521 the founder of the Jesuits, St Ignatius of Loyola, suffered a badly broken leg and being laid up in bed for seven months read all he could. Eventually, when nothing else was available, he took down a copy of the Lives of the Saints and after reading it was so smitten by the incredible lives they had led and the missions they had accomplished, he decided to leave the king's service and instead enlist in the service of Christ.

Reading various accounts of what today's heroic men and women accomplish in some parts of the emerging New World makes one well aware that this challenge is still available and as arduous as ever for those who decide to take up the challenge.

On receiving the Sacrament of Baptism, the infant is given the services of an angel to watch over him/her and it is the angel's mission to try as hard as possible to protect his care from all spiritual danger. After the boy or girl achieves the 'Use of Reason' and makes their first Confession and receives the Blessed Eucharist for the first time, their own independent spiritual desires begin to grow or wither. This greatly depends on the religious knowledge that is imparted to the young person. What trials and tribulations take place in the life of every young boy or girl growing up God only knows but casualties do happen, mistakes are made and injuries are sustained.

Even at a young and tender age the loss of God's love can be the terrible price one must pay for one's foolishness. With God's mercy however, nothing is impossible and the young penitent need only express their sorrow seek forgiveness and help is at hand. In trying to find one's way back after a long time recalling one's own personal angel who has been waiting for the call over many years is a wonderful start.

One also can also try and develop a special devotion to a particular saint whose life appeals for one particular reason or another. Enlisting such a saint to whom one may feel a particular understanding gives a great degree of spiritual help and comfort. Our Mother church teaches that 'saints' are those special remarkable people whose lives reached such a degree of perfection whilst on Earth, that they were granted immediate entry into Heaven at the moment of death. The beatified Jesuit, Fr John Sullivan SJ (1861-1933) kept this powerful prayer always close to his heart:

"Take life in instalments, this day now. At least let this be a good day.
Be always beginning. Let the past go. Now let me do whatever I have power to do. The saints were always beginning.
That is how they became saints."

The examples of the influence of saints to petition God on behalf of sinners are legion, and those who feel their own unworthiness requires an intermediary can access this route with great confidence knowing whose company they are in. If one already has a patron saint chosen at Confirmation then to pray to him or her to help one regain one's faith is also of great benefit. If on the other hand if one decides for one reason or another to pick a particular saint then one should choose a saint with great affection, entrusting them with the task of helping you to get home safely.

Preparation to re-join the Church by spending some time away from one's usual lifestyle and surroundings, is also a time of great spiritual value. Whether it is spent in solitude or on a structured, formal retreat, praying for a return to grace would be no different than practising a re-entry run on a flight simulator. This timeout enables one to prepare to make a general confession and reunion with total joy to receive the

Sacraments of Penance and the Blessed Eucharist. This homecoming would, the Gospel tells us,

> "have Heaven in raptures and the banquet feast for the returned prodigal son or daughter laid again in great glory".

To speak of the Universal Church, The Holy Roman Catholic Church as being the one true Church, is neither understood or accepted in today's culture and applies to some Catholic clerics as well as to many New Catholic lay people. Indeed there are those who, by accident, choice or design, prefer to promote an ecumenism between all Christian Churches because of what is shared 'in common.' Sharing a love of Christ may be beyond doubt, but the truth in the Mass, the Sacraments, the Immaculate Conception, and the Assumption to mention just four core Catholic truths, are in total dispute and in no way shared. The present rapour with the Lutheran Church which appears to fly in the face of catholic doctrine absolutely beggars belief. Talking then in terms of 'common ground' is foolish talk and very far short of what the Church is commissioned to teach and what Catholics are obliged to believe.

The desire for ecumenism as expressed by our Mother Church is that of the burning desire of any Mother for her missing children to return to her. New Catholics, other Christians and those who instead prefer to promote ecumenism as a form of future power-sharing exercise in a global one-size-fits-all church are lacking in Catholic truth and their vision is flawed. If the Catholic Church were to dispel or diminish the truths and sacred mysteries she holds, she would have to be prepared to lessen the deposit of faith she has received from Jesus Christ. As this is the impossible scenario that many New Catholics and some clerics are calling for a reaffirmation of the truth is not only necessary, it is crucial. Knowingly or unknowingly, New Catholics promoting this oneness in the name of ecumenism are causing great harm to the Bride of Christ and must be made aware that what they are seeking to profess and promote, is grievously wrong. When Pope Paul VI abolished The

Oath Against Modernism on July 17th 1967 the ramifications were inconceivable. The thinking behind the decision, the dark satanic forces that were in play after Vatican II led a confused and broken man down a hazardous path to his death. The results of this oath been rescinded were monumental and the damage done blatantly evident today.

In the Papal encyclical of Pius XI Mortalium Animos, (The Fostering of True Religious Unity), delivered on January 6th 1928, the pope addressed the concept of 'one flock' under the precept that it was being presented and driven by a misguided and misunderstood definition of charity. His opposition was both outspoken and adamant,

> "The Apostolic See can by no means take part in these
> assemblies, nor is it in any way lawful for Catholics to
> give to such enterprises their encouragement or support."

Less than a hundred years later, such meetings and conferences, are being promoted as mainstream Catholic ecumenism. It appears as if a majority of the hierarchy today are to collectivity ignore what was once specifically prohibited and forbidden. Today not only are many items of inter-christian churches discussed and agreed upon the formulae to leave the points on which the churches differ, are put aside for another day. This form of ecumenism and twisted theological technique, has what paradoxically has led us to where the Church finds itself today: what was once considered totally unacceptable, is now 'welcomed' in the Church at almost every level. The way forward as addressed by Pius XI in his encyclical was very simple and straightforward, in that the only true ecumenism is the sincere effort to invite all men and women into the Catholic faith.

Pope Benedict XVI in granting some dissident members of the Anglican Community their own Ordinate under his personal prelature, may have decided that this was the unity Pius XI had in mind. Sadly the unity of mankind presented by the Catholic Church based on the teachings of Our Lord Jesus Christ appears to be still a very long way off and the labourers remain few. For this reason the world will continue to self-harm and self-destruct.

Satan is determined at all costs to cause havoc and destruction with fallen man as his ally and the destruction of our Mother Church as his goal. Through whatever international disputes, national and regional wars, social injustices and religious conflicts he can use to further his aims, he will, and fallen man will wittingly or unwittingly continue to be his ally.

The Bride of Christ, Our Mother Church, has the guidance of the Holy Spirit, the Holy Mass, the Communion of Saints and the Great Mother of God, Mary Most Holy, who one day will crush the head of Satan under her heel. To speak of our Blessed Mother is to speak of a 'real mother' who is perfect in every way, the only human being ever born in the history of Mankind free from the Original Sin of Adam and Eve. This defined truth allows the greatest consolation and comfort for Catholics, who acknowledge Our Blessed Mother as such, throughout their life. Jesus in a dying gift gave His own Virgin Mother to His apostle John, and to all who take up their cross and follow Him to be their mother also. No other Christian church can ever hope of being reintegrated into the Mystical Body of Christ, without first acknowledging, Our Blessed Mother in all her majesty and splendour, as the Virgin Mother of Our Lord Jesus Christ.

The love of our Blessed Mother is one's saving grace, and as her children she implores us to listen to her Son and devote ourselves fully to Him, especially as defined in the Eucharist. The dogma of the Immaculate Conception proclaimed by Pope Pius IX on December 8th 1854 as doctrine, confirmed her natural birth as the only creature ever born, free, of original sin. From the moment of the Annunciation when the Angel Gabriel appeared to her it was clear that Mary was to be the Mother of God, Ever Virgin born without Original sin. No soul, no body, no womb unless fully perfect, could have been created to carry and bear the divine child, Jesus the true Son of God with such a stain. Mary was born to be the living tabernacle and was chosen to protect, nourish, love and feed the Divine Baby in her womb for nine months. Our Blessed Mother, as Mediatrix of all graces having brought God into the world, today brings our prayers and petitions to Him on our behalf. Every prayer every request, every cry for help, touches our Blessed

Mother's heart. She feels the anguish being laid upon her by one of her children and for whom she seeks intercession. Our Blessed Mother still stands beneath the cross at every Mass suffering for her Son, just as she did while standing beneath the cross on Calvary, 2,000 years ago.

Over the past century, especially in the recent Marian Age, over half a dozen major Marian apparitions or interventions have been made by Our Blessed Mother, pleading with Mankind to turn to her Divine Son and listen to His voice. The two most well known took place at Lourdes (1858) in France and at Fatima (1917) in Portugal and have received full Papal approval. Of the other more recent apparitions, the Church has yet to make its findings known and its approval or disapproval, official. It can be stated however that our Blessed Mother's messages, wherever and whenever given, are always virtually the same. They confirm that the power of Satan, fed by man's sinfulness is tremendous. Mankind must turn back to her Son. She emphasises His great love for us, and reminds us that it was by His sacrifice, we are all redeemed. As every creature born into this world has an earthly mother the realisation that we share a common mother, the Mother of Christ, can only bring the greatest joy to those who are prepared and ready to contemplate such an incredible gift that Christ made while nailed to the cross. The role of Our Blessed Mother must be central to one's faith, and it must be always as a devoted and loving child, one should approach her.

It is always she the Mother, subservient to her Divine Son, who cares so much that she petitions on our behalf. Our Blessed Mother who stood at the foot of the cross on Calvary and lived through every moment of her Divine Son's agony and death. She in her own role is aware and conscious of Man's constant betrayal of her Son's sacrifice; she continuously beseeches Man to atone for his sins and change his ways, so that God will bestow His mercy on us. It is Man's sin and his gross indifference which causes our Blessed Mother the tremendous pain and sorrow she experiences on a daily basis as she stood beneath the Cross, 2000 years ago in Jerusalem. Her plea today is more urgent and specific than ever and leaves no doubt that Man must repent and return to her Divine Son through the Mass and the Sacraments.

Pope St John Paul II, in his devotion to our Blessed Mother, chose as his motto the words Totus Tuus, for he indeed, offered everything to God through our Blessed Mother. He identified and shared with Her his most fervent and committed devotion. Early in his Pontificate he claimed:

> "It is especially in the Eucharist that the power and the love of the Lord is given to us."

This power and this love is given to all of us to be joyfully shared. The terrible sin of selfishness is the sin of sharing nothing with anybody, in any space, place or time. To understand then that the Eucharist is central to the life of every Catholic, it is the need, duty and obligation of every Catholic to share it as a mark of God's love. It was as a symbol of God's love for mankind that the Perpetual Eucharistic adoration in St Peter's Basilica in Rome was established, so that it could be seen that it was from the very Chair of Peter, that the present worldwide devotion to the Blessed Eucharist was spread throughout the world. Devotion to the Blessed Sacrament, the Eucharist, the Mass has more than anything else over the years become the all-encompassing call to Mankind, by both our Blessed Mother and the recent Popes of post-Vatican II. It is as if they together have united in their call, proclaiming Jesus Christ, Saviour of Mankind.

There can be complete confidence that, once Man believes fully in Jesus Christ, all Graces and Sacraments will flow into the hearts of all Mankind. To believe in Christ, one must automatically believe in His love, His forgiveness and His salvation. It would be impossible otherwise not to do so. It is a sacred truth that the Eucharist unites Man to God. In the Eucharist there are no boundaries and no limits to God's love for Mankind. Likewise it is where Man's love should know no limits in his love for God. In as much and as far as one is capable of giving oneself fully, and completely to Jesus Christ one is already experiencing Divine love. The Eucharist on Earth is where Jesus puts his arms around you, and you put your arms around Jesus. In this moment comes the ultimate realisation of what Jesus said,

"And you will know the truth, and the truth will set you free." (John 8. Ll, 33.)

'To know love and serve God in this life and to be happy with Him forever in the next.'

May Thy salvation be ever with us.
In God's name, live your life
In God's name, live your love
In God's name, prepare a welcome
For the Way, the Truth, and the Life

To shine, from Him, through you, for all to see and feel

Now and forever.
Re-Enter, rejoice and be happy, for
The Kingdom of Heaven is close at hand.

Salvation is of the Lord
Salvation is of the Lord
May thy salvation Lord
Be ever with us.

Amen.

Printed in the United States
by Baker & Taylor Publisher Services